Theatre games
A new approach to drama training

The games described in this invaluable handbook are all designed to enable anyone involved in acting to develop their technique without inhibition or artificiality. For those more interested in watching than doing, the book offers an unrivalled opportunity to explore and understand the processes by which performers achieve final performances.

As a professional actor, director and drama teacher, the author has developed his 'theatre games' system over the years and has proved its effectiveness for teachers, students and actors alike. In *Theatre Games*, after a short theoretical prelude, he sets out the details of how to play the various games and describes the acting skills which can develop from them. The games are arranged in order of complexity and illustrated with photographs and diagrams.

Clive Barker was born in Middlesbrough, Yorkshire, in 1931. Having trained in stage management at the Bristol Old Vic School, he joined Joan Littlewood's Theatre Workshop in its heyday in 1955. Here he acted and also conducted training sessions for the company. He took part in the first productions of *The Hostage* and *Fings Ain't What They Used T'be* at Stratford East, and appeared in the West End productions of, among others, *Oh, What a Lovely War!* and Tom Stoppard's *After Magritte*. Among the plays he directed were the Royal Court production of Shelagh Delaney's *Lion in Love*, the British premiere of Slavomir Mrozek's *The Police* and Marlowe's *Dr Faustus* for the German National Theatre in Weimar. He directed in Germany, the US and in Colombia, where he was Associate Director of the Teatro Libre de Bogota. From 1966–1974 he was Lecturer in the Department of Drama and Theatre Arts at Birmingham University and after a short period as director of the Northcott Theatre in Exeter he was Senior Lecturer in Theatre Studies at the University of Warwick until his retirement in 1996. He served on the boards of many arts organisations, many catering for the less advantaged in society: he was a Trustee of Ed Berman's Interaction from its inception in 1968, 7:84 (England), Geese

Theatre Company who work in prisons, and, more recently, the International Workshop Festival and The Shysters, a group of actors with learning disabilities. He had a major stroke in 2002 which limited his ability to continue working, but when he died of another stroke on 17 March 2005, it was in the foyer of York Theatre Royal after leading a workshop with The Shysters.

Dick McCaw has been teaching movement at the Drama Department at Royal Holloway, University of London since 2000. He began his career as a theatre producer, having co-founded the Actors Touring Company in 1979 and the Medieval Players in 1981. Clive Barker served on the Board of Directors from 1986–1992. Between 1993 and 2001 he was Artistic Director of the International Worshop Festival (IWF) which specialised in providing professionals working in the performing arts with opportunities for continuing training, research and creative development. Clive Barker was Chairman of the Board of Directors from 1995–2001. With Peter Hulton of the Arts Documentation Unit, Exeter, he has created eight DVD-ROM documentations of some of these figures – making their work accessible to students and researchers alike. Since 2001 he has been studying the movement principles of Rudolf Laban with one of his pupils and colleagues, Geraldine Stephenson. He qualified as a Feldenkrais Practitioner in April 2007.

THEATRE GAMES

A new approach to drama training

Clive Barker

methuen | drama

Methuen Drama

1 3 5 7 9 10 8 6 4 2

Copyright © Clive Barker 1977
Critical introduction copyright © Dick McCaw 2010
DVD copyright © Dick McCaw 2009
Produced by Arts Archives. www.arts-archives.org

Clive Barker has asserted his right under the Copyright, Designs and Patents Act,
1988 to be identified as the author of this work.

First published in 1977 by Eyre Methuen Ltd.
Reissued with additional material and a new cover design by Methuen Drama in 2010

Methuen Drama
A & C Black Publishers Ltd
36 Soho Square
London W1D 3QY
www.methuendrama.com

A CIP catalogue record for this book is available from the British Library

ISBN 978 1 408 12519 9

Printed and bound in Great Britain by Martins the Printers Ltd

The extracts from *Body and Mature Behavior* (1970) by M. Feldenkrais
are reprinted by permission of the International Universities Press, New York.
The extracts from Elisabeth Wycoff's translation of Euripides' *The Phoenician Women*
(in *The Complete Greek Tragedies*, copyright © 1959 by the University of Chicago)
are reprinted by permission of the University of Chicago Press.
The diagram of the Kinesphere from *Modern Educational Dance* by Rudolf Laban
is reprinted by permission of Macdonald and Evans Ltd; the plans of Nottingham Playhouse
and of the Yvonne Arnaud Theatre, Guildford, are reprinted from *New Theatres in Britain*
by Frederick Bentham (1970), by permission of TABS (Rank Strand Electric);
the reconstruction of the Swan Theatre is reprinted from *The Development of the
English Playhouse* by Richard Leacroft, by permission of the author and of Eyre Methuen Ltd;
Oskar Schlemmer's drawing is reproduced from *The Theatre of the Bauhaus* by permission
of the Wesleyan University Press, Middletown, Connecticut.

Reproduction of images for this second edition from The Clive Barker Archive,
Special Collections, Rose Bruford College.

To J.L., who kicked me into finding my own way, and F.C., who kicked me finally into writing it down.

The persistence of games is remarkable. Empires and institutions may disappear, but games survive with the same rules and sometimes even the same paraphernalia.

Roger Caillois, Man, Play and Games

Acknowledgements

The development of this work has been so much an integral part of my development as an actor, director and teacher that it would be impossible to list the thousands of actors and students who have significantly contributed to it, often totally unaware that they were doing so. Nevertheless, I am deeply indebted to them for the pleasure they have given me in their work and the ideas I have taken from them.

My particular thanks should be recorded to Nat Brenner and Rudi Shelley of the Bristol Old Vic School, for my early introduction to the Theatre; to Joan Littlewood and Jean Newlove of Theatre Workshop, for the basic grounding in technique they gave me; to Howard Goorney, who has always made the things I find difficult look ridiculously easy; to Brian Murphy and Glyn Edwards, for their participation in the exploratory work which formed the basis of my work; and to Paoli di Leonardis who first encouraged me to seek some pattern in the various experiments.

In later years, I am grateful to Tony Manser of the University of Southampton, who saw a significance in the work that I was blind to and contributed much to the philosophy behind it; to John Russell Brown, who encouraged me to make the work systematic, and took me to Birmingham to make this possible. I owe much to the contact I had with my colleagues in the Department of Drama and Theatre Arts in Birmingham; to Jane Winearls, who poured a sympathetic scorn on any of my easy generalisations; and to Gordon Davies and W. J. Hollenweger for showing me how insular the work had become at a time when I could see no way forward.

I am deeply indebted for the contact I have had over the years with three game-players of great genius, Albert Hunt, Ed Berman and the late Naftali Yavin, whose standards I still aspire to reach. I am similarly indebted to Christopher Fettes, Yat Malmgren and John Blatchley, of Drama Centre, for the support they have given me through their continuing belief that the work of the actor has a systematic and scientific basis. Without the determination and enthusiasm of the students of Group 8 of Drama Centre and the 'Theatre of Man' option in Birmingham the work would have taken years longer to arrive at its present stage.

Lastly, I acknowledge the help and support given by Pat Morgan in the preparation of this manuscript, and Jo Barker for making the writing of it possible. My children, regrettably, must wonder on reading this book why, when I spent so much time playing games with other people, I found so little time to play games with them.

C.B.

Contents

About Theatre Games – a critical introduction

One teaches best what one is learning oneself. Clive Barker

Since its publication over thirty years ago *Theatre Games* remains a classic for students and teachers of drama and I hope to explain this enduring popularity by examining the foundations of Clive Barker's approach to theatre training. I was a close friend of Clive's for the last twenty years of his life: our friendship began when he invited me to lead workshops in Poland with him and his great friend Albert Hunt. At first it seemed that they were just mucking about playing children's games – enjoyable, but what was the point for someone interested in 'serious' drama? I was not alone in this impression. Chris Johnston was 'training to be a Stanislavskian method actor' at Drama Centre 'when 'a short bearded man ... started throwing tennis balls around': it was Clive, and the fun and chaos of his teaching made Johnston realise that this was another, and equally valid way of teaching and learning drama.

> Pleasure was the springboard, lifting us into movement, dialogue, interaction. There was laughter. The work was accessible and lively, and the theoretical baggage light enough to carry.[1]

This was both the pleasure and the problem with Clive – he wore his learning very lightly, and since his games were opportunities for students to explore and to find out, he was always more interested in what his students thought than in expounding or imposing his own thoughts.

No surprise then that *Theatre Games* is a deceptively simple book: there are references to the movement pioneers Rudolf Laban (1879–1958), Moshe Feldenkrais (1904–1984), and theatre director Joan Littlewood (1914–2002), but overall the tone is conversational. Clive never indulged in theory for its own sake and when he did it was always tested and tempered through practice. *Theatre Games* is not a compendium of exercises and games; it is part autobiography, part reflection on the needs and nature of actor training, and part training and teaching manual. The narrative of

Theatre Games explains how he encountered certain problems and principles in actor training (in great part through his experience of working with Littlewood at Theatre Royal, Stratford East), how he developed theatre games (again from Littlewood) as his personal strategy to negotiate these problems, and finally how to understand the principles (pedagogical and neurological) underlying the playing of these games. Both at the beginning and the end of *Theatre Games* he freely admits that the necessarily theoretical form of a book is alien to his rather Socratic way of teaching:

> I have never used the work in the form in which it is set out in this book, which is simply the most convenient for presentation on the page. I would never, for instance, expose the basic principles on which the work is based before I started on it. In practice, these principles are revealed only as the actor works through various stages ... If an actor is told in advance what the purpose of an exercise is, this knowledge might push him towards doing the exercise, 'properly' or 'well' or 'efficiently' as an end in itself, and this would interfere with the experience and sensations that are encountered in simply 'trying' it. His concentration would be on the end result, instead of one the process or means, which could defeat everything I am trying to do. [8–9]*

In essence, his principle was 'see what happens when you try the exercises' [9]; in his teaching he always insisted that 'first you work then you talk', or as he put it in a letter to Chris Johnston, 'he allows himself "*three sentences before there is some action. Once we've done something then we can talk*"'.[2] Toward the end he writes that 'the form of the book acts as a limitation to free thought and response', and invites his readers to 'use it critically in the first instance; that is, to try to prove mistaken my hypotheses and explanations.' [217]

In the spirit of this invitation I intend to engage critically with some aspects of his thinking. I shall begin this overview of *Theatre Games* by looking at the history of theatre games – how Littlewood used them, and then how Clive developed them in his work with fellow actor Brian Murphy and others. For Littlewood games were one tool among many but before examining the thinking behind them, I want to consider some of the

*Numbers in square brackets refer to page numbers of this edition

different classes of game in Clive's book: those for warming up, for basic physical fitness, for posture, co-ordination, speed-of-reaction; those for finding out about Laban's movement qualities, the dynamics of space and rhythm, of ensemble and group dynamics; and those which are dramaturgical exercises.

Then I shall deal with the underpinning theory of *Theatre Games* much of which came from the researches that Feldenkrais published in *Body and Mature Behaviour* (1949). While Clive was one of the earliest practitioners to make extensive use of Feldenkrais' ideas, some of his extrapolations are, as I hope to show, mistaken. And yet when one compares their approach to teaching, we will see that they share many things in common and that Clive's theory is only faulty in its formulation: it is vindicated and redeemed through practice.

The history of games in theatre

Clive first came across games when at 'a Boy Scout Troop in Middles-borough'.[3][85] However, as he explains, it was Littlewood who showed how they could be used in the context of theatre. For example, 'The Raft of Medusa … a children's struggle game' was 'used with devastating effect by Littlewood in a projected production of *Danton's Death*'. We shall see later how and why he used children's games as a means of working on scenes and plays.

The second thing that he took from Littlewood is what he calls her '*via negativa*' (an expression more associated with Jerzy Grotowski) – that is, a form of training that works by taking away from the actor whatever prevents them from achieving their full potential. Littlewood's approach

> worked by breaking down the actor's preconceptions of himself and his work (that is, what 'worked' for him), and then tried to put him in situations where he could find a fresh, imaginative, and authentic response to the stimuli provided by the situation and by the other actors.[2]

In conversation he would describe her laying an actor bare, sometimes, in the case of Richard Harris (an early member of Theatre Workshop), quite literally. Clive's approach was less confrontational, and addressed certain resistances, limitations and difficulties within the actors:

1. The resistances of his body to carry out patterns of movement or actions which lie outside the normal use of his body.
2. Limitations placed upon his work by the difficulties of translating the intentions of his mind into physical activities.
3. The difficulties of engaging in seemingly spontaneous patterns of behaviour and social interaction, when he already knows the outcome of the action.[12]

I shall return to these principles when discussion theory later.

Clive's first step towards creating his own training came when the West End cast of Littlewood's production of Brendan Behan's *The Hostage* decided to work on movement during the day. It was clearly a difficult step.

> It is one thing to stand in a technical class and do as an experienced teacher tells you. It is another matter to try to train yourself, and yet another matter to tell someone else what they should do.[5]

Their dilemma was clarified in the following question:

> By what means can the actor train to extend his physical faculties that are pleasurable, unself-conscious, and possible for him to undertake without getting mentally and physically screwed up?[5]

His entire approach is summed up in this question, the answer to which, of course, is by playing games. We now turn to what games he used for what purposes.

The use of games in actor training

Littlewood was one of the earliest English enthusiasts of the writings and practices of movement pioneer and polymath Rudolf Laban. In her first and only year at RADA in 1933, her classes with Annie Fligg (one of Laban's pupils) gave her a lifelong taste for his approach to movement. She became quite an expert on Laban and she would give public lectures on him. Her company, Theatre Workshop, and Laban's Art of Movement Studio were both based on Oxford Road in Manchester in the late 1940s; when Littlewood moved to the East End of London, she was determined to continue her connection with Laban, and worked closely with Jean Newlove, one of his early protégés.

When Clive joined Littlewood in 1957 Laban movement was still being taught to the actors. He recognised its value in addressing 'specific movement problems directly, because they clearly revealed movements which I could not carry out, and that work attracted me more'.

> However, a major problem arose. Some of the actors could not do it, some found it impossible. The reason for their failure did not lie in any lack of physical aptitude. It lay in the mind. Faced with having to carry out technical exercises they somehow seized up and became mentally distressed. The experience created tensions within the company as it split into two groups, movers and non-movers.[4–5]

This is an incredibly subtle point: that it is the technical demands of this form of movement training which screws up actors *mentally* rather than physically. Later in the book he explains that the Laban system had 'always been for me the best basis for movement objectivisation', but then continues by making another crucial distinction: that 'the best movement teachers teach movement, not the system', and that less enlightened or less confident teachers focus on the terminology rather than the movement qualities that they refer to, and that this inhibits rather encourages movement since it supplies 'preconceived intentions and effects to be pursued'[46]. Once again, we return to his point that if 'an actor is told in advance what the purpose of an exercise is, this knowledge might push him towards doing the exercise, 'properly' or 'well' or 'efficiently' as an end in itself'.

What was the alternative to technical exercises? In a word, games.

> I have never found a technical exercise for which I couldn't find a direct parallel in the world of children's games. This by no means guarantees that the problem will be solved, but it can be tackled in a manner that is totally within the actor's experience and movement memory.[63]

A game provides a situation where the student can find things out for him or herself rather than trying to reproduce a formula given by the teacher. Once again, we hear an echo of Grotowski's rejection of recipes or instant solutions to acting problems. Games like Grandmother's Footsteps or Pirate's Treasure give the student the experience of moving in a certain way: the first 'works on the *control of quick, light movements*', the second on '*light, sustained movements*';[81] in Crossing the Ice children 'develop *quick, light, direct movements*'.[78] These are all terms that Laban uses in his theory of movement qualities: a movement can either be light or strong, sustained or quick, direct or flexible.

When it comes to providing a physical warm-up at the beginning of a work session, Clive's games are a delightful alternative to the mechanical abstraction of gymnastic exercises. Over and Under is a competitive relay game between two teams where 'the running players has to go over the head of one of his team-mates and under the legs of the next';[72] it can also be played with a ball. Although these exercises have been described in less than a couple of lines on a page, you have the stuff for twenty minutes' intense, engaged and delighted physical activity. Not only are the students engaged in a complete flexion (bending forward) and extension (reaching back) of the spine, but they are also learning how to work as a team, learning to organise themselves efficiently and to work rhythmically. They are doing the same amount of exercise as in a strenuous gymnastic work out, but are also learning how to work as an ensemble, and having a huge amount of fun at the same time. If you wanted another stretching exercise then look at his ball game on pages 74–75, which involves a phenomenal amount of stretching *without the students ever being conscious of the fact*. The student is only aware of playing the game, the physical stretching and working of the muscles and tendons is purely incidental. Barker admits to this subtle pedagogical strategy: 'All of these Games necessitate muscular activity, whilst directing the actor's attention away from the specific nature of the activity. The actor, therefore, tackles the movement obstacles through functional activities, and is prevented from becoming self-conscious about problems'.[79] Chris Johnston pointed out, Clive assumed a very 'low status' role as a teacher which might explain why he made so little theoretical capital from his wealth of practical insight. Possibly this is because he had been a working actor himself (though he actually trained as a Stage Manager and fell into Directing) and knew their needs. All his games are designed to open possibilities rather than impose technical or aesthetic rules.

The object is to make it possible for the actor to be able to produce as wide a range of movements in time and space as he can, so that he selects from these possibilities when he comes to a specific role or activity. This releases him from the restrictions of his own charac-teristics of movement. The object is not to produce a multi-potential puppet, since every human being will find new possibilities in his own way by using his own personal resources and overcoming his own resistances.[65]

The aim of developing a person's full potential was also central to Feldenkrais (one of whose books was called *The Potent Self*). Both sought to develop a '360 degree awareness of space', and three of the theatre games featured in the enclosed DVD-ROM – Tail Tag, Coins and Finger Tag address this question.

> The amount of 360 degree awareness of space, and the carriage this produces, along with the relationship patterns defined by the rules, make it possible to build gradually towards a complex social situation, and to produce a general pattern of social movement for two groups of characters.[129]

Tail Tag involves each of the players attaching a tail made from toilet roll (or a handkerchief or even a sock) into the back of their waist band, the aim of the game being to steal the other's tail whilst ensuring your own doesn't get stolen. As you can see from the DVD-ROM, Clive gets an immense amount of information from this game – it is about whether a person turns from their high or low centre; about shifting loyalties between the players; about the dynamic use of theatre space. These three games lead to the final exercise in the DVD-ROM which Clive nick-named the Clocking Game. Here we are dealing with a particular type of spatial-and-kinaesthetic awareness, one that is unique to performance. When there is a group of actors standing in a space and one of them moves, what happens to the overall feeling within the space? What do you as an actor in that space feel you need to do in response to that movement? Is the distribution of actors within the space unbalanced? The only similar exercise I know of was taught by Jacques Lecoq (1921–1999), where you imagine that the stage is balanced on a point in the centre so if anyone moves, the rest of the group has to rearrange itself to restore the state of balance. Clive's exercise works more from a sense of interpersonal dynamics as expressed in positions in space. The aim is to develop a sense of play within an ensemble, which, as Littlewood pointed out, is less like being an orchestral player under a conductor, and more like playing jazz which 'gives more scope for improvisation but it also requires more sensitivity to the other players. There is much more give and take'.[156]

When describing games which explore spatial awareness, Clive noted 'that it is possible to build gradually towards a complex social situation, and to produce a general pattern of social movement for two groups of characters'. This leads us back to the earlier discussion of how Littlewood used games as dramaturgical devices, that is, as a means of exploring a set of relationships within a particular scene or play. The two groups of characters in question are the Capulets and Montagues in *Romeo and Juliet*, and the scene is the street fight between the young men. This dramaturgical use of games is explained in the following two citations:

> In this sense the games in this book are used as parables. They are images of action, through which general principles and laws are transformed into living sensations of cause and effect, which make the processes involved easier to understand.[10]
>
> The strength of a game's structure, for me, is that the specific encounter, exchange or conflict can be isolated, worked on and taken directly into the situation of the play.[168]

'Images of action' is such a telling phrase to describe a theatre game and it has a particular application to Clive's use of blindfold games. In the DVD we see three blindfold games where an actor slashes out with a newspaper at the invisible assailants who surround him. One of these is an image of the action of Macbeth towards the end of the play when he is under attack from all sides. But Clive also suggests Bull in the Ring – where 'the "bull" has to break out of a circle of players'[87] – as a game which can provide an equally evocative theatre image:

> Macbeth says, 'They have tied me to a stake; I cannot fly, But bear-like I must fight the course.' It needs little adaptation to move from Bull in the Ring to a taunting game.'[90]

He also suggests that Bull in the Ring 'could well be used as the basis of an improvisation for *Woyzeck*'[90] and notes how Andrej Munk uses the game 'as a powerful image in his film *Passenger*':

> Among the stills in the first half are some showing a shipboard party during which the woman is attacked playfully by revellers. The image reappears in the second half when prisoners are selected for extermination in the prison camp.[87]

To explain this breadth of reference he refers to Roger Caillois' book *Man, Play Games* (1962) which had a big effect on his thinking about the connection between games and drama. These taunting games go back to the ancient 'rite of killing the old king and the bringing in of the new for the sake of the prosperity of the tribe. It is central to the concept of tragedy'.[87]

> The use of games is therefore not only a means of technical training and of exploring human behaviour and acting but a springboard for exploring the nature of drama and theatre.[88]

Later in the book he describes games as

> a tool through which I analyse and come to understand the action embodied in the text, and which I use to express, project or reinforce the psychological activities of the characters. The more I play with them, the more I learn.[153]

Anyone who has used theatre games in their teaching will know that even when no connection with a play or scene has been suggested, the situation becomes dramatic. An actor will not play a game indefinitely because it will not sustain 'attention and stimulate his energy flow for ever'. What happens is a 'gradual introduction of discipline' into the game which 'moves the playing into higher levels of skill',[79] and one moves from an uncontrolled game to a more structured drama. I remember playing British Bulldog and finally there were two actors facing a human wall through which they had to pass: there was no chance of them not being caught. The actors held that moment, and we agreed not even to play the final scene – it was already enough *as an image*.

Theory and theatre games

The section on blindfolds begins with *The Fight in the Dark*, adapted 'from a set piece in one of the Peking Operas'[57] and a rare example of a game which came from a play rather than vice-versa. The game is played with and without blindfolds to notice the very different bodily positions adopted by the actors (see illustrations 5 and 6 on page 59, and 7 and 8 on pages 60–61). Clive comments:

The major difference between the two versions is that, in the open-eyed version, the actor is concentrating on the *result*, consciously trying to create the illusion of darkness. The intention becomes totalised and intellectual; it gets in the way of the body/think processes, and the balance of his body is disturbed.[60]

This distinction between the intellectual and the bodily approach is central to Clive's notion of actor training. By body/think he means the kinaesthetic sense: 'the process by which we subconsciously direct and adjust the movements of our bodies in space, either in response to external stimuli, or to intentions arising in the mind'.[29] The *Oxford Companion to the Mind* (1987) offers a fuller definition, by explaining that since our sense of spatial orientation comes through our ears (and the vestibular system of our inner ears which provide our sense of balance), this sensory information firstly have to be co-ordinated, and then, if we are to act on this information (for example, to strike our assailant in *The Fight in the Dark*) this 'requires that sensory spatial information be co-ordinated with the motor commands which control the movements of limbs. This is the process of *sensori-motor co-ordination*'.[3] Rather than a kind of bodily thinking, the kinaesthetic is a complex process of matching and coordinating sensory input with appropriate motor output.

Clive frankly admits that he was 'pushed towards learning about the interaction of mind and body through the nervous system' after he had already worked out his theory of actor training. And he felt that he needed this 'understanding of the nervous system as an explanation for what I was doing. It seems the clearest way of explaining it *in* a book'.[8] All his information is derived from Feldenkrais' *Body and Mature Behaviour* (1949). It was from Feldenkrais that Clive drew the opposition between the front and back brain by which he distinguishes intellectual thinking from bodily thinking:

The front part of my brain I use for visualising, for reflective meditation, for precisely defining my thoughts and ideas, for thinking in abstract, and for the deliberate conscious control and direction of my actions. ... The back brain also appears to control my physical actions and reactions instinctively without my being directly conscious of what is happening.[17]

Feldenkrais made sense of what he had discovered through practical experiment. But just as his account of the kinaesthetic sense was partial, so his neurology is similarly sketchy. While it is roughly accurate to say that we use the front brain for visualising, this only after the primary data from the retina has been processed in the visual cortex at the back of the brain, and which is then fed back as information. He ignores the intricate processes of sensory perception and how this sensory perception is matched by an appropriate motor response. He defends his approach by arguing that 'the terminology used doesn't help actors':

> Terms like motor-cortex, ganglia, proprioceptive nerve endings would inhibit me from acting, rather than help me, unless I could relate them to direct physical sensations and experiences I have had.[24]

Here he muddles two roles: his job as a writer who has chosen to explain the actor's processes neurologically, and then his former job as a working actor. You cannot dodge behind one to avoid dealing with the other. While this isn't nitpicking, we must remember that the general point being made is central to the actor's work: Clive notes that 'Stanislavski is constantly trying to find ways for the actor to work through the subconscious mind/body mechanisms'.[20] Ironically, it is precisely the misapplication of Stanislavski's 'terminology' that can lead actors to 'intellectually define what they are going to do, or want to do ... instead of converting their intentions into physical reflex processes'.[45–46] This is the same argument he used in his critique of teaching Laban through terminology. Thus, if we think of 'front' and 'back brain' as metaphorical rather than neurophysiological terms we have a useful, indeed a liberating, approach to training.

> Somehow if you let the back part of the brain work, without conscious interference, the body works more efficiently. If you concentrate on making the body work, you interfere with its working. Army instructors, taking recruits round obstacle courses, will always tell the recruit not to think about what he has to do, but just do it. Those who think, fail most often to gain the objective.[18]

The words 'interference' and 'interfere' remind us Clive's approach is a *via negativa*, one which removes blocks to efficient movement.

Later in *Theatre Games* he makes a very telling distinction between awareness and consciousness and stresses that the teacher needs 'to assist the actor to be aware rather than conscious of the way the mind and body co-ordinate naturally'.[53] This subtle and opposition gets us to the heart of the Feldenkrais Method. Both men's approach to education and development share many features: a focus upon the kinaesthetic sense rather than intellectual analysis; a playful and heuristic approach to learning which focuses upon the experience of the learner rather than the knowledge of the teacher, which is about playing and listening out (actually learning how to learn); a way of working which is less about work and trying, as in Clive's adage, 'Nothing succeeds like failure, because failure causes the actor to think, re-assess, and try a different way'.[131] Both men helped their students renegotiate their patterns rather than aiming to destroy and then re-building personalities – a *via negativa* based on humane negotiation rather than destruction. Clive's discussion of balance and posture owes an immense amount of Feldenkrais, though, once again, many of his discoveries were a result of his own practical experiments rather than his reading. Both men were avid autodidacts and experimenters.

The Theatre Game is equivalent to the hundreds of lessons in Awareness Through Movement that Feldenkrais created in the 1950s, 60s and 70s; both are structured movement experiences by which the student can engage in active and autonomous learning through doing (with awareness). As Clive notes, 'One cannot teach "acting". One can only create situations in which the actor can learn and develop'.[6]

> The object of the games and exercises is to reveal to the actor what happens when he works, and to help him be aware of the mind/body processes involved in his work. What use he then makes of this understanding is up to him. One can never predict what value any individual will get or take from any exercise. One should never try to make an exercise or game 'work'; one should set it up and let it take place.[51]

Both men insisted upon students not trying, that they listen to the process rather than fixating on the goal, of playing with curiosity rather than working. Many of Feldenkrais' lessons take place on the floor where one rediscovers the infant's acts of autonomous learning-through-finding-out. Similarly, Clive considers games to be an example of a child's 'process of learning through experimentation'.[63] He goes on, 'One goes back to the root processes of learning, by which he acquired movement skills in the first place, and this helps him rediscover lost skills, or those which have atrophied. ... It substitutes for the pain of learning the joy of re-discovery'.[64] This surely has been influenced by his reading of Feldenkrais who describes the baby's movement learning thus:

> For successful learning we must proceed at our own rate. Babies repeat each novel action clumsily at their own rate until they have enough of it. This occurs when the intention and its performance are executed so that they are just one act which feels like an intention only.[4]

Put another way, once babies have mastered the movement, they can then simply do it at will; as Feldenkrais puts it, the intention and the performance become one. What characterises both men's account of child learning is that it is self-directed and rooted in the child's own experience. Their approach was *heuristic* – that is, about the student finding out for themselves, rather than being told.

> The keynote to all the work is that it is *a process of exploration and discovery*, not the direct acquisition of practical skills which the actor does not possess. The acquisition of skills is the by-product of the work.[51]

This quotation also evokes his version of the *via negativa* – a training which is about building confidence and engendering a spirit of enquiry through taking away hang-ups and resistances; a training where the actor is given autonomy. This feeds in to his vision of a theatre where

> The actor is the theatre, and the sooner we give it back to him the better.[211]

Conclusion

In this introduction I have selected four groups of Clive's theatre games: for warming-up, for developing a sensitivity to movement qualities, for spatial dynamics and ensemble, and for dramaturgy. There was no space for trust or speed of reaction games, for his theories about theatre narrative and the tenses of acting, or of speech production. The important thing is to understand why he used games rather than exercises to tackle questions of technique and physical training; games rather than improvisation or discussion to work on text; and why he drew on Feldenkrais to help articulate his theory of actor training. For all his wariness of terminology and theorising, Clive grasped the importance of this very different approach to teaching and learning – it was a theory for practice. If Clive was difficult to take seriously it was precisely because he insisted upon the pedagogical value of playful experiment; because he understood that theory must come after practice, and then be tested again (and again) *through* practice. There is a deadly serious intent behind this playfulness, and it has to be defended.

While Clive might not have developed his study of either Feldenkrais or neurophysiology any further, he points the way for future research into learning and teaching. Advances in brain imaging over the last twenty years means that his (and Feldenkrais') claims about physiology can neurology can be tested with much greater depth and rigour. Beyond understanding the specific case of how actors learn their practice, this research might help explain and defend a less coercive form of education which is centred upon the learner rather than the educator.

About the DVD-ROM – learning through watching

The DVD-ROM offers students a chance to see a master at work. Peter Hulton filmed two of Clive's workshops for the International Workshop Festival, in 1996 and 2001. About these videos Clive once said, 'It's all very well seeing me teach, but you don't know what I was thinking'. Taking him at his word I recorded his commentaries on what he saw in the exercises and what might have been in his mind whilst teaching them. In a sense, this only develops on a method that he already practised.

> Work is carried out then as an alternating process of doing, and watching others do ... One acts, one watches, one acts again, one watches again and so on.[57]

Discussions would follow these observation sessions 'to provide the basic vocabulary' – thus developing a theory from practice, one to be tested out in further practice. When doing these interviews Clive turned to me and said, 'Well, at least there's one thing I know, and that's how to observe movement'. It was a skill that he wanted to develop in his students. I hope that this helps you to understand the man and his extraordinary eye for movement and human interaction.

Page References for Games played in the DVD-ROM

Speed of Reaction Games – p. 82
Grandmother's Footsteps – p. 81
Pirate's Treasure – p. 81
Finger tag – p. 125
Coin-tag – pp. 128–9
Tail Tag – p. 129
The Clocking Game – pp. 138–9

Dick McCaw, London, October 2009

Introduction

This book is about the work and art of the actor. It is intended for actors, those who work with actors, and those who are interested in the work of actors and in the Theatre in general. In writing the book I have found it necessary in the early chapters to set down certain scientific facts and theories which underlie my work and to quote occasionally from scientific works. Readers should not be dismayed at first glance through these chapters. I have kept them as simple as possible: the quotations are directly relevant to the practical work and the book then moves quickly into the field of acting practice.

The work set down here is a stage of development reached in my teaching and acting practice after nearly twenty years' work. As such, it does not record many of the stages I have outgrown. Nor is it a fully developed programme of work. It takes its present form because it has been developed according to my own needs, and the needs of students and actors who have worked with me. I am encouraged to set it down by the fact that my own understanding of the work of the actor, and my attempts to communicate that understanding in teaching situations, or in rehearsal, have been of value and assistance to others.

The development of the work

I differ from almost all other actors in one significant way. I had no initial ambition to act. My ambition, when I entered the theatre at the age of 23, in 1954, was to write. I had no pretensions to act, direct, or do any other work in the theatre, but I had to earn a living whilst I learned to write, and I imagined that the theatre was the best place to learn how to write plays. I enrolled for a one-year course in stage management at the Bristol Old Vic School, and discovered a wider vocation: I became involved in all aspects of the theatre.

The School, at that time, was in a disturbed state. It was the first year of a new regime, and it had largely run to seed under the old. During the third term the confusion was such that I was able to suggest to the Director that he let me direct two productions with the first year students, and he was relieved to agree. It is not the ideal way to run a school but it was one way of learning. I directed Whiting's *Saint's Day* and Tennessee Williams' *Hello from Bertha*. I never saw either performed as I was carried off to hospital on a stretcher the day before the dress rehearsals, as a result of having to rehearse by day and work by night in order to pay my way.

With *Saint's Day* I had beginner's luck. I was strongly in sympathy with the play. The actors were enthusiastic and the production just grew between us. It was well-received. *Hello from Bertha* was another world for me and the actors; lacking the technique, I directed it according to the method of Elia Kazan, as culled from various books and magazine articles. By the time I came out of hospital nobody would discuss it. It was plainly a disaster. It could not have been otherwise. Luckily for me there was *Saint's Day* to discuss. Unfortunately one of the actresses in *Hello from Bertha* was turned out of the school because of her performance in it. She married a year later, so she didn't stay on my conscience for long, but her dismissal forced me to analyse what we had done together, because I had thought her work in rehearsal was very good. The analysis was not made easier by the fact that no-one would discuss the production, and my realisation that the direction had been totally misconceived. Had it not been a failure, or had I only directed *Saint's Day*, I might have had to wait some years before beginning a very critical assessment of the why, and wherefore, of the actor's work. As it was, fired with one lucky success and chastened by one disaster at the outset, I switched tracks and determined to be a director, realising that I needed to know a great deal more about the actor's work, for which I had no formal training.

When I had convalesced I joined Theatre Workshop as a Stage Manager and, in the manner of anyone who goes there to do any job other than acting, I became an actor. I had no ambitions as an actor, but it seemed that to learn about the work of the actor necessitated some experience of actually doing it, so I flung myself into it. It was a very painful experience. At that time, Littlewood made extensive use of the '*via negativa*' in training her actors. She slammed all the wrong doors in their faces until they were forced to find the right one. I realise now that she worked by breaking down the actor's preconceptions of himself and his work (that is, what 'worked' for him), and then tried to put him in situations where he could find a fresh, imaginative, and authentic response to the stimuli provided by the situation and by the other actors. She systematically destroyed all the security of past solutions to acting problems which the actor carries around inside him, and which he holds on to, applying them, in a generalised fashion, to new areas of work, and forced him to make a specific response to each new situation. It can be a frightening experience for an actor. He has certain techniques, tricks, mannerisms which he knows have been successful in the past – to discard them faces him with the fear of failing to find new responses which will be successful in the new situation. Littlewood, at that time, expressed this through phrases like 'In order to be a creative artist you must risk failure', and 'Go out to fail, not succeed. Efficiency is death in the theatre', For many actors these were exciting words to hear, but terrifying to put into practice. At the time the door slammed on me, I was shattered without knowing how to put myself together again.

In the second production, *The Good Soldier Schweik*, I played a manic Military Policeman. The easiest way to break an actor down is to first of all build him up. I was hailed as a comic genius in rehearsal. Old hands warned me I was being set up for the chop, but that was little help when the chop came. I was never able to repeat in performance what I had done instinctively in rehearsal. There must have been some performances she missed seeing, but my memory of the production is that she came round *every* evening to distribute notes. The other actors got detailed notes. All she ever said to me was, 'You weren't there' or 'You still weren't there', I was reduced to pursuing her for some explanation, which she never gave, and I was almost in despair. I encountered one of the actor's chief problems: the harder you try, the worse it gets. The more you think about what you are doing, the harder it is to do it. The more clearly you work out what you are going on stage to do, the worse the result. The more single-minded you are in your intention, the less responsive you are to the other actors. It took me eighteen months to work out that what I was doing was going on stage to make something happen, instead of going on to *let* something happen. When I had learned that lesson I never forgot it, nor the pain it cost me to learn it. In the process of trying to sort out the problem, and all the others I had to face, I learned a great deal about the actor's work. It took me so much trouble to learn it that, in the process, I became totally engrossed by the business of acting.

The initial stimulus to work lay in the problems I faced, and in the attempt to try to understand why all the other actors were better than I was, by what means they made what I found difficult appear easy.

For most actors, technique is a means to an end: performance. For me, it is a constant source of study and fascination. I enjoy acting, it is a necessary part of my life, but the core of my life is the processes through which the actor works, and the difficulties he encounters in working. What merit I have as a teacher of acting, and, largely, as a director, is because I have had to face all the problems from scratch, and I have fallen into, and crawled out of, all the traps.

Because I had no initial vocational drive to act and, consequently, no formal training, I have been forced to work it out methodically and objectively. I had no natural resources to fall back on: I have had to develop them. It is the hard way to learn. It doesn't have to be that hard to learn, and most of the training work I have developed is the result of a search for ways in which the learning can be made easier, and to cut out as many as possible of the unproductive mistakes and pitfalls that I have made and fallen into along the way.

I began to make the work systematic in 1958 and again the initial stimulus came from Littlewood. At that time the Theatre Workshop company was probably the only company which carried out training work during the rehearsal and performance periods, although many companies do so now. The work fell into two areas. Warm-up exercises and games were carried out with the general intention of loosening up the actor's body, and hopefully his imagination; and technical movement classes were taken by an experienced, Laban-trained teacher. We also did vocal work, but this was largely a disaster. I was given some of the warm-up sessions to lead.

I could see the benefits of warm-up sessions, in that they got the blood circulating and woke the actors up, but I was not happy because they seemed so haphazard. It didn't seem to matter very much what you did, it was simply a generalised, play-about activity which somehow, someway, got the actors moving about on their feet and off their backsides. I was aware that actors think better on their feet, but I felt it ought to be possible to be more specific. I tried a number of experiments, but could find no general principle behind what I was doing.

The technical movement classes, I could see, attacked movement problems directly, because they clearly revealed movements which I could not carry out, and that work attracted me more. However, a major problem arose. Some of the actors could do it, some found it impossible. The reason for their failure did not lie in any lack of physical aptitude. It lay in the mind. Faced with having to carry out technical exercises, they somehow seized up and became mentally distressed. The experience created tensions within the company as it split into two groups, movers and non-movers.

The next year, when the production of *The Hostage* moved into the West End, a number of those actors who had been enthusiastic about the movement work wanted to use the time, allowed by the run of the play, to carry on the work begun at Stratford East. We hired a rehearsal room during the week, and, because I had led some of the warm-ups and become more involved than most in the training process, I was given the job of leading the sessions. No sooner had we started than we, too, became smitten with the same mental seizures that had afflicted the other actors at Stratford. It is one thing to stand in a technical class and do as an experienced teacher tells you. It is another matter to try to train yourself, and yet another matter to tell someone else what they should do. The experience was very similar to that I had undergone in *Schweik*. The harder we worked, the more distressed we became. The question was formulated, 'By what means can the actor train to extend his physical faculties, that are pleasurable, unselfconscious, and possible for him to undertake without getting mentally and physically screwed up?' By lucky accident, and in desperation, I went back to the one physical area of training that was enjoyable – the warm-up games and exercises – and began to develop the games work that forms a large part of this book. Alongside this, I have tried to answer the complementary question, 'What is it that screws up the actor when he works?' I have been trying to answer these questions for the last fifteen years, and to suggest productive ways of overcoming the basic problems that face the actor.

The work has been developed through a number of activities. At times groups of actors have worked with me, inside the production situation and outside it. I have taught in drama schools and a university Drama Department. I have used the work as the basis of lecture demonstrations, and as a means of discussing the actor and the theatre in a practical frame-work rather than in abstract. I have spent a period training a professional company in West Germany. The form in which the work is set out reflects all the stages it has gone through. It is not complete; there is still much to be done. The work has been both strengthened and hindered by being carried out for long periods in elementary teaching situations. It has gained from the need to clarify what the basic activities of the actor are. It has been weakened because the situation concentrated too strongly on the elementary problems facing the actor. The more advanced areas of the work are still awaiting exploration. The work I did in West Germany with experienced professional actors began to open up whole new areas, as they skipped through the basics without effort and pushed the more advanced work forward.

The teaching situation

In the sense that it has taken nearly twenty years for me to develop the work through trial and error, it is difficult to set it down. Every teacher has his own way of working, and this is often inseparable from his personality, the problems he is led to face, and the specific methods he finds to overcome them. Insofar as I have tried throughout the period to understand and overcome the obstacles to my own development as an actor, I am often in a position to clarify the problems that another actor faces, and to suggest the means by which to tackle them. But, from then on, I must work strictly in terms of his attempts, using my own experience only as a guideline, but never insisting that what 'works' for me will, of right, 'work' for him. If there is a 'right' way for any actor to tackle the problem he faces, then he must find it himself. One cannot teach 'acting'. One can only create situations in which the actor can learn and develop.

Every actor has said at some time in rehearsal, 'It doesn't work'. No director, faced with this, would dream of saying, 'Make it work'. Suggestions have to be made for 'trying' another way. The same is true of teaching. Often an actor has to try other ways of tackling the problem before he can accept my invitation to try my suggestion. One must be patient, which is never easy. In the event, the actor frequently has to face a problem which he cannot overcome by any of the means available to him, before you can help him. With young and student actors this happens continually throughout their training. Their appetite for work exceeds their capabilities and they are constantly demanding help.

What 'works' for the experienced actor in rehearsal and performance is built up over the years through a process of trial and error and is rarely objectivised. We are happy when we are meeting the demands of the play and the director; we are distressed when we are not. For security, many actors cling to a limited technique which has served them well on previous occasions. They apply the same restricted means to a wide variety of situations, a process which, in part, is known as 'cutting the role down to size' or 'finding the role in yourself instead of yourself in the role'. This is also the source of 'type-casting', of an actor playing only a very limited range of roles. There are many reasons for this practice. It is, for some actors, a profitable line of work; casting directors try to make life easy, by casting an actor in the sort of role he has played successfully before; occasionally, actors are afraid of stretching beyond their known abilities, because they fear their limitations might be exposed, and failure result. Most actors resent 'type-casting', and feel themselves capable of a much wider range of roles than they are called on to play, but they experience anxiety and insecurity when asked to extend themselves beyond what they know they can do.

Many actors are conscious of a distance between their intentions and their achievements in the roles they play. Curiously, when rehearsal and performance make few demands on their abilities, most actors are unhappy. When demands are made of him that go beyond his known capabilities, the actor experiences insecurity, unless he can be shown ways of tackling the problem. When this is done, he can often produce his most creative work. With older, more experienced actors I have encountered a surprising willingness to explore alternative ways of working, providing I can work in their terms; that is, they must not be faced with an entirely new situation, which they cannot relate to past experience. Many experienced actors, who are used to a very technical way of working, panic when it is suggested that they throwaway the script and improvise. In this respect, every teaching situation for the actor has got to keep returning to a very basic level.

There doesn't exist in this country any generally accepted 'method' of acting, or philosophy of theatre. Life would perhaps be easier if, for example, there was general acceptance of Stanislavski's work as a basic method providing a terminology which could be used to discuss acting. But this is not so, and one must work always from the position of the actor's own technical means and understanding. If one can do this, one gains the actor's confidence, and one can begin to suggest, step by step, other ways of tackling the problems. I must say, though, that, whenever I have asked or been asked to work with experienced professional actors on general training, there has been eagerness to participate. This is largely because the general teaching session as opposed to the rehearsal does not suffer from the need to tackle the specific problems of the play. A rehearsal is usually concerned with *what* does and what doesn't 'work' and how to put it right; teaching is largely concerned with *why* things do or don't work. The rehearsal situation is concerned with utilising whatever resources the actor possesses in the mounting of the play; the teaching situation is concerned with developing those resources, or rather with removing the obstacles to the actor and fully utilising the potential of his mind, voice and body. Away from the pressures of rehearsal, many actors are eager to work on these problems.

The uses of this work

The work I have set down in this book has been largely used either to tackle specific problems with young actors, or to form the basis for an exploration of the acting processes with more experienced actors. It is not a 'method', except insofar as it is my method. Beyond that it can only be the starting point from which someone else might construct his own method, nothing more. It should never be accepted uncritically by someone else just because it works for me. In fact, it will probably be more productive, if anyone using it were to begin by trying to prove my hypotheses to be mistaken, rather than correct. If in this critical process, he succeeds in making it work for himself, it then becomes part of his own method. He has taken it from me, and it is no longer mine.

In any case, I have never used the work in the form in which it is set out in this book, which is simply the most convenient for presentation on the page. I would never, for instance, expose the basic principles on which the work is based before I started on it. In practice, these principles are revealed only as the actor works through various stages. I started work specifically on the actor's problems. Along the way I have read far and wide to try and understand the precise nature of the difficulties and obstacles. Slowly I have been pushed towards learning about the interaction of mind and body through the nervous system. But the work was almost fully developed pragmatically to its present stage before I came round to this. I have ended up with an understanding of the nervous system as an explanation for what I was doing. It seems the clearest way of explaining it *in a book*. Many actors who have worked with me will be amazed to read it, since no discussion of it had ever entered our work.

As a rationalisation of the principles behind my work, it is important to anyone who might want to take ideas from me and use them, but the principle does not justify the work. Nor does the work illustrate the principle. Having set it all down, I have a fear of this becoming the case. If an actor is told in advance what the purpose of an exercise is, this knowledge might push him towards doing the exercise 'properly' or 'well' or 'efficiently' as an end in itself, and this would interfere with the experience and sensations that are encountered in simply 'trying' it. His concentration would be on the end result, instead of on the process or means, which would defeat everything I am trying to do. If the games and exercises are to be used, then read the explanation, stow it away at the back of your mind, forget it, see what happens when you try the exercises, and take it from there.

The order of the exercises is not mandatory because they are used according to whatever form the problem takes when the actor faces it at a particular time. They could be the basis of a training programme, and even of a production method, but only with an acting ensemble; that is, a company which is going to work as a team over a considerable period of time, with a high level of commitment to the work as a group product. I believe that such a company provides the richest performance work, when the common and complementary abilities and needs are explored in teamwork, and not simply amalgamated or disguised by the choreographic abilities of the director. Such ensembles are very difficult to build and maintain in the theatre as it exists at the moment in this country, but there are a number of small groups and companies beginning to feel their way towards building an acting ensemble, and the work set out in this book may help them along the way.

In the meantime, no actor need ever fear that I would demand that he participate in the games and exercises before working with me in rehearsal. The job of the director is to work in whatever terms the actor is able to work. As a directing tool, the work set out enables me to be clear and objective about the specific problems an actor encounters in rehearsal and performance, and more often in training; and this hopefully enables me to help him in his work. But in working with actors, one starts with what one has, and not with an ideal. My belief in the acting ensemble is not that it is the only way of working, but that it offers the actor the greatest opportunities for developing and strengthening his work.

However, the work has been developed not only as a practical means of tackling problems facing the *actor*. The teaching situation has one other major requirement: that is, to make *non-actors* clearly and practically aware of the various means the actor uses to rehearse and perform. Having to do this has helped me make the work more objective and clear. In this sense the games in this book are used as parables. They are images of action, through which general principles and laws are transformed into living situations of cause and effect, which make the processes involved easier to understand. In this way, this book may contribute to the general understanding of the theatre, and of the work of the actor, which I see as central to any discussion of theatre.

Lastly, because the work has developed alongside my own work and understanding of the theatre, and has largely been the instrument of my own education and development, there is behind the work a philosophy which I hope will emerge in the reading.

CHAPTER 1

The work of the actor

The work of the actor may be said to fall into five main areas:

(1) He exhibits real physical skills (including vocal skills). That is, he makes demands upon his body apparatus that go beyond the general level of use and ability which apply in everyday life.
(2) He exhibits mimetic skills. That is, he simulates physical states and activities which are not real for him.
(3) He imaginatively explores situations of time, space and character which are not real for him.
(4) He exhibits patterns of human behaviour which are not natural to him.
(5) While engaging in all these activities, he interacts with other human beings, namely, the other actor/characters and the audience.

The actor's work therefore depends upon: (1) physical fitness and flexibility; (2) his ability to control the activities of his body resources; (3) the range of his imagination; (4) his ability to put the intentions of his imagination into immediate physical effect; (5) his ability to interact spontaneously with other people.

The terms in which these activities are exercised will depend upon the demands of the play, the performance situation, and the style of the production. A large part of the actor's work (and training) is concerned with the content of his work, and has to do with study of the text, study of character and situations, and study of historical modes of behaviour. From this he derives his understanding of the play, the production, and the part he is to play in it. My main concern here, however, is to examine how the actor converts his understanding of what is required of him into intentions; how he converts his intentions into physical activities; how he adjusts those activities according to the needs and responses of the other actors and, incidentally, the audience.

None of the activities of the actor is unique to him. All occur in everyday life. The processes by which he carries out his work are common to all human beings. The significant difference for the actor is that he chooses consciously to present these activities and regularly to repeat their patterns of action in the presence of an audience. Whereas in everyday life these activities are in response to economic or social pressures or stimuli, and are subject to the controlling discipline of the social and economic necessities of life, the actor chooses to express himself through the abstracted activity of play, and to subject himself to the arbitrary disciplines of an artificial situation.

The artificiality of the theatre situation creates certain pressures for the actor. His work is subject to constant public scrutiny, he lives with the fear of failure; he is regularly placed, through the exercise of his imagination, in critical social and personal situations of which he has no direct experience. He is often called upon to exhibit in public demonstrations of physical skills, or the mimetic representation of those skills, for which he has served no apprenticeship. He has to produce at will, and in a hurry, convincing representations of patterns of human behaviour and interaction which, in real life, happen spontaneously *in response* to external stimuli. He has to repeat these activities, apparently spontaneously, time and time again, at arbitrarily fixed intervals, and often in totally different locales. I am concerned with the processes through which he carries out this work, and the obstacles that have to be overcome in exercising them.

The obstacles arise in these areas:

(1) The resistances of his body to carrying out patterns of movement, or actions, which lie outside the normal use of his body.
(2) Limitations placed upon his work by the difficulties of translating the intentions of his mind into physical activities.
(3) The difficulties of engaging in seemingly spontaneous patterns of behaviour and social interaction, when he already knows the outcome of the action.

These problems occur in every actors' work and each actor devises his own ways of coping with them. The first is tackled during training by movement and voice classes to give the actor a basic technique. This work is led by specialised teachers, and I have suggested that the actor often runs into problems when he leaves the teacher, and tries to keep in practice on his own. Some actors do keep up their physical exercise; more keep up their vocal exercises; many do not keep up either. It is a normal and understandable human failing that we find it difficult to drive ourselves to do things which are not immediately necessary or enjoyable.

The actor's life often includes long periods of unemployment; solo practice of technical exercises is usually tedious, often distressing, and only very rarely enjoyable. The fact may have stung Stanislavski to demand:

> Let someone explain to me why the violinist who plays in an orchestra on the tenth violin must daily perform hour-long exercises, or lose his power to play? Why does the dancer work over daily every muscle in his body? Why do the painter, the sculptor, the writer practise their art each day and count that day lost when they do not work? And why may the dramatic artist do nothing, spend his day in coffee-houses and hope for the gift of Apollo in the evening? Enough. Is this an art when its priests speak like amateurs? There is no art that does not demand virtuosity.[1]

But the situation he worked in was different from ours. The actor, when working, works long hard hours. The rehearsal time is almost always too short for the production work that has to be done in it. There is little time and energy for technical practice. Facilities do not exist for the actor to train outside of work. Dance and movement classes are available, but the cost, however reasonable, is usually beyond the actor's means. It is very hard to make yourself keep in practice when there is not the immediate stimulus of work to drive you to it.

I know an actor should work on his voice and body for at least an hour every day, but he has my sympathy. I find it difficult to make myself work and get into condition, unless I have a direct reason for doing so. Apart from which, most of the work an actor is offered makes very little demand upon his body. He can skate through the average television play or serial without ever breaking into a sweat. Drama school gets actors into the habit of working physically, but it is very easy to lose the habit. We coast along until we hit a problem that our physical condition or aptitude does not allow us to solve, and then we have to work. Often the problem can be avoided by altering the activity until it does fall within the normal range of our body use, and in the circumstances this is often necessary, because it is too late to tackle it when we run up against it in rehearsal. Or we tackle it by the sheer hard grind of repetitive practice.

The second and third obstacles occur constantly in the actor's work and are tackled in a variety of ways, which the actor rarely, if ever, objectivises. Phrases occur in the actor's vocabulary which give some clues. 'Throwing it away' and 'winging it' are two of these, as though by ignoring the problem it will somehow disappear (which, surprisingly, it can do). The actor is encouraged in rehearsal to 'stop worrying about it, and just do it', or 'try it', or 'let it go'. Actors are told they are 'trying too hard', 'trying to make it happen' instead of 'letting it happen'. They are told they are 'working too hard'; they should 'just relax', and 'it will come'.

Watching actors work, one can often observe a physical process at work. Visually it appears that the actor is sinking the thoughts down inside himself, through constant repetition of the lines being tried, accompanied by physical actions like tapping the foot or beating the hand in rhythm. Often, the actor walks through the moves again and again, emphasising the rhythm. Frequently, one can see the actor straighten from a hunched-over position into a more erect position as though some sort of swallowing process was going on. Sometimes he will say he is 'letting it sink in'. Sometimes the activity appears to take the form of a run up: the actor technically runs through the previous lines or units of the scene hunched over in posture and then suddenly springs upright into the action and line he is working on. He often says at the end of the process, 'I've got it now, I can do it'. Sometimes he will say 'I can't get it', or 'I can't take it in now. I'll have to go away and work on it. I'll mark it for now', and he methodically walks through the shape and stages of the activity.

Perhaps the strongest clue to what is happening lies in the phrases which regularly arise in rehearsal, 'It doesn't *feel* right', or 'I can't *feel* it', or, sometimes, 'I think I get the *feel* of it'; as though the process had to be converted into a physical sensation in order to carry it out and preserve it. When it goes, the actor says, 'I've lost it'. A number of directors I have worked with, including myself, get infuriated by actors saying this sort of thing, and the extreme answer is, 'You're not there to feel it, do it'. The dispute is whether the actor must reach the physical sensation himself, in isolation, before attempting the activity, or whether the sensation will arise naturally out of the unpremeditated performance of the activity.

In either event, the process involves (and the obstacles arise from) transforming mental activity into physical actions; it also involves an awareness of the physical sensations produced by these actions, which will enable the actor to preserve the experience of the activity, so that he can later recreate it. What is also well-known in the theatre is that, when the conversion of thought into action runs into problems, the harder you try to make it happen, the worse it gets, and general unhappiness ensues. More conscious mental effort appears to reinforce the obstacles and to cause greater frustration.

At later stages of rehearsal, when the interplay between actors is inhibited by actors still having to concentrate on what they are doing, directors will often encourage them to 'trust it', 'forget it', or, again, 'throw it away', as though mental and physical concentration and effort interferes with the interaction of the group. It is obvious that an actor who still has to think hard about his lines holds up the work of the cast, because he can't work with the other actors. The terms 'Forget it' and 'Trust it' seem to presume that the activity can be safely left to some subconscious level of direction, which will adequately take care of what needs to be done, without the actor being conscious of it. It is this which I wish to explore. The theory of delegating all action to the subconscious is central to Stanislavski's teachings on acting. He advises us to put our trust in the subconscious mind.

> Do not try to find a solution of some difficulty in your part by sheer stubbornness of will. Leave it alone for a time, achieve a state of complete repose, and changes the problems of your attention.[1]

Magarshack, interpreting Stanislavski, confuses the issue:

> Another method of inducing subconsciousness to take over more and more of the actor's conscious work is for him to concentrate on his big problems, which will automatically leave the small problems to his subconsciousness.[2]

The advice is sound to the extent that it relates very often to what the actor instinctively does in rehearsal. It is a well-known simple human phenomenon that if you can't remember something, think of something else, and often what you were trying to remember suddenly pops up in your mind. I take issue with the concept on two grounds. Firstly because the actor today has to play many works which do not have the psychological *through lines* and *super-objectives*, or *ruling ideas* which are the bigger issues that Stanislavski advises his actors to concentrate upon. Secondly because, however useful the concept may be, it persists in keeping some activity in the conscious mind, which is likely to interfere with the natural functions of the sub-concious mind and the physical actions of the body. To understand how this happens we need to be more specific about how the conscious and subconscious parts of the mind work.

CHAPTER 2

The mind

The period of rehearsal, for the actor, is one in which he absorbs a great deal of material about the character he is playing and about the dramatic situation, as well as taking account of the director's intentions. He has to learn the lines of the text and remember them and the precise movements and placings in the choreography of the scene. Often he must impose upon the lines and the movements a meticulous attention to pace and rhythm – what is called 'timing'. All of this material is perceived – initially – both intellectually and as something external to his normal personal behaviour. It must be consciously apprehended, taken in, and transformed into projects of action or physical activities, which can later be re-created, subconsciously – that is, without thinking about it. If any of it does come 'naturally' to him, it is only as a result of training or experience over a long period.

What is also apparent in rehearsals is that, until the actor has fully absorbed all this material, he cannot 'do it'. It is common, in rehearsal, to have an actor say 'I'm sorry I can't *do* it, because I'm still thinking about the words'. Occasionally, with difficult texts, the action will be disrupted by the actor 'trying to think ahead'. He knows a difficult, sticky passage is coming, and he tries consciously to anticipate it in his mind and invariably finds that the flow of action is totally disrupted. He frequently 'dries' on passages of dialogue which were until then 'safe' for him. This is not an absolute law. During long runs, when the actor is absolutely secure in what he is doing, there have been many stories of actors carrying on two mental activities at once. I have seen actors 'count the house' whilst in mid-speech. I have known actors come off-stage after a scene and say 'I've just thought of something' and come out with something totally divorced from the action. Naturally the actor runs a risk by slackening concentration on-stage, but it is possible to absorb the materials of the performance to such an extent that it becomes almost mechanical. At its worst this must diminish the intensity and sensitivity of the performance but the process is the core of the actor's work in rehearsal: to absorb the external material into himself to such a degree that he can spontaneously re-produce the action without consciously thinking about it. This is the core of Stanislavski's method, the translation of conscious intention into subconscious action.

I would like, in as simple and direct a way as I can, to examine what appears to be two distinct mental processes, sometimes complementary, sometimes detached, sometimes in total and mutually exclusive conflict. I am physically aware of two modes of thinking. I feel there are two distinct parts to my brain, each with its own function and mode of operating. The front part of my brain I use for visualising, for reflective meditation, for precisely defining my thoughts and ideas, for thinking in abstract, and for the deliberate conscious control and direction of my actions. The back part seems largely to live a life of its own and I am only conscious of what it is doing when I 'stop to think', or when I hear the words I am spontaneously speaking. The back brain also appears to control my physical actions and reactions instinctively without my being directly conscious of what is happening. As I sit typing this book I am not consciously aware of what I am writing, until the words appear on the page. Only when I hit an obstacle and don't know what to write next, do I stop, meditate and form the sentence in advance of typing it. I get my thoughts sorted out in the front part of my brain, but the ideas generally come subconsciously from the back of my mind. If I slow the process down, I am aware that I can be conscious of what I am going to write approximately one word in advance of typing it. Some monitoring control is at work because when I make a typing error, I instinctively stop typing and then have a look at the sheet to find out why I have stopped.

As I understand it, I spend most of my waking life directing my actions in a subconscious way from the back part of my brain. I have just shaken the ash from a cigarette without any conscious intending on my part. It wasn't until I had completed the action, and saw the ash-tray with my eyes, that I realised what I had done. I don't have to consciously think about traffic to cross a street, I watch out for traffic instinctively. In fact, the back brain appears to get on with reacting to external situations and producing the necessary actions, to carry out my purposes in life, *whilst I am actually thinking of something else.* Frequently, I arrive at destinations without the slightest memory of how I got there. Sometimes I realise I have driven past major landmarks like motorway service stations without noticing them. My conscious mind has been meditating on some subject, or working out what I would do when I reached my destination, or just day dreaming, spinning idle thoughts and fantasy, whilst I have, almost unconsciously, been driving a car through heavy traffic. I haven't been 'thinking about what I was doing'. It also seems a general expedience that when you have all the time in the world to reach a destination, and you let the mind wander as you stroll along, you always seem to arrive at your destination quicker than you would if you were in a hurry, and had deliberately rushed. Somehow if you let the back part of the brain work, without conscious interference, the body works more efficiently. If you concentrate on making the body work, you interfere with its working.

I am aware of this principle in other areas, too. When I first learned to type and to drive a car, I had to work hard to make my body carry out the necessary movements. I was slow and clumsy and got very frustrated at the mistakes I made. I knew what I wanted to do but somehow the body reacted too slowly to my conscious directions. Now that I have learned to do both activities, I carry them out subconsciously. It is as though the back part of my brain is 'programmed' to carry out instinctively certain activities without direct control or intention.

Some of these activities, I am aware, if I ever think about it, require a very fine control of body movement. Walking downstairs is physically a very complex activity. Yet I do it without thinking, unless I perceive that the steps are slippery or rotten, or boards are missing, and then I consciously 'watch my step'. For some reason, I become very clumsy when I do this. Army instructors, taking recruits round obstacle courses, will always tell the recruit not to think about what he has to do, but just do it. Those who think, fail most often to gain the objective.

I am also aware of times when the two parts of my brain are at odds with each other and that, much as I try to control myself consciously, some process is at work within me which I cannot control. In spite of all my conscious determination to stay calm, some deeper anxiety or excitement quickens my pulse; sets my heart thumping; intensifies my breathing rhythm. The traditional advice is to stop worrying and relax. In extreme cases fear can paralyse the body functions completely and make it impossible to run or to cry out.

Sometimes, though, the intervention of the conscious front brain is necessary. The back brain appears to receive and process information about my body. I feel uneasy or depressed or troubled. I am not sure why. Often, if I am asked, I cannot explain why I feel that way. I am in a 'mood'. Sometimes it is difficult to explain, sometimes, if I sit down and think or talk, I can analyse why I feel that way on this day. I am aware that some-where at the back of my mind there is a reason. On reflection I sometimes manage to formulate the reasons. In talking, the reasons somehow emerge as the sentences take shape. Often I myself am surprised to learn what the cause of my 'mood' is. It is a general experience that at times of trouble we need to talk to someone. Schools of psychiatry have been built around the usefulness of talking as a way of revealing the contents of the mind. The use of the psychiatrist's couch is a recognition that, for this to happen, the work must be taken off the body. In effect, by making the body lie down, we relax the physical tension which is necessary to counteract the force of gravity when we stand upright. When this happens, the mind also relaxes, and becomes free to release its information and thoughts.

The complementary activity to this is to make a conscious decision to 'snap out of it'. We 'pull ourselves together', and this usually means a conscious decision to stop worrying or thinking, that is, to cease the conscious intellectual activities of the front mind, and 'just get on with it'. To brook on the causes of emotions such as anger, frustration, bitterness only fouls us up more. We are advised that the only solution is to 'forget it'. The saying 'I can forgive but not forget' seems to imply some process by which our conscious actions will take no account of the insult or offence, but the memory of it will be held at the back of the mind. It is important to establish that, in all these processes, I am physically aware of an emotional state or mood, before I am conscious of why I am experiencing it, and that for the most part, I do not bother to question or rationalise why I feel a particular way, on a particular day. I accept it and get on with living, although I am very much aware that it strongly influences what I do, and how I interact with other people.

For most of my life, I am not conscious of how or why I live my life the way I do. The back brain appears to have some relation to the processes of a computer. It holds the memory banks of information. People say, 'There's something at the back of my mind,' and, 'I always had that at the back of my mind.' The activity that I associate with the back brain is continuous, often tumultuous, and, largely, totally unconscious, until a demand is made to objectivise it: that is, to 'print out' in the conscious, reflective front brain the tape that is running through the back brain. It must also be said that the activity of the back brain constantly and continuously reveals itself in our physical actions and purposes.

My way of writing is to let everything 'stew' for days on end. The process is accompanied by restless body movements. I pace about, I twist and turn, alternately sit down and stand up again. I break off for many cups of coffee and unnecessary trips to the toilet. At a certain point, I sit at a typewriter, and write what I have to write, straight out. Then, when I can see what I have written I consciously correct it. I am aware of a similar process when I am rehearsing a play, either as an actor or director. The preparation and early work involves feeding a lot of information into my mind about the play, the characters, the dramatist, and the historical situation which is the background to the play. I experience confusion; I walk round the streets or sit restlessly in a room. For many years, not understanding what was happening, I used to believe I was avoiding work, which I understood then as poring over the script in detail, being methodical. I was very critical of the time I thought I was wasting, and considered myself lucky that, when I entered the rehearsal room, I somehow managed to cope with the situation adequately. I used to think that I would have coped even better if I had done more 'work'. It took me a long time to understand that I had actually been working very hard, processing thoughts and ideas and information, letting it sink in and settle, making order out of confusion.

I was surprised after a month of what I thought was rest and relaxation to find myself, in conversation with a friend, discussing a whole range of questions about the 18th century theatre, which had certainly not been there a month previously. On reflection I could recall things I'd read in that time but had not consciously connected to theatre. The connections had been made subconsciously. I understand Stanislavski's story of the man going for a walk and then asking the answer to his problem from his subconscious. I think he might have had a little more charity towards the actors sitting in cafés. Perhaps they *were* working, rather than idling.

The realisation that mental activity, and consequently work, is taking place subconsciously, releases the mind from a great deal of anxiety. Until I realised that was happening I was made very unhappy at the tensions caused by conscience. I kept worrying that I ought to be 'working' and this caused some form of emotional or mental distress, through the contradictions in working subconsciously and worrying about not working consciously. Having talked to other actors and directors since, I have found that other people are similarly affected. A number have said they thought it was some defect in their character which caused it. And yet the process is central to the actor's work. Stanislavski is constantly trying to find ways for the actor to work through the subconscious mind/body mechanisms. What I have described earlier of the rehearsal activities is directly related to getting the direction of the activities switched from the conscious front brain to the subconscious back brain. Every director dreads the 'intellectual' actor, the one who works it all out, who consciously thinks about what he is doing and directs his work accordingly. In fact, 'intellectual' is a dirty word in the theatre, but we must be careful not to throw the baby out with the bath water.

The subconscious processes of the back brain are not amenable to control unless we know what is happening there. It is one thing to realise that the subconscious mind will work more efficiently if it is left to work on its own, and another to trust it uncritically and blindly. Taking the image of the computer again, the back part of my brain is programmed to direct my responses to a wide range of situations. I am largely the person I am, because I have at some time chosen to respond to situations in a certain way, often by inhibiting certain responses which I believe are unproductive. When I am angry I don't throw bottles through windows. When someone picks a quarrel with me I tend to get up and quietly walk away. Once upon a time I used to stand my ground and fight, but I gained no benefit from it, so I changed. I have learned to control myself and my behaviour. The programme, from which my back brain subconsciously directs my actions, had been built up throughout my life, and has been subject to continuous adjustment and modification, most of which is so far in the past that I have no recollection of it. The programme is in any case so complex that it cannot be simply understood, because of the interlocking checks and balances built into it. It would be very tiring to rationalise our reasons for taking more than a few of the decisions we make during every day and only when it fails to function effectively do we 'rethink' it, or, more usually, part of it! Social learning and development in Man is closely integrated with this process. We experience; we objectivise what we have learned from that experience on reflection; we consciously decide to change; we reprogramme the mechanism to react in the light of that decision the next time we meet a similar situation. When the programme totally fails to fit the problem we often experience an emotional crisis.

These crises form the core of most of the world's drama and provide the climaxes of many plays. The active project embodied in the programme comes into conflict with the external environment, human or material, or encounters a contradictory project within the programme. Comedy is largely concerned with attempts constantly to re-adjust the programme so as to deal with a changing situation. Tragedy and farce deal with either the inability to find a programme that will suit the situation, or the single-minded pursuit of a project that leads inevitably to disaster. The type of play called 'drama' centres on the processes of adjustment necessary to the programme; it is usually more concerned with the experience of being human than with the values or purposes of the projects pursued.

The ways in which these crises are experienced are obviously specific to the individual and the nature of the problem encountered. We say, 'I could kick myself', when we realise we have yet again walked involuntarily into an unhappy situation, 'I must have been blind', 'I can't understand how I could have been such a fool'. When the programme lets us down, we 'made a mistake', or 'we didn't think'. We resolve 'never to make that mistake again'. That some form of conscious intellectualisation is necessary is revealed when we decline to tackle the problem immediately, but say 'I'll have to think about it'. In order to change the programme some conscious decision is necessary. It is at all times possible to make the conscious decision to change but we do not usually do so until a crisis reveals to us the inadequacy of the present programme, or the problems it is running us into. To make the change we have to become conscious of what the programme is. At times of crisis we say 'I don't know my own mind', or 'I must *make up* my mind'.

Contradictions in the programme are expressed as 'I'm torn both ways', 'I don't know what to do'. The problems frequently arise when we make minor adjustments to the programme, when the basis of the programme is wrong. When this happens we can't 'make sense' of it, or 'whatever I do seems to be wrong'. Many people, myself included, experience physical and mental torment when reading books in which the author uses a rarified or idiosyncratic language. The same is experienced in the theatre when members of an audience encounter particularly obscure or advanced examples of dramatic form or structure. 'I couldn't make head nor tail of it', 'It was double-dutch'.

Usually we manage to walk away from the problems of adjusting the programme to deal with situations like this. Only when we are driven to tackle a problem, and can find no acceptable or productive course of action, do we re-think the basis of our programme. This always involves an analysis of the problem faced, and the means we are using to tackle it. The concept of lateral thinking is based on the understanding that the wrong means may be being applied to the problem. Central to the concept of improving industrial skills through work study is the question, 'Why is the job being done in the first place?'

All of these processes are experienced regularly by the actor in rehearsal and performance, although, naturally, he prefers not to question them or even consciously to think about them. If he did, he would usually inhibit his work. He trusts that his experience and technique will 'instinctively' transform the conscious mental work he is doing into subconscious projects of action – although actors are born worriers and are constantly afraid that it won't happen.

Many highly skilled and technically proficient actors persist in believing that acting is an instinctive or intuitive process, which cannot be described or objectivised. They carry on working non-reflectively. Or, as every director has said at some time, 'Don't tell me about it, show me'. That is, reveal the project through your actions. There is wide disagreement about the amount of discussion that should take place during the rehearsal period. Jean Vilar, for one, believed that a great deal of discussion was necessary in order to establish what the actor was going to do, before he got on with doing it. That is, to be absolutely clear about the content of the programme, before the actor begins to assemble it and try it out in action. Joan Littlewood uses the discussion period to explore the wider aspects of the play, preferring to build up the actor's programme in the active rehearsal situation. In doing this, she takes a great deal of the actor's intellectual work upon herself. Many actors are very unhappy with discussion, they prefer to get straight on with it, often characterising the intellectual work as their 'homework', preferring to incorporate it into the process of learning the lines. What is common to most actors and directors, except a very few, is that they resent discussion during the active rehearsal period. Conscious thought and discussion have little place in a rehearsal; they get in the way of work.

But here we hit a snag. If an actor runs into difficulties, and these difficulties are caused by fundamental misconceptions in his approach to his work, that is, the overall programme is wrong, how do we get him out of it? The theatre today often demands of an actor a technique that is flexible and wide-ranging enough to cope with Ibsen, Coward and Sam Shepard in quick succession. Actors frequently cling to what has 'worked' for them in the past although this might be at variance with the demands of the play. Actors do 'get lost' in their work. Every director has at some time despaired of an actor who cannot, in some way, take direction. You tell him time and time again what you want and it always comes back the same, or something totally different appears, which bears no resemblance to what you asked for. The actor often apologises profusely for not being able to do it 'for some reason', and becomes depressed and distressed. He knows what you want but can't give it to you.

There is a phenomenon among some student actors who have pre-conceived some idea or programme for what 'acting' is, i.e. a distinct activity in its own right. Whatever they do is subjected to irritating mannerisms which have nothing to do with the situation or character or dramatic activity. These often manifest themselves in a particular carriage of the body, or highly stylised movement, or in false or exaggerated patterns of inflection in the voice, or a falsely elevated style of delivery. They cannot get rid of these mannerisms simply by being told to drop them. This frequently occurs with young people who have undergone elocution training in their teens. It is difficult to stop them using their 'elocution voice', when they perform or rehearse. The mannerism has become deeply ingrained in the mind programme, and reveals itself in every action made. Some way has to be found to enable the actor to be aware of what he is doing, without interfering with what is, for him, the natural and correct way of working. Simply to make him conscious, intellectually and reflectively, of what is going wrong, will only inhibit him and distress him more. Some active physical way has to be found to lead him out of the problem.

This chapter has set out a hypothesis derived from my own personal experience and sensations. It is not scientific, for two reasons. Firstly, the processes of the brain and its connections with the body are still not definitively understood. Secondly, the terminology used does not help the actor. Terms like motor-cortex, ganglia, proprioceptive nerve endings would inhibit me from acting, rather than help me, unless I could relate them to direct physical sensations and experiences I have had. It is also clear that the exact way that any human being functions is never quite the same as any other human being with similar physical apparatus. For an actor to be able to understand the workings of the mind and body, and consequently to control them and use them more effectively, he must be led to the physical experience and sensations of himself in action. Scientific terms he cannot connect directly to action push him towards reflecting on the terms, and take him away from *doing*. However, I feel obliged to enter some scientific evidence in support of what I have written, and this can be found in the Appendix at the back of the book.

CHAPTER 3

Thought and action

In the previous chapter I have described problems that occur for the actor when the normal subconscious co-ordination of the mind and body is disturbed by the intrusion of conscious reflective thought. I have suggested that the effective tackling of these problems needs some method of working that avoids the pitfall of making him conscious of the problems, since this simply leads to more conscious reflective thought about the problems and thus increases them. With the experienced actor, whatever method we choose, it is largely a matter of preventing interference with what he has already learned to do naturally. With the young actor it is largely a matter of helping him to find, through his training, the natural way of working. There is also a case to be made that, with the changing demands made upon the actor by new forms of drama, the experienced actor sometimes finds himself in need of re-training. Whatever the problem, the method of tackling it must centre on the activities of the subconscious reflex activities of the back brain and it is these we must examine now, before proceeding directly to the training of the actor in the next chapter.

Mind and body

There is one function and activity of the back brain, which I have not developed far enough in the last chapter. It controls the muscular movements and co-ordination of the body. There is a direct connection between the programme in the subconscious mind and the muscular activities of the body, through which it reveals and pursues its purposes.

The processes of mind and body are inextricably linked. There are, and have been, several systems of psycho-physical therapy which seek the cure to mental distress and unbalance through the actions of the body. It is a recognisable fact that body use affects the mind, and that states of mind are reflected physically in the body. Mental depression is often reflected in a slumped body position. A slumped, depressed body position induces a listless state of mind. The two are sometimes self-reinforcing, and it is difficult to break out, 'to snap out of it'. Inhibitions to physical action go hand in hand with indecision in the mind. It is not a question of which causes which, although there may be a prime cause, but rather a self-reinforcing vicious circle is set up, until some means can be found of breaking it. It is a well-known fact that recovery from illness often depends upon the patient's will to get well. Emile Coué, the apostle of auto-suggestion as a means of curing disease, built a system around repeating the phrase, 'Every day, in every way I'm getting better and better'. No doubt he had some successes.

With me a very simple factor like weight affects my work. I have learned that it is difficult for me to work if my weight is over 11st. 4 lb. It is not only that my body is unfit and sluggish over that weight, but my mind doesn't function effectively either.

The value of psycho-physical methods of therapy lies in their ability to break the vicious circle of interaction by tackling the problems at their most tangible and easily apprehensible point – the physical use of the body – rather than at the least tangible and apprehensible points – the psychological state of mind, or the social relationship patterns, or other environmental factors. A complete recovery would have to entail some solution or adjustment in these areas, too. However, in working with the actor we are not dealing with cases of pathological illness, merely with problems he encounters which hinder the effective functioning of his normal processes. But since acting is above all a physical activity, rather than an intellectual one, we begin working on the actor's problems through the use of his body, and the psycho-physical sensations that come with using his body.

It should also be made clear that there is a distinction to be made between consciousness and awareness, and between what is subconscious and what is unconscious. Whilst making love, I am very sharply aware of what I am doing, but if I stopped to think about it, I would no longer be making love. I engage in a very subtle process of demand and response with my partner, on a number of levels, physical, mental and emotional. My awareness of what is happening to me and what I am doing, might be subconscious, but it is a long way from being unconscious. It takes all my powers of physical and mental concentration to juggle three oranges, but I haven't time to think about what I am doing, whilst juggling. The difference between thinking *about what* one is doing, and thinking what one is doing, is the difference between the conscious and the subconscious. The former can take place *before* or *after* the activity, but not *during* it.

Jean-Paul Sartre indeed gives primacy to the thought processes of the subconscious back brain over the conscious front brain. The claim he makes is that every instance of being conscious is also one of being in some sense self-conscious. Sartre's explanation of this is as follows:

> If I count the cigarettes in this case, I have the impression of discovering an objective property of this group of cigarettes: *there are twelve of them.* This property appears to me as one existing in the world. It is possible that I am not aware of myself as counting them. I don't 'know myself counting'. The proof of this is that children can make a spontaneous addition without being able to *explain* how they set about it; Piaget's tests which show this are an excellent refutation of Alain's formula: To know is to know that one knows. However, at the moment when the cigarettes are revealed as a dozen, I have a nonthetic consciousness of my activity of adding. If I am questioned, if someone asks me 'What are you doing?' I would immediately reply 'I am counting' and this reply does not only include the momentary consciousness that I can get by reflection but also those consciousnesses which have passed without being reflected on, those which are forever *unreflected* in my immediate past. Thus reflection has no primacy over the consciousness reflected on; the former does not reveal the latter to itself. On the contrary, it is the non-reflective consciousness which makes reflection possible . . .[1]

Sartre is describing precisely the processes I am dealing with, although his use of terms is slightly at variance with my own. What is very interesting is that he attributes to the non-reflective, back part of the brain the functions of conceiving intentions, making decisions and putting them into action. This is possible because of the direct connections between the old back brain and the muscles of the body.

> It is no more possible to separate the intention from the action than thought from the language that expresses it and, as it often happens that our speech reveals our thoughts to us, so our actions reveal our intentions, that is to say they allow us to separate intentions, to schematise them, to make them into objects instead of limiting us to living them.
>
> When the will intervenes, the decision is taken and its only real function is that of making the announcement.[2]

Which may go a long way towards explaining the point made earlier that a lot of highly skilled and technically proficient actors persist in believing and saying that acting is an instinctive or intuitive process. It gives a philosophical justification to the heart-cry of the director, 'Don't think about it, show me!' Reveal to me your project through your actions.

Body/think

If we proceed from my assumption, that to by-pass the reflective, conscious interference of the front brain, we must concentrate on the co-ordinated body/think processes which are revealed through the muscular movements of the body, and are amenable to improvement by working on the body actions and activities, then we are trying to train the sense through which these processes are perceived.

A few questions arise:

(1) What is it that enables those who use the proper or better way of doing, to distinguish it from the other ways, and so to continue in it?
(2) Why is it that those who have adopted an inferior procedure usually stick to it in spite of seeing examples of better use around them?

Is it that 'je ne sais quoi' that some people seem to have, sometimes spoken of as an instinct, a kind of sixth sense? Indeed, a sixth sense it is! – *the kinaesthetic sense*. It is the sense by which muscular motion, weight, position in space etc., are perceived.[3]

The kinaesthetic sense, or *body think* is the process by which we subconsciously direct and adjust the movements of our bodies in space, either in response to external stimuli, or to intentions arising in the mind. It is the process by which physical purposes are carried out effectively for the greater part of our lives; it is the process by which we practise habitual physical skills naturally and unselfconsciously; it is the process by which we constantly take in information from the external environment and react to it without reflection, and by which we comprehend and respond to information being sent to the brain by our own bodies. It is the process by which, in all these areas, we are aware of what we are doing and what is happening to us. Only when it fails to achieve our purposes, or we fear it may not be able to, or we wish to change our behaviour patterns or acquire new skills, or when there is some disturbance in its working, do we connect the front brain to it and supply an overriding conscious control. Such a 'disturbance' occurs when illness, drunkenness or physical fatigue interferes with the normal function of the kinaesthetic sense, which is to orientate the body successfully in space in relation to other people or objects. That is, we lose the sense of where we are, and stumble, bump into objects, confuse distances. When this happens, the normal righting reflexes in the back brain are cut out, or become subordinate to the optical righting mechanism, which relies on a direct connection between the eyes and the front brain. We deliberately focus, consciously and hard, upon physical objects. That is, instead of orientating our body in space, from our instinctive perception of those objects in relation to our fixed centre, we orientate our body in relation to the fixed centre of the object we focus on.

It is clear that the kinaesthetic sense is more finely developed in some people than in others, but it is there in everybody. It is arguable that actors ought to be people with a finely developed kinaesthetic sense; they enjoy physical activities, they respond easily and imaginatively to physical stimuli, they rarely like intellectualising about what they do. It is almost possible to equate talent in the actor with a good intelligence and a finely developed kinaesthetic sense: that is, the powers to conceive complex imaginative intentions and the ability to realise these in action. The rest comes with experience and the acquisition of discipline.

Magnus claims that the kinaesthetic sense, or body/think, acts automatically unless it is disturbed, and that it is regularly disturbed by impulses from the front brain. Conscious thought regularly disturbs the working of the body/think, which automatically rights itself when, and only when, conscious thought and direction cease.[4]

Feldenkrais describes what happens when the natural coordination of mind and body are seriously disturbed, and the directives from the mind to the body are inhibited or disrupted.

> People in the unfortunate situation described live on an intellectual level. All their body functions are interfered with by voluntary directives. Conscious control, when properly directed, often improves details here and there, but intellect is no substitute for vitality. A sense of futility of life, tiredness and a wish to give it all up is the result of over-taxing the conscious control with the tasks the reflective nervous activity is better suited to perform. The conscious control is paramount in integrating all the functions fitting the immediate circum-

stances. The internal mechanisms enabling him to succeed should be left to the self-regulating nervous co-ordination. At least, in the present state of our knowledge of the nervous system, we can do no better than follow the best adjusted and mature specimens, and they do not abuse the conscious control.[5]

If we accept that the subconscious, back brain body/think processes are automatically self-righting, we are looking for three factors. Firstly, what are the means by which we can by-pass conscious control, to allow these processes to work naturally? Secondly, what inhibits or interferes with these processes acting naturally? Thirdly, how do we make the actor aware of how his body/think works, so that we can help him prevent interference and remove inhibitions? But first let us examine some of the physical ways the body/think manifests itself.

Use and balance

The bulk of stimuli arriving at the nervous system is from muscular activity affected by gravity. Therefore posture is one of the best clues, not only to evolution, but also to the activity of the brain.[6]

If all movement is the constant shifting in space of the balance of the body's weight, then the first factor we must consider is how balance is maintained, and how shifted. It is not an accident that the physical metaphor of balance is taken to describe someone of a mature mind – a balanced person.

The processes of balance, and shift of balance, are normally achieved physiologically, by the constant flow of fluid through the vestibular apparatus between the ears, and the balancing contractions and relaxations in the anti-gravitational muscles. The body makes no move that is not accompanied by an intention in the mind, conscious or subconscious. No thought in the mind takes place without some corresponding movement in the body, although this may be almost imperceptible to the eye. Standing still involves a complicated set of actions to control oscillations to either side of the supposed centre. There is constant muscular flow throughout the body to control balance and to control movement, and this is the constant shift of balance of the body's weight in space.

There is no such state as stillness, until the organism ceases to move entirely at death. Even in abnormal states, such as paralysis of parts of the body, movements occur along the lines of communication, until they reach the point of paralysis. The amputation of a limb is frequently ignored by the brain and amputees can still 'feel' the limb there, through the actions of the nervous system.

Flexible shifts of balance involve an optimum of tonus or tension in the anti-gravitational muscles, and is closely tied to a properly co-ordinated erect posture. Feldenkrais again:

> As no segment of the body can be moved without adjustment of all the others to a new configuration, the description of any act must necessarily be extremely cumbersome. Any act involves so many muscles and so complete an activity, that it is more useful to describe the function than the mechanism. And this is:
>
> (1) that the proper posture of the body is such that it can initiate movement in any direction with the same ease;
> (2) that it can start any movement without a preliminary adjustment;
> (3) that the movement is performed with the minimum of work, i.e. with the maximum of efficiency.
>
> People with proper body control do, in fact, carry themselves in such a way that no preliminary adjustment or movement is necessary to pass from standing to walking or from walking to running. They can also reverse any undertaken movement at any time more easily than other people. All directions are accessible to their inspection while in locomotion without an intermediate preliminary adjustment.[7]

What happens in every human being is that certain patterns of use have been set up which inhibit or contradict this process. The mind adjusts to the new situation, until 'use' becomes 'habit', and what is abnormal, is experienced as normal, through habitual use.

I don't think there would be any general disagreement that there is an appalling proliferation of bad posture in our society, and that, in a wide variety of cases, we can see people with hunched shoulders or slumped shoulders, twisted spines, contracted necks and a mass of other mal-co-ordinations of the body. Yet to these people, through use, these conditions are experienced as normal, and are very difficult to break down. In another sense, the classical dancer trains to achieve a particular co-ordination of the body, because of the abnormal demands made upon the body by the ballet, and this learned use becomes second nature. The mime artist trains himself to isolate or accentuate actions in various parts of the body, to make them clear. The value of mime training, for the actor, lies in the fact that once actions have been isolated, they can be re-synthesised again. In fact, until some aspects of movement have been isolated or experienced in their specific sensation, the task of working on the body is difficult.

The complicated patterns of use are fused in the actor's mind into a totality, and he experiences it as a body-image which defies analysis. One of the biggest difficulties with technical physical exercises is getting the actor to carry out only the body function or activity that the exercise requires. He finds it difficult, say, to bend the knees without nodding his head, or sticking his backside out to the rear. Made conscious of what he is doing, he consciously tries to prevent it happening, and the interference of the conscious processes of the brain only makes it more difficult, and he gets frustrated.

The principles of co-ordination

Most of the early games work, laid out later in the book, is designed to provoke better co-ordination through natural processes, which can then be objectivised, after it has been experienced. Before then, it is necessary to look at some of the important areas of movement co-ordination. Prime among these is the relationship between the head, neck, spine and pelvis, and the tension-stops along the way.

The spine, in early childhood, is practically straight, and the cervical curve begins to form before the lumbar curvature. Thus the shoulder, neck and sacro-lumbar regions are those in which most incomplete, or otherwise faulty learning will find its halting barrier. These are mechanically the regions in which the greatest muscular adjustment is necessary, because very heavy masses have to be properly aligned with great precision. Also many of the muscles of these regions act on more than one joint, and their control is more delicate. Moreover, twisting of the body around the vertical axis, through the centre of gravity, for which the human frame is predominantly fitted, and which is a special advantage of the human erect posture, takes place mainly in these two regions.

With the head prevented from turning right and left on its support and lumbar vertebrae made rigid too, turning of the body becomes an awkward, laborious and slow operation, necessitating at least three steps.[8]

Let us consider some of the factors that inhibit flexible coordinated movement. The causes of these inhibitions often go back to childhood, often to encouraging a child to stand upright, before the necessary strength is present in the muscles. Often they are due to social and educational pressures put on the child. A child is told to hold his head up straight at school. The child interpreting what this means, holds up the front part of his head, and in doing so shortens and constricts the muscles of his neck. This disturbs the natural relationship between the head and the spine. In holding up the front of the head, the child throws the balance of the body's weight backwards, off-centre. To stop himself falling backwards, he takes a counter-tension in the small of the back, and this is counteracted by a further counter-tension above the knees to stop himself falling forwards. This is counteracted by a final counter-tension in the feet, which brings the whole pillar of the body forward (*illustration no. 1*). The result is that high

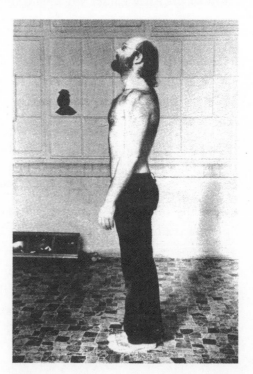

1 '... Head up and straight'

pressure points of tension are built up which inhibit the relaxed and flexible control of the body's movement by the mind and have to be overcome by preliminary adjustments before locomotion can take place.

In most people, the processes of adaptation become confused with nature. In the course of an exercise, Barlow discovered that out of 105 subjects, all but one clenched the muscles at the back of the neck when sitting down, and only eleven were able to stop themselves doing so when it was pointed out to them that that muscular action was superfluous to the movement they were making.[9]

Every drama school has to deal with this problem in every student to a different degree, since it is so rare as to be unforeseeable that any student should not have acquired some pattern of misuse and mal-co-ordination of the body by the time he arrives at training. The problem is compounded by an increase of tension in situations of anxiety, like a performance, where the individual feels he has to prove himself.

Tension in the actor

On stage, the problems tend to manifest themselves principally in two ways, a general stiffness of movement, and a tightening of the voice, with a corresponding rise in pitch or tone, as the neck tension forces the larynx to rise against the vertebrae of the top spine. If one works in isolation too soon, the removal of tension in one area tends to be counteracted by an increase of tension in other areas. The relaxation of the throat muscles is often accompanied by an increase of tension in the intercostal (rib) or stomach muscles, or in the legs. It is totally impossible to have a single major tension-stop in isolation: one would fall over. A major tension-stop is always accompanied by counter-tensions elsewhere in the body, to preserve the balance.

The resulting effect of these tension-stops is to distort the natural shape of the spine, and produce a serpentine, exaggerated line through the body, and a restricted range of movement (*illustration no. 2*). This is not only because of the necessary adjustments that have to be made before mobility, but also because the communication of intentions from the brain down the spine (which is the communication channel) is inhibited at various points in the process by the resistance of the tension-stops.

The two principal areas of tension which inhibit the actor, along with

2 '. . . Producing a serpentine, exaggerated line through the body'

other people, are in the neck, and the pelvis. The neck is the first major
tension-stop along the chain, from the brain to the trunk and limbs. Pressure
applied with the finger and thumb to the sub-occipital neuro-muscular centre
at the base of the skull can almost immobilise a person. The pelvis is
important because of the restriction of mobility in the pelvic joints.

> The pelvis is articulated on the femurs by ball and socket joints that
> are free to move in all directions. These joints alternately support the
> full weight of the body. The necessary rigidity is obtained in these free
> joints solely by muscular support. The pelvis on which the spine rests
> is therefore a link of major importance in locomotion. If the top is
> tilted forward [as it is when the spinal curve is exaggerated], the
> lumbar curvature is increased and the centre of gravity is lowered.
> This tilting forward of the upper end of the pelvis is made possible by
> lengthening the extensors of the hip joints and the deep muscles of the
> lower abdomen. The lumbar curvature is further increased by the
> thorax being tilted backwards to compensate for the mass moved
> forward by the pelvic tilt. In order to maintain the head in its habitual
> relation to space, the thoracic flexion must be further increased.[10]

Acting, it can be said, is the one athletic pursuit that does not begin by placing the player in the right position to function effectively. A balanced, controlled swing, with the right co-ordination of muscles, is essential for golf; getting in line with the ball, and getting to the pitch of the ball, is central to cricket; a flexible balance, and the ability to move easily and swiftly to the bounce of the ball, is essential for tennis; and boxers spend hours in the sparring ring, co-ordinating reflexes. Acting demands no less of a human being in the way of mental and physical concentration and co-ordination. It is well recognised in all other athletic pursuits that it makes no sense to put more energy into what you are doing, if what you are doing is basically wrong or contradictory. All other athletic pursuits demand a heavy commitment to correcting basic errors in stance, balance and flexible movement. In acting, we tend to let the actor work from whatever physical configuration he is in at that moment. We tend to work on the peripheral actions, instead of the central actions from which they flow. Hand gestures are more easily defined and corrected than the total balanced movements of the body, which support and originate them.

Fundamental to any consideration of easy flexible balance, and shifts of balance, are erect carriage and a relaxed natural centre of gravity.

The centre of gravity in the body

I have dealt earlier with the tension-stops along the spine, which cause displacement and restrict ease of movement around the vertical axis. A hypothetical line of the central axis has been advanced in a chart, referred to as the Harvard University Chart, for grading body mechanics. I reprint this here (*illustration no. 3*). It can be seen that the most potent posture for flexible movement, with maximum accessibility to all directions with a minimum of necessary pre-adjustment of posture, is present when a vertical line can be imagined passing through the body from the front part of the ankle joint to the entrance of the ear. Where this line passes the top edge of the pelvis is the body's natural centre of gravity. The spine and upper body balance on the pelvis and the lower limbs articulate out of it. The proper co-ordination of any body movement, therefore, relies physically upon impulses originating in the pelvic regions, which effect a co-ordination of movement in both the upper and lower body simultaneously.

On purely mechanical grounds it can be proved that the best way to initiate movement forward is obtained with the upper part of the pelvis leading the movement forward.[11]

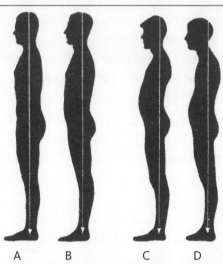

Fig. 3 The vertical parallel lines were drawn by the writer

In the cases where standing is maintained in conditions close to the potent posture, a vertical plane through the centre of gravity, and parallel to the shoulders passes approximately through the anterior part of the ankle joint and the entrance to the ear (external auditory meatus). On measuring the angle formed by a line joining the entrance to the ear and the anterior of the ankle joint, with the vertical at the ankle joint, people may be divided into four groups:

A	B	C	D
0°–0°15'	0°15'–0°45'	0°45'–1°30'	1°30'–2°0'

In practice, it is more convenient to measure the horizontal distance between these lines to a line at the level of the ear, and divide it by the vertical distance of the ear from the floor. This gives approximately:

A	B	C	D
0	15/1000	25/1000	35/1000

These are, however, tentative figures, as the number of measurements made is too small from a statistical point of view.

It may be interesting, in this connection, to state the following: There is a chart referred to as the Harvard University Chart[1], for grading body mechanics. This chart gives four silhouettes, reproduced in Fig. 3, corresponding to four grades.

Grade A. Excellent mechanical use of the body
1. Head straight above chest, hips and feet.
2. Chest up and forward.
3. Abdomen in and flat.
4. Back, usual curves not exaggerated.

Grade B. Good mechanical use of the body
1. Head too far forward.
2. Chest not so well up or forward.
3. Abdomen, very little change.
4. Back, very little change.

Grade C. Poor mechanical use of the body
1. Head forward of chest.
2. Chest flat.
3. Abdomen relaxed and forward.
4- Back curves exaggerated.

Grade D. Very poor mechanical use of the body
1. Head still further forward.
2. Chest still flatter and further back.
3. Abdomen completely relaxed, 'slouchy'.
4. Back, all curves exaggerated to the extreme.

3 The Harvard University Chart

Because it is often difficult to sense exactly where the top of the pelvis is, until work has been in progress sometime, it helps to think the centre of gravity corresponds to a point halfway between the navel and the top of the pubic hair, though of course it lies in the body behind this point. When acting in productions that have called for violent energetic movement, I have found it useful to tie a piece of elastic around the line of the centre, under the costume, so that I am always physically aware of it.

The effect of tension-stops along the spine, which throw the weight of the trunk and head off-line, and off-balance, is that the centre of gravity of the body has to be lowered, through tension in the legs and feet, in order to keep the body upright. The resulting effect can be seen in those people who start walking by throwing the top part of the body forward, and just managing to get their legs under it to stop falling (with a resulting series of shocks to the rigid muscles of the thighs). The reverse can often be observed: that is, off-balance is counteracted by a massive tension in the upper body, increasing the spinal curvature and throwing the chest forward, which has the effect of producing an unnaturally high centre of gravity. The movement then appears to be initiated by thrusting the leg forward and dragging the body after it, with a resulting strain on the back. Actors, in my experience, more usually have a low centre of gravity.

In working with actors, it is difficult in the early stages to make them aware of the low centre of gravity. The tension-stops along the spine are relatively easy to experience, and to observe in others, but the centre of gravity is a somewhat abstract concept. In practice I have found it more useful to point to the principal observable effect of a low centre of gravity, which is that the pelvis appears to be joined with the lower limbs, and the body seems to split in two at a point higher than the top of the pelvis. This point is the centre, or hinge, of the curvature of the lower back (*illustration no. 4*). For this reason, in working with actors, it has always proved more productive to refer to a *high body centre*, rather than to a low centre of gravity. The high body centre can usually be observed clearly. It can always be discovered by moving your hands up and down the spine and the abdomen, feeling at what point the spine hinges flexibly. All other vertebrae of the spine on either side of the centre point are usually held rigid by tension. In working to get the body centre lower, the centre of gravity rises towards its natural placing.

4 'This point is the centre, or hinge, of the curvature of the lower back'

Pushing

The effect of the high body centre in inhibiting potent, flexible movement, can be demonstrated quite simply by throwing a tennis ball against a wall, catching it, and repeating the throw several times. All movement is naturally based upon an alternating flow of impulses in and out of the centre (in Laban's terms 'gathering' and 'scattering'). That is, strength is maintained because each outgoing action is interspersed with a recovery of the balance over stance. The more violent the movement, the greater the recovery necessary, and the more spatial the oscillations back and forward across the centre. To achieve a strong throw after a catch, the body must return over centre, in order to gather strength, for the impulse of the next throw. Failure to complete this recovery leads to a weak throw next time. The effect of inhibiting this recovery, because of a tension-stop in the upper body, or a high body centre, results in weaker and weaker throws, and more tension in the body to compensate for lack of strength. If the stop is a particularly violent one, or the vertebrae on either side of the high body centre are rigid, it can result in an attempt to produce strength through contractions of smaller groups of muscles, along the line of the movement, which produces enormous strain overall with diminishing effect.

Which is why inexperienced actors have a problem sustaining strength at the ends of lines in difficult passages of verse. They push, push harder, and push harder still, without taking the necessary recoveries in between, and all they produce is light, quick, staccato rhythms with decreasing strength, which is all that is possible using the body this way. The problems this process causes are well understood in other athletic pursuits. The quick left jab may score points, but never knocks anyone out. To get the knock-out, the boxer must 'get his weight behind the punch', that is, he must gather his strength by recovering over centre before delivering the punch. Successive left jabs must maintain strength by moving the centre forward continuously, or else the boxer overbalances. Acting is a much more complex combination of human activities, involving all aspects of the human personality. The effect of 'pushing' is to throw the weight of the top body forward, which has profound effects on the actor's work and the performance at large.

In spatial terms, the effect of 'pushing' is to direct attention away from the actor, in the direction in which he is pushing. He thus ceases to be the centre of his own space area, and stands on the periphery of the space area towards whose centre he is pushing. When two actors do this, the high point of interest on the stage is usually found in the centre of the empty space between them. It becomes difficult, if not impossible, to look at the actors, and to let the eye travel naturally, from centre to centre.

The activity of pushing is one of constant giving out. Reaction we associate with recovery. Extreme shock reactions are sometimes characterised as 'I was taken aback'. When everyone on stage is giving, and no-one is taking (the physical and mental activities cannot be divorced in practice), the normal to-and-fro of interaction between characters/actors cannot take place, and the movement of the action of the play is broken up into disjointed statements and single actions. These appear to have no effect on anyone else on stage, since no-one responds or reacts to them, except in terms which are themselves actions and not reactions. Comprehension becomes possible only in literary terms. The audience does not respond physically, but sees, reflects and interprets intellectually. Sitting in an audience, I have the experience of being talked at, or more usually talked past, as I observe the other characters/actors being talked at, and not *to* or *with*. I feel pushed into a position of sitting back and listening (occasionally into getting headaches). I am unable to respond to the natural flow of action, and am therefore discouraged from participating in the action in any other than literary terms. I hear and understand the words, but since the processes of communication rely for any depth of understanding upon sympathetic muscular movements made in the listener and the watcher, the significance of the words is lost, because the sympathetic response is inhibited.[12]

> Initially, the give and take occurs between the physical activity of presentation and the sensitized organs of perception in an audience. Gradually the sensory response expands into the imaginative . . .
>
> From actual experience performers can sense whether or not a 'house' is with them, principally because the degree of muscular tension in the audience telegraphs, before any overt sign, its level of attention. We might well say that an audience does not see with its eyes but with its lungs, does not hear with its ears but with its skin. All of us are aware of the ionization of feeling throughout our bodies when we are absorbed in a play and the quick rush of sensation when we react to a critical moment. Nor do we have to discriminate the dramatic signals mentally in order to react. Perception includes

subception, bodily response to stimuli before we are focally aware of the stimuli. In theatre, this means that our bodies are already reacting to the texture and structure of action before we recognize that they are doing so.[13]

The same process that I understand as the subconscious working of the back brain takes place in the audience during the performance. I am not usually conscious of what is going in, until, later, I consciously think about what I have seen. I am aware of mental effort, but not conscious of what is taking place inside me. I am aware that when I am paying attention I sit upright, alert. When my attention is lost, my body slumps, and my conscious mind wanders off to think of other things.

Pre-conceived intentions and playing results

The particular configuration an actor's body takes may to some extent be the result of his personal physical development and habitual body use. It is also strongly conditioned by mental activity. I have explained the activities and functions of the old, back brain and the new, front brain and their connection with the muscular activities of the body. One thing further needs to be said: that is, that the predominant use of either part of the brain materially affects the co-ordination and configuration of the body. When the human being is alert and responding to all external stimuli, we associate this with an erect posture, the head held upright. There are phrases for describing this in metaphorical terms: 'with ears pricked' presumes a lengthening of the back neck to raise the ears higher than usual; 'all eyes' presumes a maximum flexibility of rotation of the head. It may be harmful to tell a child to 'pay attention and sit up straight', if you don't show him how to achieve this efficiently; paying alert attention is associated with a straight spine. On the other hand, the processes of meditation are associated with phrases like 'sunk in thought', 'deep in meditation', and 'wrapped in thought'. The verb itself – to 'reflect' – has associated meanings of being bent or folded. The statement 'let me think' is often accompanied by a lowering of the head. Rodin's *The Thinker* is a definitive example of the reflective process. In conscious thought, the relationship of the head, neck, spine and pelvis is displaced from the optimum upright configuration; the head comes forward, the spine becomes a convex curve, and the pelvis retards. When this happens in the actor, he usually tries to contradict the process by shortening the muscles at the back of the neck through contraction, in order to raise the head to its normal position. The result is once again the serpentine spine seen earlier. The clues to why this happens are at the very beginning of Chapter 1. 'The actor has to *produce at will*, and in a hurry, convincing representations of patterns of human behaviour and interaction which, in real life, happen spontaneously *in response* to external stimuli; he has to repeat these activities, apparently spontaneously, time and time again, at arbitrarily fixed intervals, and often in different locales.'

The central part of the acting process embodies the paradox of recreating spontaneous patterns of action and activities, when the outcome is already known, and doing this wilfully. Nothing in the performance takes place unless the actor is instrumental in setting the processes in motion. But this should not be confused with 'making it happen', which is what sometimes occurs, and from which many of the problems spring. The actor tries *consciously* to make things happen, which is in direct contradiction to the processes by which the actions take place in everyday life.

We have seen earlier that consciously directed intentions interfere with the normal mind–body co-ordination, resulting in loss of flexibility and mobility, in tiredness and over-anxiety. Closely associated with the conscious intention, in the acting processes, is *'playing the result'*. That is, the actor understands consciously in his mind what he wants the ultimate effect of his action to be; the conscious mind *concretises* and *totalises* the *end* to be achieved, or the *result* that should be the conclusion of his action, and he tries to make it happen without going through the natural mind/body process that will help him arrive at it. Because the end result is held consciously in the front of the brain, the body is pulled off-balance into a reflective configuration, and the normal reflex actions of the back brain, as well as the mobility of the body, are interfered with. The result is never achieved and can never be achieved. The harder you try consciously to achieve, the further you get from allowing the natural processes to happen.

The process is self-reinforcing, and causes some distress among young actors. It is also the cause of the phenomenon that a good show is usually followed by a bad one. The actors, encouraged by one performance that happened spontaneously to take flight, go out the next evening and try to repeat what they had found their way to the night before. They try to re-create the *effect*, not the *process* by which the effect was achieved. It is a problem which often arises with young actors between rehearsals. In the course of the rehearsals, instead of absorbing what he has learnt into the reflex activities of the back brain, and trusting that he has absorbed it, he goes home and thinks about it, concretises it into a fixed image, which he then tries to repeat at the next rehearsal. It is a depressing experience for directors that each rehearsal seems to start at a lower level than the level at which the previous one ended.

Since it is not possible to interact with other people and to intellectualise at the same time (which is what the actor is doing when he has a conscious intention or fixed result in his mind), actors often find it difficult to look at other actors on-stage, and have to fix glassily just past the ear or on the breast-bone. In everyday conversation, too, when we need to think consciously what we are saying, or to reflect on what has been said to us, we lower the head and eyes, and withdraw from direct contact.

Directors have various ways of coping with this in rehearsal, usually through phrases like 'Don't play the result, play the process', 'Don't go on to do, go on to be', 'Don't work so hard, throw it away'. Understanding what this was about was the result of my eighteen months' search, described earlier, to understand what Joan Littlewood meant by 'not being there'. One of the most important statements I have ever heard from an actor on his work was when Harry H. Corbett said to me that his ambition was just to give one performance in which he had only one conscious objective or intention, and that was the one that took him out of the wings on to the stage. The rest should come from reflex reaction to what happened out there.

Acting methods

It is a cruel irony that Stanislavski, who should be the greatest help to an actor, since he devised the first and only systematic examination and explanation of the actor's ways and means, should become, through bad teaching and misunderstanding, an enormous stumbling block to many actors. Stanislavski explored the processes of acting and set them down, using an objective terminology to explain what he understood (and central to his work is the understanding that acting is a psycho-physical process). Actors sometimes seize on this terminology as a crutch. They intellectually define what they are going to do, or want to do, and then, instead of converting their intentions into physical reflex processes, they totalise them as a result, an end to be pursued. Once embarked on this course, the failure to produce the right effect in rehearsal or performance forces them back consciously to re-examine their 'intentions', 'motivations', 'given circumstances', and 'images', and to concentrate even harder on what is a purely intellectual activity, and one which inhibits them from physical action. Every director has come to dread the young actor with a 'method' or 'technique', in terms of which he can earnestly explain everything which he cannot do. It constantly leads to arguments, misunderstandings, verbosity and frustration in rehearsals. I think the troubles encountered often cause a number of very talented and intelligent actors to abandon Stanislavski and their drama school training, since it becomes clear to them, in practice, that what they are trying to do doesn't work. Every actor, sooner or later, wants to get to the point of forgetting technique, of meeting each situation as it comes, just getting on with the job, 'going out and just doing it'. Too many adopt this position before they are ready, before they fully understand the job, and what exactly it is that they are 'just doing'. This seriously inhibits their development as actors.

I believe Stanislavski provided the strongest basis for any actor training, although I would question whether the fifty years that have passed since he formulated his ideas do not necessitate some re-examination of his concepts. In nearly all the teaching I have done, I have had the support of other people training the student actors in Stanislavski technique. The work is often taught very skilfully. The problem comes usually when either it has been half taught, or when the actor finishes his formal training and is left to carry on the work without guidance. None of my work is intended to supplant Stanislavski, simply to cope with the problems that arise in practising in a very difficult and usually isolated working situation.

I think these problems arise in other areas of actor training, as well. The Laban system has always been for me the best basis for movement objectivisation. Laban-based or not, the best movement teachers teach movement, not the system. The system exists, and is useful, as an objective terminology by means of which physical human activities can be explained and talked about. But the terminology again sometimes begins to assume paramount importance, and as such it becomes a fixed concept and a rigid discipline which can inhibit movement expression by supplying preconceived intentions and effects to be pursued.

The director's role

Often because he has already conceived the effect he wants from a production in his mind's eye; often because he does not know sufficient about the actor's ways and means to translate his objectives into active processes which will stimulate the actor to work without prior reflection; and, often because time in any production is at a premium, *the director in rehearsal gives the actor the result.* He tells the actor what he, the director, wants to see, rather than what he wants the actor to do. Directors owe more than they will often admit to actors, who, time and time again, get them out of trouble by their own innate technical ability to analyse the *result* the director gives them, and convert it into working processes. When they do this, what they produce is always richer than what the director at first envisaged. It is required of an actor to do this, 'to take direction'. If the actor has difficulties doing this, and young actors often do have difficulties, since drama school allows the luxuries of lengthy rehearsals and recourse to experienced teachers who will help them, then the result is the dead repetition of the choreographic patterns of the director's intentions. The actors are playing the production, not the play.

It also leads to actors having problems in rehearsal because they cannot make the bridges or transitions between the insecure position they start from and the final effect the director describes to them. They know what he wants, but not how to give it to him. This leads to frustrated directors, resentful actors, and to dead, mechanical productions. Sometimes it leads to directors accepting what the actors can do naturally and ignoring the demands of the play. This, at least, is alive and theatrical, if intellectually unsatisfying for an audience, but it is still an evasion of the problem.

The director's job after all is to work with the actors. His concepts and ideas are his justification for being there, but not the total justification. The actor sells the product on the stage. In order to do his job, the director must engage with the actor's ways and means, and work in terms of them, in a situation of mutual exploration and discovery, and refinement of choice. The director who brings his finished concept of a production to the first rehearsal leaves the creative work by which he arrived at it behind in his study. The production becomes eighteen people illustrating the results of one man's imagination. An ensemble production utilises the imaginative work of nineteen people functioning co-operatively. The actors understand their contribution to the whole, and their work is that much richer and more alive. It is not generally realised that, towards the end of his career, Stanislavski expressed the wish to arrive at the first rehearsal knowing just as much as the actors knew. The process of mutual imaginative exploration and discovery, and its subsequent recreation in performance by the acting ensemble, is the theatre's greatest strength and asset. Pedantic directors often substitute the 'play' or 'the dramatist's intentions' for their 'concept'. This is really no better. These are the disciplines within which the actors work, but not their strait-jacket. The audience does not come to see a series of moving tableaux, illustrating scenes from the play. It comes to see the actors performing or re-creating the action of the play.

The director's job could be defined, like the teacher's, as creating situations in which the actor is free to make discoveries, which can then be objectivised and worked upon. At some point the director working with the actors will realise that the opening night is approaching and that he must consider the audience. If what the play demands in clarity and articulation is not there, he must, by direction, put it there; he must 'head for home'. The mark of the creative director is to hold up this moment as late as possible. Which means, he must also be technically a highly proficient director in order to do it at a late stage of rehearsals. Working this way is harder, and more rewarding, than heading for home on the first day with a fixed and finished concept.

Giving to the actor a totalised result leads him to reflect on the self-defined and self-limiting image, and, in trying to reproduce it without being able to explore the possibilities inherent in the situation, he is bound to produce clichés and stereotypes. Reflection leads naturally to definition, and definition of limited and totalised concepts and images is precisely what clichés and stereotypes are.

The process by which an actor 'builds a character', to use Stanislavski's phrase, is essentially one of growth. As the actor acquires more information about the part and the relationships of his character with the environment, human and material, his understanding of the content of the play and of his part in it grows, and his work deepens and becomes more complex. To give the actor too much external, pre-defined information too soon inhibits the processes whereby he explores each stage of development and absorbs it into his performance. Given the result, he is sometimes led to 'externalise': that is, to apply to his behaviour exterior actions which are not supported by a structure of inner feeling and sensation. He is led to split himself in two. He is both in the role, and standing outside it, trying to direct it. This sometimes happens with actors playing results. They look as though they are standing two feet behind themselves, pulling the strings of a puppet. The mind is divorced from the body.

No actor should ever be asked a rhetorical question such as 'Didn't we decide we weren't going to do that?' as this invites him to split himself into a reflective mind, considering his physical activities. Something similar occurs when directors give direction to actors in terms of the resulting feelings and emotions which are expressed during the action, for instance: 'Do you think you should be angry at that point?'

A. J. Manser, examining Sartre's conception of reflection, says:

> In this sense, 'reflection poisons emotion' by radically altering its character. This is because to reflect on anger or on any other violent emotion is to take up towards it the same position as another person might take. In reflection I consider my anger as I would consider your anger. No reflection, however, need be involved in an emotional or mental state. To express one's anger does not require reflection, for it does not involve contemplating or analysing the state. If a man were to consider his anger coolly, then to that extent he would no longer be really angry. Sartre also puts this in terms of intentionality by saying that there is only room in the mind for one intention at one time; there cannot be both anger at Peter's foolishness, something which is directed to an external object, *and* consciousness of that anger, something directed on an internal object.[14]

The task of the acting teacher and director is to take the pressure off the actor and allow him to work freely within the programme of his role and the situation he has at that point in time. Then he will make discoveries about the situation which can be discussed *afterwards*, analysed, modified and disciplined by a further, deeper understanding of the action of the play. To give the actor a load of instructions too early in rehearsal, about his part and the situation, is destructive, because, until he has had time to digest the information and let it sink in, and turn it into active projects, one is simply emphasising the distance between what he can do, and what he ought to do. In these circumstances the actor usually opts out and marks what the action is, and this demotes the rehearsal from a period of creative exploration to a dead and tedious choreograpic session.

CHAPTER 4

Actor training

None of the foregoing would I ever reveal to an actor working with me, certainly not before we had done a great deal of work together. The sequence of events should never run: let us understand how the mind/body mechanisms work; let us be aware of how they work; let us apply that knowledge to the problems of acting and actor training. It must always be, for me: let us tackle the problems of acting and actor training; now that we have defined the problem and tried to tackle it, let us understand what is involved in overcoming it; if you like, I'll explain this in objective terms as scientifically as I am able. Most of the work I do stays in the area of tackling the problems by whatever means that I have at my disposal. The means are entirely practical and providing they help the actor to work I feel no obligation to reveal the principles. With actors who work with me over a long period of time, the principles are gradually fed into the work so that they can carry on the work away from me.

If I encounter 'pushing' in an actor, I would ask him to throw a ball against a wall several times, to objectivise what he is doing and then try to find some game or exercise to invoke the sensations of the fluctuating flow of movement over the centre of gravity. I would deal purely with the physical aspects of the activity, and let the mind take care of itself. That is, I would try to balance the actor's body so that the natural mind/body processes could work instinctively. If the principles are, or need to be, understood, they should emerge from the work in progress. If the work is carried out on the basis of the principles, however correct they may be, it implies that there is a 'correct' or 'right' way of doing it, and inhibition sets in.

The ideal of the completely flexible actor is Utopian and detracts from the main purpose which is to enable the individual actor to find the best use of his mind/body resources. In this respect, there is no such state as 'normality'. A complex pattern of use in the body exists in every human being differently (although certain general patterns can be established). Secondly, to establish a principle of 'normal' use of the body takes us back to the concept of the 'noble savage' and obscures the central issue which is that the body be trained to perform the actions that we require of it here and now. The only valid question is: what can he do and what does he find difficult?

I make one promise to every actor who works with me. Everything I ask him to do during training, I will, if challenged, relate directly to the work done in rehearsal or performance. The object of the games and exercises is to reveal to the actor what happens when he works, and to help him be aware of the mind/body processes involved in his work. What use he then makes of this understanding is up to him. One can never predict what value any individual will get or take from any exercise. One should never try to make an exercise or game 'work'; one should set it up and let it take place. Afterwards one can discuss the experience. Because I have been through all the processes and have shared discussion with many other people who also have, I have some clear guidelines to what is happening; but in the last analysis the only person who can say what happened to him, in often the simplest situation, is the actor himself. The merit of the leader lies in his ability to use his own subjective and objective experience to help the actor articulate what he has experienced. In practice, the range of experience is neither infinite nor anarchic, because the games and exercises are being carried out within the framework of learning about and exploring the work of the actor. This provides the structured vocabulary for discussion and focuses it.

The keynote to all the work is that it is a process of exploration and discovery, not the direct acquisition of practical skills which the actor does not possess. The acquisition of skills is the by-product of the work. By starting with this premise we concentrate on the processes of action and not on the results we want to achieve.

> In our education stress is laid on the result, and not on the way of achieving it; even though it be at the expense of greater effort than is really necessary. At the higher level of effort, one cannot detect small differences [in the body sensations]; therefore, it is impossible to improve beyond a certain stage. Thus, things are self-perpetuating; the crude kinaesthetic sense tends to become cruder and cruder, the finer one tends to become finer yet.
>
> Activity becomes habitual with repetition to which consent is given. The habitual mode of doing feels right because of repeated approval.[1]

If Feldenkrais is correct in his assumption that, once the actor embarks on the hygienic path, the work becomes self-reinforcing and leads naturally to further improvement, then we have opened the way for self-development in the actor.

The present situation, which allows the actor so little opportunity for training and development once he has finished the formal training of drama school, demands that we find some way by which the actor can find his own way forward. The process of learning and development in the actor is, in any case, directly related to the process of growing up and moving towards maturity. The understanding of what he is taught in drama school is limited by his terms of reference, and the ability to apply it to his living and working. However skilful the teacher, problems always arise with student actors because what they are taught at the beginning of their training only makes sense to them after they have undergone a large body of other work. My experience as a teacher has involved a continuous permutation of elements in my work to try to find the most productive sequence. Almost invariably with every group I have worked with, I am told at the end of the training period 'If you had done this work first we would have understood the earlier work much better and got more benefit from it'. It is an illusion. Almost any permutation of elements produces the same reaction. As the student actor's terms of reference develop through the work and through the normal processes of growing up, so does his understanding. Young actors invariably run into problems of adjustment moving from the special situation of the drama schools to the professional working situation, in trying to apply the lessons they have learned.

One's development as an actor is, in any case, inseparably bound up with a growing understanding of oneself and one's fellow men through personal and social relationships. To restrict the concept of education to a short period of learning facts and basic skills, at a somewhat immature period of one's development, is to inhibit the processes of learning. The essence of any discovery about oneself, or one's relationships with other people, is that things can be changed. But often, because of the continual tactical nature of adjustment that takes place subconsciously in the mind, change cannot take place until the discovery has been objectivised, and a conscious decision to change has been made.

On a purely physical level my body does not respond to my intentions in the same way that it did twenty years ago. This is not a decline. What I have lost in physical strength I have made up in more economical ways of working. Whereas before I achieved control over my body through concentration of physical energy, I now work for control through a relaxation of tension. I don't work nearly so hard and the changing body activity has affected my mental processes. Throughout the period I have been working, there have been moments at which I have quite suddenly found myself able to make certain movements that I could not previously. These have never come when I have been working hard at that area of movement, but usually when I have been working in other areas for some period of time and returned again to the original problem. Once the breakthrough is made, the possibilities of movement in my body change. After long periods of teaching, when I return to work professionally as an actor, I have to work hard physically to change my body/think activities. This has nothing to do with physical fitness. In teaching one strives to reveal clearly and technically the means by which one works. Performance demands that, to a large extent, one conceals the technique from the audience. The concentration has to be taken away from 'how' one works and centred on 'what' one is doing, and this demands making changes in the relationship between mind and body.

Basic teaching techniques

I have already laid stress upon certain aspects of the teaching situation; the need for the teacher to avoid the temptation to pursue predetermined goals, to make exercises 'work'; the need to find exploratory processes to by-pass the conscious brain mechanisms and allow the automatic body/think processes to come into play; the need to assist the actor to be aware rather than conscious of the way his mind and body co-ordinate naturally; the need to work always in the strict terms of the actor's immediate experience, rather than setting up some ideal state for him to which he may progress.

The rest of this book sets out the means I have used in trying to do this. But before going on, there are a few 'tricks of the trade' to be listed, and one major process, central to all the work, which must be examined first.

Tricks

In basic training, when one is not dealing with specific problems faced by experienced actors, but rather setting out a pattern of work for inexperienced or student actors, it is often easier to begin by showing them what they *can't* do, instead of starting straight into work. This is one way of arousing motivation and commitment in the actor to the work. Sometimes actors need to be shown the reasons why the work is being done, before they can agree to take part in games and exercises which have no obvious result. I often ask actors to repeat a complex dance step, which I demonstrate for them. The one I usually use is a vaudeville hoofing step. The step is basically an alternate crossing of the legs and arms, and a spreading of the limbs in a sideways movement across the stage. It demands a coordination of the upper and lower limbs, through a central impulse from the pelvis. Given the step to repeat, the actor usually tries to think about what he is doing (since he has no experience of how to do it) whilst actually doing the step. The result is that the head comes forward, the balance is disturbed, and the step cannot be done. Often the actor tries to look at where he is placing his feet whilst moving them at the same time, with the same result. The first lesson of ballroom dancing is to stop looking at your feet.

I also use a gunfighter's speed-of-reaction game to demonstrate the two modes of thinking. Place a biro or pencil in your pocket, with the end of it protruding far enough to be grasped easily by the hand. Balance a matchbox on the back of the hand, and extend the arm parallel to the ground, at shoulder height. The object of the game is to take the hand away from under the matchbox, grasp and draw the pencil, and hit the matchbox before it hits the ground. With a little practice it is relatively easy to do, providing one doesn't look at the pencil. The essence is speed of reaction and it can only be played successfully if one doesn't think about what one is doing. If the eyes turn to look at the pencil, as one goes to grasp it, the body loses balance as the head comes forward, the eyes signal the position of the pencil to the front brain, which directs the back brain to make the necessary impulse to grasp the pencil. By this time, the matchbox is gathering dust on the floor.

It is often possible to get actors to experience the differing activities of the two brains by asking a question like, 'Do you know what the front of the British Museum looks like?' and then, 'How many pillars does it have?' Most people asked these questions are clearly aware of a general picture in the back of the mind which is then thrown forward into the front brain in search of definition (which never comes – one knows or one doesn't know; all the conscious reflection in the world will never produce a sharp enough version of the first picture to enable one to count the pillars). The switch from the back to the front brain is usually accompanied by a physical nod of the head and a lowering of the eyes.

Beyond this I would, sometime during the post-session discussions, introduce the material outlined earlier – how I experience the two brains working – to see what common or complementary experiences the actor can recall from his own life.

Observation

In the early stages of work, it is very difficult to help the actor be aware of how he is working without reflecting on what he is doing. His habitual way of objectivising is to stop and think consciously about what he has done, and then to change what he is doing as a result of a conscious intention. This brings in all the problems detailed earlier. Discussion is necessary, after the working session is over, in order to be clear and objective about what has been done, but some link is necessary between subjective subconscious activity and detached conscious objectivisation. If we do not want the actor to reflect on what his experiences are, then the only other way of objectivising them is to observe how they manifest themselves in others, and to apply the knowledge gained from observation to the control of his own subjective activities. He tries to do what he has seen someone else do. This takes the attention away from himself. It extroverts it instead of introverting it. The actor is aware of what is to be done, rather than conscious of what *he* must do.

This is a part of every actor's work, to observe behaviour patterns in others and to try to recreate them in himself imaginatively. Where this sometimes goes wrong is when the actor observes a certain behavioural pattern, forms a total image of a result he wants to achieve in the reflective part of the mind, and tries to repeat the totality, instead of working through the subjective kinaesthetic sensations. Thus an actor observing in an old person a certain cramped and semi-collapsed stance and restricted range of movement, tries to reproduce these phenomena at will, and does so by a violent contraction of the muscles through tension, without observing analytically that the original state is produced by the collapse and over-relaxation of certain muscle groups. The stage provides many examples of tense 'old men'. Life provides many examples of old men restricted in their movement by a *lack* of strength and tension in various groups of anti-gravitational muscles. The stage effect comes from working off a generalised image in the mind. The correct effect can only be achieved through the processes of analysis and re-synthesis.

When first working in this area, the actor Brian Murphy and I spent many hours standing on railway stations and street corners, in libraries and art galleries watching people, and then putting ourselves imaginatively in their situations. We looked at pictures, browsed through books, rushed for trains, loitered in waiting halls and on street corners. We observed each other's attempts to recreate the original, criticised and compared notes, and tried again. We isolated activities in the bodies of the people we observed, and from this we learned the primary importance of the connections between head, neck, spine and pelvis. I would still advise this simple but arduous process to any young actor who works with me as a necessary part of his learning. But my observation has led me to understand the necessity for possessing certain analytical tools, and also to appreciate the fact that these analytical tools can be developed and used in laboratory situations, where one can isolate parts of the process from others, and study them accordingly, in the same way that the chemical scientist isolates processes in a complex chain reaction in order to study their interaction.

In order to do this, some instruction has to be given in observation. I have said earlier that when the normal righting processes are disturbed in the body/think, the conscious mind takes over through the optical righting mechanism. Something similar occurs when one *looks* instead of *watches*. That is, when one consciously searches with the eyes for information, rather than allows the eyes to take in the information. Sight has developed to a predominating position over man's other senses. It is through the eyes that we draw in most factual information about the world outside us. Normally, this information is not reflected on unless we are either surprised by the information we receive, or consciously looking for something or someone. The act of consciously looking for something often restricts our response to the wide range of information that is present in any situation. The nearest I can get to a practical example of this is picking blackberries. My experience is that if you go out to look for blackberries someone always comes after you and finds a lot that you have missed. The technique is to watch the bush and the blackberries leap out at you.

This is after all how we experience and respond as an audience. We watch a play, not look at it. Whilst watching, a great deal of complex and often diffuse information is taken into our minds without reflection, and we respond to the external stimuli non-reflectively and instinctively. Only afterwards do we reflect on the experience, and assess the significance. Post-performance discussions have always seemed a disaster to me because they short-circuit the period of necessary reflection. It takes a great deal of experience and often training to be able to give an objective assessment shortly after a complex event. Sometimes with critics writing to tight dead-lines, the notices seem to reveal that they have been looking at the play, and not watching it. They write up all the obvious facts about the production but little of the significant content of the play. It is often said that critics are a special audience, but it need not be so, and isn't so with serious critics, that is, those who are prepared to watch the play, respond to it, and then write their notices out of their post-performance reflections. It is a question of degree of articulation.

Work is carried out then as an alternating process of doing, and watching other actors do. In the early stages the two processes are followed by discussion which involves conscious reflection. This is to provide the basic vocabulary. As soon as possible, the exercises continue, switching repeatedly from one role to the other. One acts, one watches, one acts again, one watches again and so on. It is only at this point that one tries to outline a predictable or pre-conceived form for the exercise. The exercise can be deliberately destroyed, to see what happens when one tries to carry out the activity by different means. The exercise is always thrown open to the group to suggest alternative ways of structuring it, or to explore the activity in any way they wish. The whole process is a complex interweaving of exploration and observation, repetitions, imitations and experimentation with alternative ways of acting in a given situation. Through this, rather than mechanical exercises, the actor learns and develops.

The Fight in the Dark

Although most of the games I use take a long time to wear out their usefulness, because the actor returns to them at different stages of his development and, therefore, makes different use of them, there is one game which holds a very important position in my work, and to which I return time and time again. The game is valuable both as observation training, and in the wider training of the kinaesthetic sense and body/think. This is

The Fight in the Dark. I have adapted it from a set piece in one of the Peking Operas.

A square is formed by chairs facing outwards, leaving a small gap in one corner. The chairs are occupied by the observers. In the centre of the room formed by the square is a precious object, say, a jewel. One player is guarding it. The other is a thief who enters the room through the gap to steal it. The room is imagined to be in total darkness.

The thief tries to find the jewel, which he cannot see, whilst avoiding the guard, whom he cannot see. The guard cannot see the jewel and, therefore, cannot be sure where it is. Once he has been able to react to a sound made by the thief, he must find the jewel and guard it, and/or find and kill the thief. The options are left open until the game has been played a number of times. The actor is left, first of all, to find his own way of playing the game. After this, disciplines are fed into the game, either to help him select from the alternative strategies open to him, or to examine particular strategies possible within the game. The first playings, though, are straightforward and open.

The game is played by successive pairs of players, so that each actor has the chance both to play the game, and to observe it being played. At first

the game is played with the eyes open in full light (which is how the Peking Opera stage it), and then blindfolded.

The differences between the open-eyed and blindfold versions are usually widely different, physically. The observable manifestations of this are usually that in the open-eyed version, the head, neck, spine, pelvis relationship forms a convex shape with the pelvis retarded, and the head dropped (*illustration nos. 5 and 6*). In the blindfold version, the head becomes more erect, the base of the spine flattens, and the relationship between head, neck, spine and pelvis becomes much straighter (*illustration nos. 7 and 8*). There is usually a marked improvement in balance when the players are blindfolded, much more use of extensions in space as they feel around, and a dramatic change in the relationship between them.

In the open-eyed version, the space in which the players move is very loosely defined. Because of the configuration by the body, each player appears on the periphery of a space area without a clear centre. The two players have little connection with each other beyond being incidentally inside the square. In the blindfold version, they appear concentrated in the centre of their own very clearly defined space, which always, because of their use of extensions in space, includes the other player. The distance between

5–6 The Fight in the Dark: the open-eyed version

them becomes very clearly defined as dangerously close, and yet they are clearly detached from each other. This increases the dramatic tension for the watchers, and heightens both their concentration and excitement.

The major difference between the two versions is that, in the open-eyed version, the actor is concentrating on the *result*, consciously trying to create the illusion of darkness. The intention becomes totalised and intellectual; it gets in the way of the body/think processes, and the balance of his body is disturbed. Often an actor has in the front of his mind a fixed image or picture of what he is trying to re-create.

In the blindfold version of the game, the actor does not have to reflect on the circumstances, as they have been created for him (as they never are in the theatre). His body/think processes become predominant, and he pursues the physical intention of search and evasion. The other senses sharpen, once sight is removed, and the physical and imaginative centres of the brain take over. He plays a game, instead of pursuing an effect.

When playing the game, one must always be critical of what is happening. Inexperienced actors and people with poor habitual body use

often go on trying to achieve pre-conceived results, even when blindfolded. This area of work is the best training I know in the actor's task of re-creating, imaginatively, areas of physical action. It is important because it can move into areas of high mimetic skill, such as is exhibited by Chinese actors.

It is impossible to predict the outcome of the game, because so much depends upon the experience and ability of the actor in recreating situations instinctively, rather than in conceiving thought or pre-conceiving intentions. Experienced actors frequently manage to produce instinctively the imagined reality of a pitch-dark room, in which event, the exercise is repeated deliberately using the intellectual mechanisms so as to demonstrate the difference. If the actor can instinctively find his way to the imaginative recreation of the room in darkness, then the way is open to move on to other Peking Opera games, such as the one where the ferry-man punts a boat across a stream, carrying a passenger, without a boat, pole, or stream.

7–8 The Fight in the Dark: the blindfold version

CHAPTER 5

Games theory and games sessions

My early use of games work was entirely confined to the practical problems of movement training. It arose out of the situation described in the Introduction, when actors became distressed by the difficulties encountered in trying to carry out technical exercises.

Perhaps those of us who were able to train had a finer kinaesthetic sense than those who couldn't, but ultimately this didn't help us when we tried to exercise on our own initiative. I found it impossible not to pursue the totalised result of the exercise, which is like trying to direct what one is doing from a position outside one's own body. Physically, the effect is that, if one continued the dynamic line of the body reflected in the curvature of the spine, the head would enter the body somewhere between the navel and the rectum. The head is thrown forward and the pelvis retarded and the body is in the wrong position to undertake any exercise or activity that requires a relaxed and balanced co-ordination. It requires a great deal of blind faith in processes for the novice actor to inhibit the search for results. With the result in mind, he knows what he is after and can intellectually monitor his progress (always poor). But it is the changing sensations in the body which are the balance of the action; through them we find our way again (though never quite the same) to the re-creation of the action. Until the actor is aware of these sensations, it is difficult in movement classes to prevent him from going after the result. Technical exercises tend to make the actor self-conscious and (in the early stages of work) to introvert his energies.

The classes became an emotional nightmare for me and we soon abandoned the exercises and started playing with warm-up games and improvisations. However, we were left with the shame of having given up. By accident we stumbled on a way. We were working on extensions in space, and somehow just sticking our arms out didn't appeal to us. I suggested we marked a goal against a wall and that we threw tennis balls against it. The goal-keeper had to stretch to catch the balls, not moving his feet away from stance. The idea appealed, people enjoyed themselves, one actor at least was working, a tremendous relief came over me. All I had to do to lead a session was introduce more and more games. I ransacked my memory for games, and a way of working began to evolve. Since then, I have never found a technical exercise for which I couldn't find a direct parallel in the world of children's games. This by no means guarantees that the problem will be solved, but it can be tackled in a manner that is totally within the actor's experience and movement memory.

Children's games and play are a very complicated area of human activity, and psychologists are right to remind us that the child is not just a small adult. Nor is he the simple blank page on which an adult character will later be writ large. He is a human being in the process of learning by experimentation. Mobility is one important part of his learning. Through games, the child explores the range of movement possibilities open to him. He tests his progress by leaping at tree branches, jumping streams, walking on walls. He devises often quite complicated structures for developing control over his movement, and perfecting skills. Later, in response to personal, parental and social pressures, he selects those skills and movement patterns which he thinks will best express his purposes in life, or which suit the persona he conceives will best present himself to the world. What is clear is that by adolescence the child has lost many of the skills which he had at an earlier age, though those that he does still possess are much more finely developed. Like all learning processes, it is liable to inhibition at various stages.

The achieving of ends begins in the gymnasium, with thirty children being told to vault the horse, without close enquiry into why some can and some can't. The assumption is that the exercise is beneficial in its own right and everyone by an act of will can perform it successfully. The results prove this manifestly untrue. The haphazard nature of children's play, combined with a developing sense of relationship to others, often inhibits the child from exploring those areas of movement which are difficult and therefore dangerous to him. The exploitation of skills already learned earns approval, failure brings criticism and, since the mind and body/image are inextricably linked in the young person, failure reflects on the personality. It is a general characteristic of actors I work with that they look back to school and say 'I didn't mind jumping from heights, but I hated hanging from my knees. I could never do it'. Physical inhibitions are set up, and physical education too often attacks these with a head-on, block-busting approach that only serves to demonstrate the deficiency more clearly and hence to intensify the inhibition. I believe firmly that children learn more in the playground and the street, than they do in the gymnasium.

In using children's games as an approach to training the actor in mobility, one gets completely away from the concept of teaching someone a set of skills he does not possess, and knows he does not possess, and which produces an anxiety situation for him. One goes back to the root processes of learning, by which he acquired movement skills in the first place, and this helps him rediscover lost skills, or those which have atrophied. The strength of this approach is that he returns to a low level of achievement to find the place where his development stopped or became inhibited, and it then allows him to use his adult powers to overcome those obstacles. More important than this, though, it takes the actor back in his memory to a period and process that is associated with pleasure, and often delight, and that was free from anxiety. It substitutes for the pain of learning the joy of re-discovery. It also reinstates the non-reflective body/think mechanisms, since the child does not consciously reflect upon, or direct his play. Allowing for problems that arise out of habitual mis-use, the games approach leads the actor to the optimum use of his present mind/body resources.

As a broader principle, having done this work in demonstration classes, and at weekend schools, with a wide variety of people from all walks of life, I am convinced that the inhibition of play processes among adults is one of the great social crimes of our society. The release of emotional energy and free, uninhibited movement patterns that come when one asks respectable, middle-aged, middle-class citizens to take part in one of the conflict games described later on is both exciting and astonishing. Primitive societies understood human needs and processes better when they incorporated their moral, social and spiritual education into the dance form. Our society is physically and emotionally inhibited. Children's games are a readily accessible, and seemingly acceptable, framework for releasing physical and emotional energy. Pressure is released, and the human being is to some extent made free, in a framework which is not susceptible to social criticism – provided the sessions are billed under some such intellectually acceptable heading as 'Exploration of Theatre' or 'The Processes of Acting' . . .

Games sessions

Games can be used to tackle specific movement problems. Hopscotch is a game through which the child develops a skilful control of shifts of balance using one leg. Skipping develops stamina and breath control. In working with actors it is more usual to construct the work around extended games sessions rather than the use of single games. The changes of activity allow all the muscle groups of the body to be exercised, and the interest of the actors is sustained.

The leader needs to study children's games and build up an extensive repertoire. With experience one is able to define clear areas of work which are either basic or arise frequently. The number of times one has to find a new game becomes fewer and fewer. One can begin work with a limited repertoire and extend it as new exercises are needed, or as the group becomes bored with the same games.

In the extended games session, the actors, participating unselfconsciously in a flow of activities, reveal themselves in action. Every human being has, naturally, differing strengths and weaknesses and clear movement characteristics. In the playing of games one is able to 'read' the class, to get what information one can about the people one is working with; what areas of physical work come easily to them, and where they need to develop. The object is to make it possible for the actor to be able to produce as wide a range of movements in time and space as he can, so that he can select from all these possibilities when he comes to a specific role or activity. This releases him from the restrictions of his own characteristics of movement. The object is not to produce a multi-potential puppet, since every human being will find new possibilities in his own way by using his own personal resources and overcoming his own resistances. There are no pat formulae. *The first object of the games sessions then, is to reveal something of the actor's movement problems and possibilities.*

Games sessions are also important because it is often hard to approach a physical problem at first shot. Often, to persuade an actor to venture into areas which are unknown territory for him, or which he thinks are dangerous, one has to construct stepping stones so that he can approach the problem gradually and without anxiety, in the way that the child moves from simple games to more complex and difficult versions of the same activity, as he develops skills. 'Danger areas' develop, for example, when children are told: 'if you go on doing that you'll hurt yourself'. Repeated, the injunction establishes disastrous consequences in the child's mind, and this can inhibit him from that area of physical activity. The inhibition is the stronger because it is imaginary and not the result of practical experience.

Fortunately, no game ever fulfils only one purpose. Games are a mixture of elements combined to create a structured activity. Alongside the use of more skilful variations of the same activity, it is possible in games sessions to move naturally from one area of movement to another, through common elements in games, without interrupting the flow of activity. *The second purpose of games sessions is to lead actors to physical experiences and sensations that they could not find directly.*

The experiences and sensations of movement areas which he has explored in the past, can lead the actor to learn about himself and his bodily and imaginative faculties and processes. A complex network of pleasurable sensations are recalled from the actor's memory. The framework in which he works is richly evocative and emotionally and physically stimulating. The actor is much more interested in his past, and the stages through which he grew up, than he is in what often seems an abstracted activity – technical exercises. Wider areas of personality come into play. *The third purpose of games sessions is to initiate in the actor a process of self-awareness and discovery.*

This does not happen in isolation but through relationship with the session leader and the rest of the group. *The fourth purpose of games sessions is to create a shared body of experience which one uses to build up relationships within the group and to develop the ensemble.*

This shared body of work enables the ensemble to define and discuss its group and individual problems and its approach to work. *The fifth purpose of games sessions is to create a common vocabulary, based upon shared experience, with which to discuss the processes of human action and interaction and the work of the actor.*

Obviously all these purposes need a sustained period of work in order to bear fruit. The one-off games session is useful for releasing energy in individuals, which is not to be devalued, and for provoking thoughts in people's minds. Perhaps occasionally, it may inspire someone to go away and start working in his own way. But little more can be gained than this. Only a regular and sustained period of work can produce deep or lasting results.

It was clear to me before I started this work that a warm-up games session before rehearsal was beneficial for the actors. It patently got everyone moving and released energy which carried over into the rehearsal. As I have gone on working, it has become clear that a more systematic approach to games is capable of yielding much more benefit than *ad hoc* warm-up activities.

In running games sessions I never have more than the first game in my mind, and this is always a release-of-energy game. From then on I improvise. That is, I trust my subconscious mind, instead of working out a sustained pre-conceived pattern of work. Like all meetings, the games session runs on a pattern of demand and response. I make a suggestion or issue an invitation and the group responds by playing (each group tends to throw up its own specific character; if it doesn't, I don't have a group, just a collection of individuals, and the first task is to use games that will bring them into contact with each other). Working instinctively, I watch the first game played and the second forms naturally in my mind. It is important that this instinctive response be trusted, and this is only possible if one participates physically in the session. A games session cannot be conducted from a chair. I once pulled my back badly and was unable to lead games sessions, since I could not tell what was happening to the players. One does not need to play all the games. In fact to take information about the group one often has to pull out of games, but by being physically aware of what the group is doing, one's body responds sympathetically to their activities (principally through rhythmic communication) and this makes it possible for the body/think to operate. If one has a pre-conceived programme of games, it is interfered with.

Like all improvisations, the richer the understanding of one's material, and the wider the range of alternatives one can choose from, the richer will be the improvisation, but this is not a prime consideration. The sessions I run now are fed by fifteen years experience. At the beginning they were fed only by a desperation to learn and by what I could remember of my childhood play patterns. A games session led by an experienced and creative teacher can be a constant source of discovery and delight, but it is arguable that one learns more in struggling than in being flown along. One teaches best what one is learning oneself. Having led sessions for fifteen years I find myself faced with a problem I never had at the outset. I have led so many sessions that I have to rid myself of preconceptions of what is going to happen. It needs more concentration to remain open-minded. I watch in the hope of seeing something new and outside my previous experience. I hope to have experience contradicted so that I might learn something new.

Occasionally you get lost. There are two ways of coping with this. Do not try to continue by consciously directing the next stages. Either cut back to a simple release-of-energy game and start again, or throw the session open to the group. They have been through all the stages of the session so far and, if they are working, they will be able to produce the next step. This makes it possible for anyone to start leading games sessions tomorrow. Let the group work out its own session.

Occasionally the session is a disaster and you cannot hold the interest of the group or stimulate them to action. Give up. You cannot make things happen and the harder you try the worse it will get. Discuss why the session has failed if you like. Go away and think about it yourself but never press on regardless. In my experience such occasions are rare. In fifteen years I have had only one total disaster. The experience was salutory. I was forced to go back and re-examine everything I was doing and had done in that session, and to try to discover whether the reason was in them or me. It is arguable that you learn more from the less successful sessions than from the successful ones, since you are pushed to analyse the comparative failures in retrospect.

The most successful sessions are when a group takes the session away from you, and spontaneously begins to throw in their own games; or, more often, a game grows on a group, and they will go on playing it and getting value from it long after you might have moved on to some other area.

CHAPTER 6

Simple movement games

There are five principle ways of taking the pressure off the actor in simple movement games. All of these methods direct the actor to focus his attention outside of himself, and so extrovert the flow of energy instead of introverting it, and by so doing, break down selfconsciousness and free the actor's body/think mechanisms.

Aims and objectives

The first of these methods uses games with *simple aims and objectives* for the actor to reach for which take his mind off the movements he is making.

In **Tag**, which everyone knows, one player chases all the others, until he touches someone else who then becomes the pursuer. The aim or objective being to catch someone or to avoid being caught. The game leads to a violent release of energy with players running wildly all over the playing space – usually with enjoyment.

Various forms of Tag can be introduced which, through rules, produce a refinement of movement patterns. If the rule is made that the touch can only be made on the head, and only when the pursued has his feet on the floor, the movement alternates between running and jumping. If the rule is made that the player touched must hold the part of his body that was touched, until he is released by touching someone else, obstacles are introduced that he must overcome. In **Cat and Mouse** the pursuer runs after only one opponent. The other players join hands in a grid, forming alleys through which the chase may be pursued. On command the players change the direction of the grid so that the alleys now run at right angles to the previous lines, and control of running and changes of direction are introduced.

Tag is a good starting game because of the violent release of energy. One must first of all release energy before one can work to control and discipline it. The length of the game depends on where you want to go later. If you want to move quickly towards some form of disciplined work, then a long game of Tag tires the actor slightly and takes the top energy off, making it easier to concentrate and be still.

Two-circle Tag is a cooler version of the game, and lets you begin a session without too violent a release of energy. Players stand two deep in a circle. Again, the hunter pursues the quarry, but the quarry can escape by standing in front of any of the pairs in the circle. When he has done this the rear member of what is now a trio becomes the quarry and must evade capture. The game allows an alternation of violent activity and rest. As the circle gets smaller, by adding to the front of the pairs and taking from the back, the players are brought closer together.

Tee-ak-ee-allio or **Team Tag** This game produces such a violent release of energy that it virtually exhausts the players. It is useful at the end of sessions involving detailed or concentrated work, when a violent release of tensions is called for. The players divide into two teams. Each team has a base in a corner of the room. The object of the game is to capture the opposing players by tapping them on the head and calling 'tee-ak'. Once touched, the captive goes to the enemy base and can only be released from there by one of his own side running through the base shouting 'tee-ak-ee-allio'. He can then rejoin the game, which continues until one side manages to capture all the opposing players at one time.

Red Rover is a form of one-legged Tag, but also relates to several other games, particularly British Bulldog. In Red Rover, one player is in the centre of the room whilst the others line up against one wall. At 'Go', the players hop from one wall to the wall opposite, evading being touched by the player hopping in the centre. If caught, they join him in the middle and the game continues until no-one is free.

The purpose of the game is hopping, which is a shift of the balance of the body's weight in space, controlled by one foot. The child is exploring and developing his powers of balance. The game structure adds obstacles to be overcome in the interests of perfecting the skill. In another version of Red Rover, the players fold arms and the object is to knock the free players off their balance in order to capture them, thus intensifying the necessity of controlling balance by the opposition of outside forces.

In **British Bulldog** the players are on two feet and have to be lifted clear of the ground. This creates a trial of strength, in which the players are trying to overcome or use the force of gravity, in lifting or avoiding being lifted.

As an example of the development that is possible in these games, let me give a sequence of three games, to show how one can move out into complex areas of human relationships.

The sequence starts with **Red Rover** which is a skilful but simple release game. The next step is to refine the rules, so that players are caught, not by touching, but by stealing a handkerchief tucked into the back of the belt. This increases the dimensions of the spatial movement, and also calls for more evasive skills in twists and turns around the central axis, rather than speed of dash to the other side. The next step is to change the framework of the game so that, instead of a dash from one side of the room to the other, it becomes a group game. All players are opposing all other players in an open situation. The object is to steal as many handkerchiefs from other players as one can. Once the handkerchief is stolen, the player retires from the game until a winner emerges. Actually the game is best stopped at two remaining players, as one against one rarely ever produces a victor. The area of dangerous space has been totalised in this way, and the player is forced into a position of all-round awareness, with quite violent shifts of balance in response to a number of external stimuli.

The game moves into an entirely new area when there are only three players left. In order for one of them to be put out of the game, since surprise is no longer a factor, two must make an alliance against the third. The third can break the alliance, if he can change his position in space, so that the balance of forces shifts, and he is in a position to make an alliance with one of his opponents against the other. What usually happens in the game is a shifting sequence of alliances and betrayals, as the players manoeuvre for positions which will take them out of danger and put another player in it. The game thus becomes a laboratory for studying human relationships in space. When games are played at this level, they form the basis for new games and further exploration. When they are played at this level, I would never involve the whole group but split into alternating players and observers.

I hope it can be seen that the last game described brings attention to bear upon the nature of relationships on the stage, and leads the actor to an awareness of space as a factor in relationships.

Competition

The second of the methods for taking the pressure off the actor focuses the energy in *competition*. This is the simplest of the methods but probably the one that has the widest use, since the framework is so loose that you can include whatever physical exercise you like within it. However, it will not usually sustain for very long. You can keep it going by introducing 'best of five' contests, or even seven, but competition palls very soon as a stimulus to a group and the method is best kept for areas of movement that it is particularly suited for, or when you can find no other way of tackling them, which is very rare. I find relay races useful for certain areas of movement. I use them for movements which employ contrasting and opposing directions.

Over and Under is one of these. A simple relay game in an extended line, where the running player has to go over the head of one of his team-mates and under the legs of the next, before returning to his place and touching off the next man. As he too starts 'over', all the team are continually going up and then down. I use it for passing a ball, between one's feet, over one's head, to the man behind, who takes it with his feet (sitting down, of course). The ball is passed up the team and then down again. If the ball is dropped it returns to the front man for a new start.

The most important area in which I use **Relay Games** is for walking exercises. I make the game a walk to the opposite wall and back, using a sequence of steps that involve, for instance, reverse shifts of balance. A sequence of two steps forward, one step back, would do this. The reverse turn of the waltz involves the following sequence:

Left foot forward
Right foot forward
Left foot back
Right foot back to join it
Left foot forward and so on.

Any pattern of movement such as this brings the actor into the problems that I demonstrated in the vaudeville dance step. He tries to think about what he is doing, or looks at his feet and becomes uncoordinated. Players are instructed to say out loud what they are doing as they do it. 'Left foot, right foot, left foot back' etc or 'Forward, forward, back, together'. In this way they think *what* they are doing and not *about* what they are doing. It is an important stage in the co-ordination of mind and body.

I also use an extended team-interweaving relay which employs various modes of uncoordinated walking. The intellectual leads with his head; the sailor rolls his shoulders; the hairy athlete pushes out his chest; the horse-walker prances with his knees leading; the fashion model leads with the back of her pelvis, shoving her crotch out without opening the pelvis. The game leads to an exploration of wrong or uncoordinated forms of walking and how these relate to projected character, and to an examination of balanced walking. Many children's play exercises can be utilised in this structure, such as frog and kangaroo jumps, or walking on all fours, stomach uppermost.

I also find it useful to use a fireman's lift relay, where number one in the team carries number two to the far end of the room, and stays there, while number two runs back for number three and so on. This is a violent introduction to the problems of handling the weight of another person's body, and leads to more exploration of co-operative balance and control.

External object: ball games

The third method of taking the pressure off the actor focuses upon an *external object* such as a ball. In one way this is fundamental. In the Middle Ages, the medical pioneer, Galen, constructed a whole system of therapeutic and hygienic exercises around a small ball, on the grounds that it was the cheapest piece of apparatus and well within the means of even the poorest to obtain. One of the earliest training exercises used by children (which trains the co-ordination of hand and eye) is catching a ball. There are a wide variety of rules introduced by children specially to improve this co-ordination. A ball is thrown against a wall and the hands must be clapped behind the back, first once, then twice, and then three times, and so on, before the ball is caught. The thrower sometimes has to perform a 360 degree turn before catching the ball. In another game a ball is thrown against a wall, a name is called, and the person named must run and judge the bounce so that the ball passes between his legs. Skipping ropes perform a similar function for children in training rhythmic co-ordination and judgement of distances.

The exercise which finally clinched my belief in the usefulness of children's games was the one shown in illustration nos. 9–12. In the early stages, the one technical physical exercise that I was unable to replace with a game was the pelvic whip. This is a very difficult exercise involving a circular revolution of the pelvis from high front open to high back closing, to low back closed, with a sudden impulse through to low front opening. The exercise involves a revolution of the pelvis on the front/back–high/low axes, with a gradual closing of the pelvic joints and an opening impulse at the lowest point. This exercise, more than any other, proved impossible, because, like most people, the mobility of our legs in the hip socket was severely restricted and the position of the pelvis, through use, was retarded. Three pelvic whips, performed by a beginner clutching the kitchen table for support, are enough to turn him into a neurotic wreck. But the game of standing with the legs apart and throwing a ball through the legs against the wall, to be caught on its return demands an alternation of closing and impulsively opening the pelvis. Children – and adults – can practise the exercise for long periods, without getting in the least bit anxious.

9–12 The 'pelvic whip' as a simple ball game

In the second game the players sit in a circle with their legs spread wide and straight, and with a foot touching the nearest foot of the player seated on either side of them (*illustration nos. 13 and 14*). The ball is lobbed underhand to bounce somewhere within the triangle made by another player's legs. The player on the receiving end must catch it before it bounces, or have a point against him. The most effective way to score points is to bounce it just inside the ankle, which requires the maximum stretch to catch it. The exercise covers the same ground as the physical education exercise of pressing to touch the toes or the space between the feet, with two significant differences. The players are prepared to go on for long periods, enduring the physical discomfort for the sake of the game, and, because the ball is used, the player stretches to reach an external object, and the energy flows from the centre out to the periphery of his reach and beyond. In the physical education exercise (*illustration no. 15*), because the exercise is self-

13–14 'The players sit in a circle with their legs spread wide and straight . . .'

15 'In the physical education exercise, the actor allow the back to droop over . . .'

contained and self-justifying, the actor often allows the back to droop over, in pressing towards the space, and in doing so he introverts the flow of movement and energy. If the dynamic line of the illustration is continued, the actress appears to be about to disappear up her own rear entrance. Instead of the energy flowing directly from the centre to the periphery, it flows from the centre, round the periphery and back towards the centre. The more energy the actor puts into the exercise the more self-inflicted violence he causes himself.

A very important ball game tackles the problem of the low centre of gravity and all the other encumbrances to erect posture. A tennis ball is held as high as the arms will comfortably stretch without lifting the shoulders. This usually is just about the place where the forehead and the hair line meet. The ball is dropped. As the ball drops, the base of the spine and pelvis collapse to fall with it, in a straight line between the heels. The ball is caught just above the ankles. The ball must not be watched but must be caught through reflex reaction.

If the spine does not drop straight, that is, if the pelvis swings to the back, either the ball hits the chest, or the top body overbalances and the arms are too far forward to catch the ball. The game is very like an uncontrolled ballet plié, and works on the same muscle groups. I use it to try to induce the actor instinctively to release tension in the anti-gravitational muscles by collapsing the centre of his body and letting it fall straight to the floor under the force of gravity.

Other people

The fourth way of taking the pressure off the actor is by using *another person or persons*. A number of these games are included in later sections of the book, as they tend to fall into very special areas of work, where the simple games lead to explorations of relationships and interactions. The second game above, though, can be replaced by having two people place their feet against the feet of their partners, with their legs opened wide and turned out. They join hands across and pull and relax in a rowing action. This tends not to be as stimulating as the ball game, but it has the virtue of relaxation during the stretch, with the partner supplying the effort.

Strong *gathering* movements can be worked at by drawing a line down the centre of the room, and dividing into two teams on either side of the line. The object is to grab the hand of an opponent and drag him across the line to join your side. Groups of players can join forces in tug-of-war style.

Many of the games I use involving partners and opponents are used to work at whichever Laban action dominates the particular game chosen. Thus **The Raft** described under 'Trust Games' in Chapter 8 works at *floating*. The **Two-man Somersault** (*illustration nos. 16–18*) is a game which tackles the fear of falling. Exercising the calf muscles by stretching and

16–18 Two-man Somersault

relaxing them can be tackled by the game of **Fox and Grapes**. One player holds an object high above his partner's head and he must stretch to try to grab it before it is removed from his extended reach. The player holding the object tantalises his partner by lowering it and then raising it out of reach. The player reaching must keep both feet on the floor.

I use games and exercises involving partners when working to free the voice. The production of sound to no purpose seems to inhibit actors more than anything else. Sound directed towards a partner, or drawn in response to a partner, is easier to produce, and when produced, is easier to control and work on. An exercise I use frequently in this area involves two partners standing back to back. The basis of a children's game is used. One player puts his arms under those of his partner; places the small of his back under his partner's buttocks; and, by bending at the hip joints, lifts his partner on to his back. In order to support the partner, the supporting back must be flattened, and the back of the lifted player is correspondingly flattened. The head, neck, spine, pelvis relationship becomes that which allows no tension stops along the spine, and there is therefore no pressure on, or tension in, the voice producing organs, and the voice can be released freely in either player.

Imagination

The fifth and last way of releasing the actor is to create some structure where he takes the pressure off himself by the use of his *imagination*. This is probably the most important category and is an area of children's play in which many elements and processes interact. Children use the **Crossing the Ice** game to develop *quick, light, direct* movements. The mime games of flying an imaginary kite, or holding on to a helium balloon are useful; I use these in conjunction with playing at being a balloon, and then a drunk, and on to an exercise of being a man ten days in the Kalahari Desert, without food and water, with just enough strength to stay upright, and knowing he won't get up if he falls. All these games work on taking tension out of the anti-gravitational muscles, particularly the muscles just inside the thigh above the knees. The exercises explore *light sustained movement*, and the minimum necessary amount of anti-gravitational tension.

I use the idea of a motor-powered model aeroplane, on a control wire looped round the finger, for explorations of extensions in space around the periphery, and also for pure 360 degree revolutions of the trunk. If the revolution is not pure, the orbit has a hiccough in it and the plane crashes. With one early group this exercise was performed by actors varying the extension of the orbits, and working in different planes of movement (high, low, middle), and at varying speeds. With a sense of awareness of each other's rhythms, a ballet was created of some beauty and with a striking likeness to Chinese painting.

A combination of using the imagination and other people can produce a game like **Climbing the Matterhorn**, which also uses competition. Two teams race to the top of the Matterhorn, by crawling over the bodies of the previous climbers in the team, to stand balanced on their shoulders. They then pull up the following team climbers. The first team to get a man to the top wins. The game is played lying on the floor, which is taken to be the face of the Matterhorn.

Imagination games can be combined with object games to good advantage. Throwing a ball and, through the imagination, varying its character, so that it is a lead cannon-ball, or a fragile bauble from a Christmas tree, or a time-bomb, is an exercise which I often use as an introduction to games and exercises which require strong, sustained concentration. I usually try to combine these games with the production of vocal sound, as a means of co-ordinating physical and vocal efforts, when the actor has other things to think about.

All of these games necessitate muscular activity, whilst directing the actor's attention away from the specific nature of the activity. He is given something else to think about. It is worth pointing out that these games allow cheating and short cuts (most games do), and that in playing the games the habitual body tensions of the actor leading to faulty posture are only minimally reduced. In the teaching process, if, after a game has been played several times, it is analysed and its pure purpose and function are revealed, most actors have no difficulty in incorporating the technical purity of the exercise into the game the next time they play. During later sessions the leader can correct posture in the interest of playing the games more effectively. The actor, therefore, tackles movement obstacles through functional activities, and is prevented from becoming self-conscious about problems, as he always is if you tell him, for instance, that he hunches his shoulders and should relax them: he immediately becomes more self-conscious about his shoulders and the tension increases. It is very difficult, if not impossible, consciously to relax any group of muscles in the body in isolation.

The process of introducing technical discipline into a games activity is necessary because a simple children's game will not sustain the actor's attention and stimulate his energy flow for ever. The gradual introduction of discipline into a game moves the playing into higher levels of skill, and the adult needs this to sustain the activity. But it is important that the game be played first simply for its own sake and for the enjoyment it gives through release of energy, otherwise the technical considerations will become inhibiting. It is almost always true to say that, until a game begins to become stale or boring to the actors, it is difficult to introduce technique into it, because until that point the game is enjoyable in its own right and for its own sake. That being the case, why should anyone want to change what is enjoyable already? The development from game to technical exercise often has to be allowed to take its time. Rushing destroys the value that can come out of it. When the energy flow in a certain game begins to diminish, the time has come to start introducing discipline.

CHAPTER 7

Categories of games

The majority of children's games involve movement of some sort, and it is in this area that they are of particular use to the actor. Instead of attempting any formal categorisation of games, I will try to explain some of the elements in games which are of use to the actor.

Movement

Since the majority of games involve movement, they therefore contain at least one element of interest and use for the actor, the facility to train the specific movement quality the game includes. **Grand-mother's Footsteps** is interesting in this respect. One player stands with his face to the wall. The others creep up on him and try to touch his back. At short intervals, he suddenly turns round, and anyone he sees moving is sent back to start again. The game works on the *control of quick, light movements*, including speed of reaction in inhibiting movement. **Pirate's Treasure** is a development. One player sits on a chair blindfolded, surrounded by coins or small metal objects. The others, in turn, creep up on him to steal the objects and return to base. If the Pirate hears a sound he points to where he thinks it comes from. If he points accurately that player is dead and retires. We used to play this game as children with a bucket of water and a large water-pistol so that there was no doubt about the matter. This game works on the *control of light, sustained movements*.

Many other games can be found which work on different movement efforts, but to show the links between games, which can be utilised in constructing games sessions, I want to mention two possible follow-up games to Pirate's Treasure. When we were children we used to construct mazes of dangerously balanced objects and obstacles. Blindfolded players had to find their way through the maze without disturbing the objects or making a noise. This requires an even finer control of *light, sustained* movements than Pirate's Treasure. It also takes the game from the area of sensitivity of hearing into the area of sensitivity of touch, and also that of sense of direction and orientation in space, without the use of the eyes. As such, it becomes an exercise to train the body's sensitivity to the environment and to develop physical awareness of space. We could maintain the aural element, and also the light sustained movements, by moving to a version of **Blindman's Buff**, in which the victims are caught in open space by the blind man, if he hears them and points towards them. Since he can move, they must move to avoid him bumping into them. Once caught, he must guess by the feel of them, who they are. Rules can restrict the area of contact from which he can draw his information. The game has now crossed into training sensitivity of touch again, and links up with the building of mazes.

Senses

There are many children's games concerned with sharpening the senses. Blindman's Buff is probably the most obvious. The game where a coin is passed from hand to hand among a group, whilst one person guesses who has really got it, which hand he holds it in, and who is faking, is a training game for sharpness of eyesight. The Boy Scouts' **Kim's Game** in which a tray of objects is shown for a short period of time to the players and then removed, leaving them to list as many of the objects as possible, also trains the memory to work off short exposures. The attraction of the game is demonstrated weekly on television. The studio player actually gets the prizes he can list from memory, but the audience enjoys the competitive element: how many can *they* remember? A widely used actors' game which trains hearing involves pairing off the players, giving each pair a distinct rhythm to clap which is different from the other pairs, separating the players, and then asking each, with eyes closed, to find their partner again by separating his rhythm from all the others.

Speed of reaction

There is one type of game which seems to hold a special attraction for the human race: games involving *speed of reaction and coordination*. **Musical Chairs** is a classic example of a speed-of-reaction game, and this element occurs in many simple forms from **Jacks** to flipping match-boxes or beer mats off the edge of bar tables and catching them before they fall on the floor. There are many variations of the children's game of **Knuckles**, the object of all of them being to move from a static hand position to hit your opponent's hand or knuckles before he can move them out of the way. The gun-fighter's game of passing a gun hand between the outstretched hands of a partner before he can clap them shut is an example, as is the other gun-fighter's game with the pencil and matchbox described earlier. Almost any book of children's or party games will reveal many more.

Control of reaction

Closely related to the speed-of-reaction games are the *control-of-reaction* games. These can be both physical and verbal, and sometimes emotional. Games involving control of *physical* reaction include **Simon Says** and **O'Grady Says**. Basically, these games work on a specific formula of instructions which the players must follow. The leader changes the formula at times, and the players must inhibit reaction to any but the correct formula. If the formula is 'Do this' and the leader says 'Do that', anyone who moves in reaction is out.

Games of control of *verbal* reaction include the banal example, exploited very successfully on television, of asking a victim quickfire questions to which he must never answer directly 'Yes' or 'No'. They include many rhythm games in which a certain period of time is given for a player to make his contribution to a list of items, or to respond to something said by the previous player. The time allowed is usually marked by a clapped rhythm. **My Aunt went to Market** is one such game. **Matthew Mark Luke and John** is another.

Players sit in a circle and number off Matthew, Mark, Luke, John, One, Two, Three, Four etc. The game is governed by a rhythmic sequence in which all players hit the left knee with the left hand; hit the right knee with the right hand; snap the fingers of the left hand; snap the fingers of the right hand, in sequence. The rhythm goes faster as the game progresses. The game is a form of verbal Tag and begins always with the highest numbered player (who will be sitting next to Matthew to complete the circle). If there are, say, ten players, allowing the four Apostles, the highest numbered player would be number six. He begins by saying 'Six to Three' (or whatever number he fancies). Before the next rhythmic sequence is completed, number Three must pass the Tag on to someone else: 'Three to Mark', for instance. The object of the game is to get to Heaven. Any player who fails to pass to someone else in the rhythmic sequence loses his place and moves to the lowest place. All players in between the place he has left and the bottom move up one place and assume a new number or name.

The use of rhythm in training the body/think processes extends to many other games and activities. I was taught to type to music to stop me thinking about the keys.

To show how complicated children's games can get in their rules, we have to move to *control-of-emotional-reaction* games. On a simple level, these include a number of games in which the player has to undergo a certain ordeal without laughing. At their most complex, they include **The Court of Holy Dido**. The rules of this game are so detailed that they had better be listed rather than described.

1. All the players sit in a circle. One player is nominated President of the Court. On his left sits the Vice President. The other players number from the Vice President round the circle – Brother number one, Brother number two, and so on. At the President's feet lies a rolled and trussed newspaper – the 'Holy Dido'.
2. The Court is declared open by the President saying 'I now declare this session of the most honourable Court of Holy Dido well and truly open'. From this point on all Brothers must sit with legs and arms crossed. They must issue no sound and make no move without permission of the President. They must not smile, laugh, sneeze, cough or make any other sign during the proceedings. They must not avert their eyes from the Court, nor close them.
3. If any Brother breaks any of these rules, then he may be punished by the Court for doing so. The normal procedure for this is that another Brother raises his right arm. The President will say 'Brother number so and so you may speak'. The Brother asks 'May I stand?' The President gives him permission to do so. He may neither speak nor stand without permission of the President, otherwise he too has broken the rules and may be punished. Once on his feet, the Brother asks 'Mr President, may I take the Holy Dido and punish our most unworthy Brother number so and so for daring to laugh/smile/smirk/uncross his legs/arms/speak without permission or whatever in this most honourable Court of Holy Dido?' The President adjudicates whether or not he may. If not, the

Brother must ask for permission to sit – 'Mr President, may I sit?' – and sits when he has permission. If the decision is to punish, he must ask to take the Holy Dido, and when given permission, he must ask the punishment. The President will decide so many strokes on the Upper (hands) or Lower Deck (rump). The Brother to be punished must wait for permission to stand before doing so.

4. After punishment has been administered the punisher must ask permission to replace the Holy Dido, which he must do with honour and dignity. They must both ask permission to sit before doing so.

5. The game continues in these terms. In cases of offence where no other Brother asks for punishment, or in cases of mass dereliction the President may instruct the Vice President, or any other member of the Court, to carry out punishment.

6. The Vice President is open to be punished as is the President, but the motions to punish or unseat the President are dangerous since the President's powers are absolute. Justice is arbitrary.

7. Any member of the Court may ask permission to commit an offence such as sneezing or coughing. The President will adjudicate, often allowing this to provoke laughter or other misdemeanours in the Court.

8. Any member may ask permission to carry out any ritual with the Holy Dido that he may conceive, such as taking the Holy Dido for a ceremonial procession round the outside of the Court. In all cases the framework of the formal manner of address outlined above must be followed.

9. The Court continues until the President declares 'This session of the Court of Holy Dido is well and truly closed'.

I learned this game in a Boy Scout troop in Middlesbrough as a child, where the Holy Dido was a knotted rope, which, with the terms Upper and Lower Deck, clearly points to its adult naval origins. No child anyway could, or would, have invented such a complex set of rules. Of all the games I play, this is the one that is requested over and over again by every group I have worked with. Of all my games this one has most frequently been taken by other groups.

The game normally passes through three stages:

1. Controlling one's own emotional and instinctive impulses.

2. When control has been achieved, watching closely the behaviour of others for signs of failure.
3. Inventing comic actions, within a highly disciplined structure, that will provoke reactions in others without breaching one's own self-control.

It is a rare training ground for comedians. We used the game in Birmingham as the framework of an improvisation in Court procedure during rehearsals of Cervantes' *The Divorce Court Judge*. Two couples came to the Court suing for divorce whilst the game was in progress, and were forced to give their pleas within the framework of the ritual of the Court, and within the laws of evidence.

The emotional element enters into a number of children's games. A very simple example, which raises curious delight amongst adults, is **What's the Time, Mr Wolf?** One player is designated Mr Wolf, and he stalks the room with all the others following him. The group taunts him 'What's the time, Mr Wolf?' and he turns and answers in progression 'One o'clock', 'Two o'clock' and so on. At some point unexpectedly he says 'Supper time' and, at this, all the other players run to the safety of a wall, while he grabs someone to eat. The player grabbed then becomes Mr Wolf. On one level this is a speed-of-reaction game involving quick, direct, strong movements but it also offers a framework in which the child can explore the emotional sensations of rising tension and fear in a safe release situation, which is enjoyable. There are many other children's games in this area.

Vertigo games

Many children's games and adult activities explore the emotional sensations that accompany loss of control over one's actions. The simplest example in this category is when two people join hands across, keep their feet close together, and swing violently round and round. (The Viennese Waltz is a refined form of this game.) A variation is played in which the two players join hands straight across and twist round independently on their own central axes, without letting go of the other's hands.

The experience is also invoked by playground and fairground apparatus like swings, teapot lids, switch-backs and roller-coasters. It reaches the high cultural form of a religious ceremony in various parts of the world. The inhabitants of the New Hebrides build 120-foot scaffolding towers from which initiates drop headlong, with only tree creepers tied to their ankles to break their fall. In Mexico, a similar ceremony involving Eagle Men has been stopped by the authorities as dangerous. The horror movie exploits our appetite for 'voluptuous panic', the intention being to take the audience to the point of almost screaming out in imagined terror. The experience is sought transcendentally in all societies, through the use of drugs.

Victim games

This is an important category of game, which fundamentally springs from the same roots as the theatre itself. These 'Victim games' rely upon one player agreeing to become the victim of the group, so that the roles of tormentor and tormented can be explored. The simplest is probably **Pig in the Middle**. Two players throw a ball to each other whilst a third tries to intercept it. The game involves teasing and deception to increase the frustration and discomfort of the odd man out.

In **Bull in the Ring**, the 'bull' has to break out of a circle of players. Andrzej Munk uses Bull in the Ring as a powerful image in his film *Passenger*. The film is incomplete as Munk died in a car crash whilst filming, and the screened version was put together by associates from the material he left. The first half is in stills only, the second half in film. A woman, who has been a guard in a concentration camp and has married and lived since the war in America, returns to Europe for the first time on board ship. At Southampton she thinks she recognises a woman coming up the gangway as a former inmate of the camp. The second half of the film explores the relationship between the two women as it was in the camp. Among the stills in the first half are some showing a shipboard party during which the woman is attacked playfully by revellers. The image reappears in the second half when prisoners are selected for extermination in the prison camp. Forced to run naked along a path lit with floodlights, those selected are hooked off the path and thrown into a circle formed by SS Guards and Kapos from which in vain they try to escape.

The role of the victim of society is directly linked to the origins of theatre because it is an integral part of the rituals from which theatre developed – the initiation ceremony with its running the gauntlet, the rite of killing the old king and the bringing in of the new for the sake of the prosperity of the tribe. It is central to the concept of tragedy.

Theory of games

Games are much more than just children's diversion. They are an essential part of social life. In our time they have tended to become institutionalised and less creative. Participation becomes vicarious through the predominance of spectator sports and the mechanical communications media; the predominance of professional sport with its embodiment of competition within rigid frameworks of rules is itself a contemporary phenomenon which points to our social and cultural values.

Roger Caillois sees the structure and values of society reflected in the way that combinations of certain elements in games gain prominence over others at various times in history. He identifies four elements; *vertigo, simulation, struggle or competition* and *chance*. The combination of vertigo and simulation he sees as 'in principle and by nature in rebellion against every type of code, rule and organisation. Whereas games of struggle and competition call for calculation and regulation and are conservative of the social structure.'[1]

Caillois identifies the properties of play activities and games as follows:

The need to prove one's superiority;
The desire to challenge, make a record, or merely overcome an obstacle;
The hope for and pursuit of the favour of destiny;
Pleasure in secrecy, make-believe or disguise;
Fear, or inspiring fear;
The search for repetition and symmetry, or in contrast, the joy of improvising, inventing, or infinitely varying solutions;
Solving a mystery or riddle;
The satisfaction procured from all arts involving contrivance;
The desire to test one's strength, skill, speed, endurance, equilibrium, or ingenuity;
Conformity to rules and laws, the duty to respect them, and the temptation to circumvent them;
And lastly, the intoxication, longing for ecstasy, and desire for voluptuous panic.[2]

He finds that 'these attitudes and impulses, often incompatible with each other, are found in the unprotected realm of social life, where acts normally have consequences, no less than in the marginal and abstract world of play. But they are not equally necessary, do not play the same role, and do not have the same influence.'

The elements of play, as defined by Caillois, are also the seeds of drama because they are expressive forms of human personal and social behaviour, and because drama is itself a game or a play activity. The use of games is therefore not only a means of technical training and of exploring human behaviour and acting, but a springboard for exploring the nature of drama and theatre. This creates the bridge over which one may cross in rehearsal from improvised games to the performance of the structured play.

Improvisation

Many directors realise the value for the actor of being taken away from the pressures of the specific scripted dramatic situation and into improvisation, where he can explore aspects of character and situation freely without subjecting his work immediately to the limiting discipline of the script.

Many directors are extremely skilful at constructing parallel and analogous situations for these improvisations. Others, I find, trust improvisation as though it were a panacea for all ills. Among young directors, and occasionally actors, improvisation is sometimes a way of escaping from inadequacies of technique. There is an almost magic faith that improvisation will solve the problems without having to work at them. The use of improvisation, which I believe is productive and creative, encounters certain problems, the major ones being:

1. There is often no bridge from the improvisation to the rehearsal situation, and what is achieved in one area cannot be carried over easily into the other. This sometimes intensifies the actor's problems by producing a sense of loss.
2. What is learned in the improvisation is then totalised as a result to be achieved in rehearsal. It can't be. In trying to do so we often return to the point from which we started – the destructive and inhibiting use of the front brain over the body/think.
3. Improvisation is seen as a total solution to the problem. In one way it is, if one understands by improvisation the ability to programme the back brain body/think to react instinctively and leave it to make the

necessary adaptations to the other actors and to the environment. The fallacy lies in believing that improvisation is a process of pure inspiration and intuition. The body/think will only react as it has been programmed to react. If it has not been programmed with a mass of material about the play, the situations, the characters and their inter-relationships, it will only produce the material it has, which will naturally relate directly to the here and now, the situation in which the actor is actually present, along with a mass of cliché responses he has learned from other situations.

This is not improvisation. It is 'mugging', 'fooling about', a totally self-indulgent activity. There is one paramount law of improvisation, which musicians know well. The stronger one's technique, knowledge of the ground material, and alternative possibilities of development, the richer will be the improvisation. Improvisation always demands more and harder work from the actor than playing strictly within the limits of a scripted situation. Setting up improvisations, as a director, requires great skill in providing a structure which leaves the actor free to work, but at the same time focuses his work and directs his attention. Too much 'freedom' wastes the actor's time and energy, by allowing him to ramble all over the situation, running up blind alleys all the time and never knowing what he is actually doing.

If we accept the importance of games, as detailed by Caillois, then games can provide a limited but very strong structure for improvisation. This may be their prime virtue for the young director, who can use the security of the games structure until he acquires the confidence and ability to construct more complex improvisations. I give a number of examples later in the book of how, by the introduction of rules and disciplines, a simple game can be developed towards a scripted dramatic situation, and often directly into it. Since I have already touched on victim games, let me just say by way of an example of this development that these games are valuable as a basic structure for externalising the internal pressures on a character. Bull in the Ring could well be used as the basis of an improvisation for *Woyzeck*. Macbeth says, 'They have tied me to a stake; I cannot fly, But bear-like I must fight the course'. It needs little adaptation to move from Bull in the Ring to a taunting game.

CHAPTER 8

Release of physical inhibitions

One major aspect of children's games, and social games, is the release of energy to dispel psycho-physical tension. Its most common form is 'horse play'. It is at the root of almost all children's games, and many adult activities. In some games it is the predominant element. It is the motive force by which the child overcomes difficulties and inhibitions and, unself-consciously, takes physical and emotional risks.

It is not possible to say what causes inhibitions in any individual. The reasons are usually hidden in the past and are an important part of the personality development of the individual. The reasons are usually not that important. What is important is to reveal to the individual in what areas he is inhibited, so that he may make a conscious decision to change, or to overcome the obstacle. There are, however, some broad areas of inhibition which seem to arise out of the common history we share. They are all characterised by a fear in the mind of consequences arising from an action or situation that we will not be able to control.

Because we fear the consequence, we hold back from committing ourselves to the action. In cases of extreme inhibition this usually amounts to a refusal to participate at all. In most cases it results in counter-tensions in the body. The human being makes the move, or performs the action, whilst, at the same time, holding back from it. The full strength and direction of the action is, therefore, *inhibited*, or subject to a contradictory movement in the muscles of the body. It is tantamount to taking out an *insurance policy* against failure, and this is the term I use in preference to 'inhibition', which is too abstract a term for me to apply to physical actions. The counter-tensions in the body are the principal cause of injury in any energetic physical activity.

Insurance policies against physical failure

There are areas of movement in everybody's life which are dangerous. Take any group of people and ask them to make a running jump. Some will be able to make free and quite extravagant leaps using a wide area of space.

Others will instinctively trail their take-off legs behind them in close proximity to the ground, as an insurance policy against falling. In some physically inhibited people, a hop is as much as they can manage. Their movement is restricted or 'bound' by tension.

This phenomenon crucially reveals a problem that is inherent in human evolution. I have argued that the erect posture and a relaxed centre of gravity are the necessary conditions for optimum free mobility in human beings. I have also, in quotation, said that the bulk of the stimuli arriving in the old back brain comes from the anti-gravitational muscles which support the erect posture. The major area of physical inhibition will, therefore, be the fear of the anti-gravitational muscles and mind/body mechanisms not functioning effectively in the course of movements. That is, we are afraid of falling down, so we take out insurance policies against it.

Feldenkrais, citing a number of authorities, argues that this fear of falling is inborn in man, and that the evolution of the species has been through a certain reaction to the fear of falling in those who survived the pre-human period.

> . . . a new-born arboreal primate falling off a tree, as they probably all did in violent earthquakes, has a fair chance of survival if the thoracic cage is made resilient by a violent contraction, holding the breath with the head being flexed in the general flexor contraction [that is, pulled down and forward]. This not only prevents the head from being smashed against the ground, but also insures that the point of contact with the ground will be somewhere in the region of the lower thoracic vertebrae or in the lower region, precisely where the top of the arc is formed by the flexor contraction of the abdominal region. The shock will therefore be transformed into a tangential push along the spinal structure, on either side of the point of contact, and absorbed in the bones, ligaments and muscles, instead of being transmitted directly to the internal organs, and so injuring the body fatally.[1]

To fall this way is the instinctive inborn reaction of a child. The response to all other anxiety states is affected or conditioned by this, because the basic pattern of *all* fear and anxiety is the irritation of the eighth cranial nerve. The instinctive body position is taken up when active resistance to a situation is withdrawn and the person takes up a position of passive protection. The limbs are drawn nearer to the body to protect the loins, throat and stomach. The position necessitates pulling the head down and forward and/or bringing the hip joints abnormally forward, retarding the pelvis. The position is held through tension in the muscles. Seeing some degree of this posture in another person, we would probably identify him as an introvert. There is no doubt to adopt this position, especially lying down, produces a certain sense of security. The implications of this phenomenon are profound and complicated. All I want to say here is that, in tackling movement inhibitions, over-coming the fear of falling is a major factor, and can also be used generally to release free movement.

The value of judo to an actor is that it teaches him how to fall with safety. There are other ways in which he can explore gradually the sensations of falling. One of these is the rubber judo mat. The actor is allowed to fall from a low crouch, and is gradually encouraged to stand upright, and then to move on to the various stage falls, running falls and tumbles. There is a children's play activity which helps. The player stands with both feet together, body straight, and falls backwards. His partner stands behind him and catches him as he falls, by putting his arms under the armpits of the falling player, allowing him to fall on to the catcher's chest. It is essential that the catcher does not advance one foot very much in front of the other, or his knee intrudes, and that the falling player's shoulders fall into the catcher's elbow joints, and not into his hands. The falling player can then be lowered to the ground. The distance of the drop is gradually increased, as the security of the falling player grows. In the extreme drop, often exploited by farce, the body is caught just off the floor by the catcher's two hands cradling the neck of the faller. The reverse exercise to this one is for the prone player to lie rigid, whilst his partner lifts him to the vertical, with two hands, from behind the neck.

Both the drop and the straight lift have been an important element in farce for more years than anyone can remember. It would not be difficult to argue that falling is an essential part of any actor's training.

The use of another person, to whom one trusts the security of one's body, is an important part of the work of building a group. Here are some examples:

1. Six players line up in pairs, facing each other at one end of the room. They join hands, thus forming a narrow channel, framed by the upper bodies of three players on either side, and with a floor of linked hands

and forearms. The other players, in turn, run and leap in a fish dive to land on the arms of the catchers. On landing, the six turn the leaper on to his back and slowly raise him above their heads with extended arms. At a signal, they drop him, join hands again, and catch him as he falls. The player being lifted is usually asked to close his eyes during the lift and drop.

2. Two players stand facing each other. One leaps straight into the air. The other catches him, by putting both arms round his partners legs, to catch him behind the knees, and pull him on to his own chest.

3. Various circus stunts are slowly introduced such as the pyramid of kneeling people.

4. Practice is given in various strong-man lifts, using bodies for weights. These are difficult to describe and need to be taught by an expert. The significant point is that they all depend upon an erect posture in the body and cannot be performed with a serpentine configuration of the spine, in fact, without the body/think posture we are trying to induce.

These are all violent, exciting and enjoyable to try out and work at. In most people they release energy, and the fear of falling is often surprisingly forgotten. They also help bring a group together.

There are two rather more sensitive and restrained games that I use. **The Trust Circle** (*illustration nos. 19–21*) uses five or six people to make a circle with one other person standing in the centre. The centre man keeps his eyes closed and his feet together. His body is held straight but not unduly tense, certainly not rigid. His body leans over to one of the players in the circle, and from then on he is passed round and across the circle with all the players co-operating to prevent him from falling, by a smooth transference of weight from one to the other. Each player takes his turn in the centre. I find that if the concentration breaks either through someone laughing or talking, or because the centre man opens his eyes or bends his body, or moves the position of his feet, he should immediately be replaced and not to try to resume until several other players have taken their turn.

The Raft Two players stand back to back. The lifter places his arms under the armpits of the person to be lifted. He bends his knees to place the small of his back under the other person's buttocks. He straightens his knees and bends at the hip joints so that his partner is lifted to lie along his straightened back. It is important that the initial position is balanced to give the person

19–21 The Trust Circle

the security he needs to relax. The lifted player closes his eyes. Other players support his arms and legs, and if necessary his head, and blow sea breezes gently across him (*illustration no. 22*). The supporting player begins a series of gentle oscillations and lifts and falls, using his knees to create the effect of a raft being carried to sea by the tide. The original intention of the game was to work on light, sustained, indirect movements – the most indulgent movement characteristic, the *float*. It has since become an important experience in the work of any actor who works with me. The sensations are very beautiful, and the giving and receiving of an experience of pure pleasure within a group is very helpful to building group relationships.

Insurance policies taken out because of physical self-consciousness

Almost everyone is, in some way, self-conscious about their own bodies, and there are many complex reasons for it. We construct in our mind's eye a picture of ourselves, the body image, which is highly critical of our short-

22 '... Other players support his arms and legs, and blow sea breezes gently across him'

comings and deficiencies, and includes little appraisal of our strengths and positive assets. A history of failures to do certain physical actions successfully is reinforced by our refusal to try to perform them on other occasions. We become convinced we 'can't do' this or that. It may well be that as children we were inhibited by being continually told 'You'll hurt yourself, if you do that', until there is ingrained deep in the subconscious an instinctive fear of dangerous consequences if we try. Sometimes the body image memory of what we could do once, and haven't gone on practising, makes us say 'Oh I couldn't do that now', and this is in part due to the memory of how difficult, for instance, movement classes were in drama school when we first seriously trained. Perhaps we were asked to undertake difficult movements without being shown how to perform them. The failure becomes indiscriminately fixed in our minds. One reason for developing my work the way I have is the understanding that, in taking actors who are even eager to train their bodies again, you risk losing them and reinforcing their fears if you expose limitations without at the outset showing them how they can overcome the problems. In my experience, many actors are only waiting for some chance to train, providing that the introduction doesn't frighten them further.

The core of the situation is that, alongside the critical image we have of ourselves and of our physical limitations, there exists some entirely imaginary idealised image of what we would like to be. With young and novice actors particularly, one of the first tasks is to persuade them to accept their own bodies as being a starting point and not an obstacle; an undiscovered country rather than a mountainous barrier; a mine of untapped resources rather than an arid landscape. The first stage is to reveal to them what they can and might do rather than what they can't (which is one of the justifications and reasons for games work). And, related to this, they need to understand through sensation the workings of their own bodies. To eliminate the inhibiting factor of gravity, the exercises are performed on the floor. To eliminate the inhibiting factor of conscious intention, they are first of all carried out by another person.

Shake-outs and Massage The group splits into pairs. One lies on the floor. The optimum position of relaxation is with a straight spine; the hollow of the back flat against the floor; the head balanced so that there is no contraction of the back neck muscles; the shoulders allowed to fall outwards; the hip joints relaxed so that the legs fall outwards. Since it is often difficult for people to let the leg turn outwards and lie flat on the floor without raising the flat of the back off the floor, it is probably better to begin with the knees bent and the soles of the feet flat on the floor. The free partner begins slowly and gently to massage all the joints and muscles in the body to relax them. The joints are moved through the whole range of directions open to them. Limbs and joints are gently shaken out. The spine is shaken out by crooking the legs over the elbow joints (*illustration no. 23*) to shake out the vertebrae one by one. The vertebrae above the one being worked on rest on the floor and act as a pivot, against which to work. The spine is tackled again by placing the hands or arms under the armpits, care being taken not to whip the head violently or let it knock against the floor. An easy sequence is to start with the toes and work up to the hips; then take the fingers and work up to the shoulders; then the head and neck; then the spine. The passive partner then turns over and the back muscles are massaged and tension teased out of them. The passive partner tries to be aware of the sensations in the specific part of the body being worked on, but must not do anything that will assist physically. The passive partner may be asked to make sound during all or part of the process, if he can release sound without becoming self-conscious. If this is the case, percussive massage of the whole rib cage, front and back, and the shoulder blades,

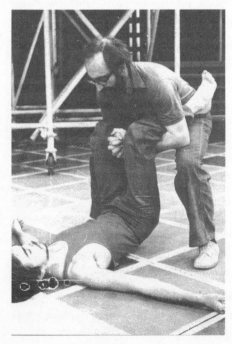

23 'The spine is shaken out by crooking the legs over the elbow joints . . .'

may be introduced. The spinal column should never be percussed. Later the percussive massage can be worked on in a standing position. The partners then change over. The whole process is lengthy, often taking over an hour for each person, but it should never be hurried.

Relaxation and Isolation In the same prone position the group is asked to imagine the tension in their bodies as a liquid substance which can be drained away. With the group settled, I talk them through draining the tension out of the toes, through the feet, ankles and into the legs, leaving the muscles heavy, limp and inert, and the joints no more than dead hinges. The tension flows slowly up through the lower limbs and hips to gather in the small of the back and remain there. The fingers come next, and the tension flows, in the same way, through the hands, arms and shoulders, to gather between the shoulder blades. Then the tension in the head and face muscles drains down through the neck to join the tension between the shoulder blades, and all this tension drains down through the chest and stomach and back, to join with the tension in the small of the back. When this has been achieved, the tension is drained away, as though through a hole in the floor boards. It is essential to take time over this process, and to be as specific as possible about the areas the tension is draining from. The voice quality and rhythms help smooth out the process. When the voice quality is right, it is surprising how relaxed the person leading the class can also become. The physical power of thought and words is astonishing.

As a next step, the group is asked to perform isolated actions of the body, such as moving the little finger of the right hand. These can be extended to a range of movements in the body, again the leader taking the class through the sequence. It is necessary to do this. If the actor is asked to conceive and carry through the movements himself, the process is clogged by the totality of his body image coming back into his mind. Only when he has practised isolation for some time can he be safely left to work on his own body. One of the difficulties of technical exercises is getting the actor to exercise only that part of his body that the exercise works on. He frequently finds it difficult, if not impossible, to bend his knees without bending his back or nodding his head. The totality of the body image brings into play all the habitual tensions of the body which he is trying to overcome.

It is possible to work at relaxation through the isolation exercise alone, but, for me, this is a later stage of the work. At the early stage of the work, the leader moves through the group, during the exercises, moving the actor's passive body to correct tense or contradictory configurations, and to try to bring the body into a harmonious co-ordinated line. At a later, more advanced stage of the work, the actor may be asked to 'think' making the movement several times before actually doing it. This in no way involves making a conscious decision to move, or thinking *about* moving, but asks the actor to try to be aware of the chain of movements involved in the action without actually following through to the movement itself. The natural kinaesthetic processes are stopped at the exact moment of doing. The precise number of times which he must stop the movement before releasing it must be given to the actor, or his conscious mind processes will come into play. He can be asked to speak his thoughts.

The actions that the actor is asked to make should not be phrased in terms of muscle groups or muscle activity, which he finds very difficult to contact, but should be in terms of joint movements which are easy to contact.

At the conclusion of all these exercises the actor does not rise from the prone position until he feels he is ready to do so. He can be asked to accomplish this in stages, if it is felt he has reached a stage of being aware of the sensations of his body/think. The first stage is to ask him to rise to sit in a chair. He should sit by placing his feet on either side of the seat of the chair, with the hip joints relaxed to turn the legs outwards. He should sit, not just on the chair, but into the back of the chair, allowing his buttocks to slide down the back, and without allowing the pelvis to slide under him when he reaches the seat of the chair. On a normal mass-produced hard chair, this means the spine at the top of the pelvis is supported directly by the back of the chair, and the rest of the spinal column balances easily upon that point without undue curvature. The feet are shifted so that the line from the knee to the ankle joint is vertical (I usually make this adjustment for the actor myself) and the shoulders fall out and back, allowing the arms to hang beside the hips. When ready he is asked to preserve the feeling of the sensations in his body whilst rising to a standing position.

Working regularly this way, I am sure the range of an actor's movements and control of his body could be greatly increased. It takes a great deal of time, and time is usually very short. In the long run it probably is the correct way to work, but we rarely have a long run to work in, and one is forced to take short cuts. The exercises above have to be done simply when one can get the time.

Insurance policies taken out from fear of lack of emotional control

The actor is, by nature, a private person in public, and any inhibition of any sort diminishes the full expressiveness of the actor's work. It must, however, also be allowed that the actor is a thinking, feeling human being and should be allowed the same liberty of conscience that anyone else is allowed. There are many things I would not do on a stage, not because I am inhibited, but because I hold certain personal and social values, which would be offended. For reasons of personal integrity, I make a deliberate decision not to participate. I am unlikely, I hope, to be asked to work in or on a play which advocates genocide, but I would refuse if I were.

However, there is often a reluctance on the part of actors to engage in areas of human behaviour which have become dangerous for them, through the history of their own development. I often have to say to actors, in plays which demand the full range of human passion and commitment, 'I don't believe you have reached the limits of your own cruelty, sexuality, revulsion, let alone the limits of the character in this situation'. Protest drama sometimes leads to a working out of these inhibitions. One is faced with young actors who want to make plays about contemporary violence from a position of commitment to non-violence. The commitment inhibits the drive to violence in themselves, and the inhibition of feeling inhibits the work.

There is often a tacit understanding built up in acting companies not to engage in certain areas of human interaction with other actors. We all have to work with people whom we do not personally instinctively like, or about whom we feel strong emotions of one kind or another. The tacit understanding not to meet in certain areas turns into a passive tolerance, which carries over from the private relationship into the rehearsal situation, and on to the stage.

Our society, anyway, is inhibited physically and emotionally. There are barriers of feeling, contact, and particularly touch, which we all experience, to some degree or another, because of the world we live in. The growth of encounter groups, touch therapy groups and the like is a direct manifestation of a widely felt social and personal need. There are a number of quick release exercises and games I use to break the ice and lower the barriers in a group quickly, but it must be made clear that this work simply breaks down the inhibiting barriers. The task of building up relationships is often a slower and more difficult procedure.

I was made particularly aware of the dangers of violently breaking down inhibitions when watching the work of a number of experimental theatrical companies a few years ago. They were attempting to break down barriers both between themselves and the audience, and between individual members of the audience. Most of the companies had some device, such as working towards a rhythmic climax accompanied by loud music, the culmination of which was an invitation to the audience to join with them, embrace, take their clothes off, love each other. Their first objectives are relatively easy to achieve, but love is a different matter. Bringing people into close relationships with one another is a difficult task. At least three of my students who took part in the ceremonies at these performances later suffered some nervous distress and withdrawal symptoms. Having had their inhibitions broken down, no secure and responsible structure existed for them to re-integrate. The group or ensemble can supply this structure.

Mature relationships with other people are only possible when an individual has enough self-confidence to stand alone on his own feet, without clinging to someone else for security. To be mature means to be open to offers, to be able to react fully to the flow of demand and response implicit in all relationships, controlling one's responses, but neither inhibiting them, nor responding so completely to the other person that one obliterates one's self-awareness and sense of separate identity.

Adolescence on the other hand is a period in which we are faced with many challenging, adult situations which constantly reveal our inadequacy to cope through lack of experience. It is marked by self-consciousness, which makes us constantly judge ourselves in terms of an external watcher or critic. We imagine that if we have a spot on our face, everyone is looking at it. We are painfully conscious of a gap between our actual patterns of behaviour and the idealised behaviour patterns we would like to pursue, and which we erroneously believe others exhibit – in being able to cope with problems which daunt us. We want to be other than we are, but we see this in terms of difference rather than development. Many of the physical problems of the critical body image described earlier arise in this period.

The core of the situation, and the cause of the pain, is the distance between ideal and unrealisable possibilities and restricted means of action. One of the first tasks with young actors in training is to persuade them to accept their own personalities and their current stage of development as a starting point for further growth.

But to expect that they should be able to accept this position straight away is also an idealisation. The gradual process of breaking down can provide potent lessons, and it is often an essential stage to be passed through before the actor can concentrate on the means instead of the ends. It is necessary to provide some structure that will at the same time (i) help the actor discover where his blocks and barriers lie; (ii) help him explore different facets of his personality, which are normally subdued, in situations which are sufficiently strongly structured to be 'safe' for him; (iii) build up a pattern of relationships within a group which will give him the security to take risks.

The task is not to allow *full* reign to one's feelings and desires, but to release them in play situations so that they may be *controlled* instead of *inhibited*. The massage work described earlier brings actors into very close personal physical contact and often releases sexual feelings. When I first found this happening to me I inhibited the feelings as not being part of the work. I then found it very difficult to carry out the work – I held back, taking out an insurance policy against arousal, by conscious control. The work was hedged by restrictions and hampered by filters and barriers. If one accepts that these feelings are sometimes released by the work and if one refrains from consciously inhibiting them, it is surprising how easy they are to live with and control. Since I am never going to sexually assault an actor in class, why be afraid of it? Most of the emotional insurance policies are taken out against things happening which could never happen in the normal course of events, and certainly never within a theatrical context. All fears are precipitated by the projection of imagined results. They may be justified in the world outside, where real actions have real consequences, but the play areas are safe. Control achieved through release in play frequently creates a confidence which can be carried over into real situations in the world outside. Games are a means of education and personality growth.

'Breaking down'

The elementary stages of breaking down a theatre ensemble or training group are very simple and often quite violent. They rely heavily on 'horse play'. The area of work is at first purely physical and although this, in dealing with the body image, brings many complex areas of the personality into play, it does not expose them directly before a person has found some security in the group. All the previous games work contributes to the process, but there are a number of games in which 'breaking down' is almost the only element.

Log-rolling The players lie on the floor side by side touching each other, alternating heads and feet. Beginning with the first player levering himself up on to the man next to him, bodies are rolled over and over along the line of supine players until they reach the far end. The line progresses like a giant caterpillar, everyone rolling over everyone else in a continuous wave.

Rocks and Snakes is a more controlled and sensitive game, for which I am indebted to Joan Littlewood. It was the first thing I ever learned from her. All the players except one combine to form a honeycomb rock shape, interlinked and mutually supporting. The remaining player snakes in and out of the cracks and crevices, over the whole surface of the rock, inside and out. Very soon, everyone has touched everyone else, everywhere.

The Raft of the Medusa In origin this is a children's struggle game. A series of squares are drawn on the floor with chalk. All the players crowd into one square. At the word 'go', they push and shove until only one player remains in the square. Players who touch the ground outside the square with any part of their body are eliminated and become sharks, grabbing at any part of any player still in the square which crosses the lines. When only one player remains, the other players move to the next square, or repeat the game where they are. The only successful way to compete is to drop to the floor and become part of a squirming mass. Standing up, with a high centre of gravity, lessens one's chances. Shoes must not be worn, or rings, watches or spectacles. I learned this game in the Boy Scouts, but I have seen it used with devastating effect by Littlewood in a projected production of *Danton's Death*, which never reached performance. We played the game for over a week in rehearsals, moving from it to an improvisation of the real situation of the Raft of the Medusa, which drifted for weeks around the Equator, overcrowded, and with insufficient supplies to sustain half the life on it. From the improvisation we moved to a realisation of Géricault's Romantic painting of the scene. The stylised movement arrived at was carried over into rehearsals of scenes in the play.

The Plague is a general theatre training game which has also been used in performance by the Living Theatre. It is advisable to introduce it only after the group has been working together for some time as it is more advanced than the previous three games.

Two players remain outside the group. The others explore through free improvisation the sufferings and death agonies of plague victims. Upon the death of all the players, the two outside players take the rigid bodies and make a pile of them, starting with the largest, strongest bodies. Each layer of the pile consists of two bodies lying side by side, at right angles to the pair underneath them.

Contact work

If the process is running smoothly, the move from horse play to discipline should take this work into areas of tactile exploration and contacts with other people. The work in these areas must be prepared through release, horse play, games work and massage work, which begin to bring actors into physical contact with each other.

A free situation is set up in which players can make any type of contact they choose with any other player in the group, through any of the senses. Players have the freedom to refuse contacts, or evade them, or break them. In order to concentrate on other senses than sight, these exercises can be performed in the pitch dark. For some reason, people have a strong illusory belief that they are anonymous in the dark and are, therefore, free to explore without normal restraint. For one other reason this is important. I would not carry out this work and take part myself in the early stages. The group can then rely on the security of one person standing outside the activity, as a guarantee that the activity will not get out of hand and lead into areas where they cannot control what is happening. For this reason, at the early stage, the leader is detached from the group and a curiosity is aroused. Contacts and relationships between him and the group are inhibited by factors outside the work itself. When there is an age gap between the leader and the group, this is intensified. Performed in the dark the exercise gives an opportunity for the group to approach and contact the leader in a safe situation.

Often work done for any length of time in the dark in one session is best concluded by taking the group straight from the dark into the open air, and suddenly restoring the faculty of sight, which invites an intensive investigation of the world outside. Colours and shapes appear more vivid and sharp. Just putting on the lights at the end of a session is often like the end of a party and provokes a depressed reaction.

The contact work done in this way is simple but enjoyable, and very productive in the release of psycho-physical tensions. It needs to be returned to at several stages in the overall work. The more work a group does together, the more use they can make of the activity, as their awareness of themselves, and the other members of the group increases.

Sometimes the work hits a barrier. The ease with which the physically uninhibited cohesion of a group can be built sometimes creates an illusion that the group has moved a great deal further than it has. This can usually be observed in the quality of the contacts between members of the group. They touch and submit to being touched but little real *meeting* or *encounter* takes place. It is a self-centred physical activity which takes little account of the other people in the group. It is necessary to remind the group that the body is not the totality of the human being. A programme of games which invoke more considerate contacts (such as the narrative work or the communication improvisations described later) will sometimes administer a salutary shock if it is led directly back to the physical contact work.

The better the contact work is going and the freer the contacts are that are being made, the more opportunity there is for making the problems of relationships clearer without inhibiting the work. Release must proceed to objectivity and discipline as soon as, and in whatever ways, it can be done. The meeting games and explorations described later (in Chapter 10) are my means of doing this. Without this objectivity and discipline, the release work is an invitation to the individual to merge his identity into a group identity.

There is another general release game which I have only used with a group of university drama students who had been together for a lengthy period of time, and then only within the framework of an extended session which tried to pull together a number of strands running through the work. All players wore hoods, for supposed anonymity. Buckets of sloppy polyfilla were mixed and coloured with gravy browning and players were allowed to sling it around at will. It was an end-of-session event and was a group analogy of the Abbot of Misrule – anything went. No two actions or reactions seemed exactly alike. Some sloshed the muck over other people; some wanted to he sloshed; others to slosh themselves; some used it as a true period of misrule and mucked up the leader. The release of energy was remarkable; everyone seemed to find it extremely beneficial, and it was an occasion of enjoyment and hilarity. I don't offer it as a serious training exercise, but the experience was clearly significant and I am still pondering on it and trying to think of less messy ways of achieving the same degree of release.

Violence

It has become almost a cliché that violence is inhibited in our society. I have never found it so in work. Violence is relatively easy to release. Tenderness is much more difficult. The sensitive contact work and the massage work help to release tenderness and respect. Violence is simple to release, although it is then difficult to help people control it. The usual pattern is for it to be inhibited again afterwards. Probably I have not carried on enough work in this area, since I personally inhibit those drives towards violence in myself.

To release feelings of violence all one needs is an intermediary instrument which can be wielded with full intention of outright murder, but which one knows at the back of the mind will not hurt at all. Pillows and balloons are both excellent. Violence has, throughout the ages, been released in the theatre through the slapstick. Rolled up newspapers can be used. Many children's games involve some sort of running the gauntlet or pursuit with a deadly weapon. I will describe one. All the players but one form a circle facing inwards with eyes closed and both hands extended behind their backs. The remaining player walks round the ring with a rolled up newspaper in his hand. He places the newspaper in one of the outstretched hands. The player receiving the newspaper opens his eyes and proceeds to beat the player next to him on the same side as the hand in which the newspaper was placed. The victim has to run a full circuit of the circle to regain the safety of his own place. The game is resumed, with the new owner of the newspaper walking round the circle.

Clown games Work on violence can be explored through clown structures. These all involve master–slave relationships. The master has the newspaper or slapstick. I use two of these games in the main. In one there are two players. A typical plot would be that the master gives instructions to the slave how he wishes the room to be redecorated or refurnished. The slave takes the instructions. The slave can use any ploy he likes to poke fun at or score points over his master. He can pull faces, he exaggeratedly polite, make a nuisance of himself. If the master catches him poking fun or scoring points, he is beaten. It is a simplification of the old Commedia situation. It is useful for exploring overt and covert violence, and situations of power.

The second game is simply an extension of the first. A situation is defined in which some action has to be taken. For example, the Duchess of Kent is attending a reception, and the hall must be laid out in readiness and in a hurry. The slave is instructed to do it and is expected to get on with it. He is beaten if he does not. Once the activity is started a hierarchy of masters is fed in, one at a time, to make sure that the work is being done. At each point in the hierarchical chain of command the lower members are expected to score points off those above them and get beaten if caught. The game moves into very complex areas of exploration of the violence inherent in power structures and bureaucracies. The game follows the normal pattern of doing, observing and discussion. One examines the ways in which the individual can release his violent feelings *towards* the 'system', and how he protects himself from the violence done to him in the system. It examines loyalty, treachery, sycophancy, responsibility and the ways these manifest themselves in social structures.

The major importance of games and structures like this lies in the game being an opportunity for examining the rules and conventions of areas of social behaviour, and a major strength is that information can be fed in by everybody in the group from their own personal experiences. For instance, twice when I was in the army an officer ordered a troop out on parade and proceeded to call them all the names under the sun. On both occasions the Regimental Sergeant Major interposed himself between the officer and the troop and said, 'I am sorry, sir, but I cannot have you speak to my men that way.' His position of command over the men depended upon the respect they had for him. He dare not stand by and not intervene, even if this meant a direct confrontation with his superior. In both cases the officer realised this and backed down. It is a well known fact in the army that the lance-corporal is more dangerous than the general, because you never come into direct contact with the general. Facts like this can be fed into the exercise as clarification.

The exercises are played flat out, at first, with uninhibited slapstick violence to release the latent feelings. Later the slapsticks are removed and the strategies become more realistic by being largely restricted to words, facial expressions and physical gestures. Later the strict rules of the situation are applied and adhered to, and the strategies are forced to become more subtle and the violence restrained or controlled within the realistic limits of the situation.

From Albert Hunt I was given another exercise in the discipline of violent feelings. Two speakers take opposing views to argue. They can be as abusive of each other as they wish but must not use any sort of physical violence or interference. A further body of players demonstrate noisily against the speakers, and stage a sit-down demonstration. Again they must not use physical violence. A third body, the police, carry away the sit-down demonstrators. The police can handle the demonstrators how they like, but must not leave themselves open to any charge of violent conduct. The demonstrators may hamper the police as much as they like, but must not leave themselves open to charges of violent behaviour. I used the exercise as a preparation for the last scene of a production of *The Workhouse Donkey*, when Butterthwaite and his protesting mob are ejected from the opening ceremony of the art gallery.

Say Something Nice There appear to be greater inhibitions to the spoken work than the deed, especially in the areas of violence and tenderness. Given an intermediary instrument like a pillow, physical violence is easily released. The sensitivity of physical contact is not difficult. Getting people to say things in these areas is often very hard. A game can be set up where the players stand in a circle and in progression say something nice or beautiful, to the person next to them. The person addressed then says something nasty or vicious to the person next to him. The game progresses round the circle, nice alternating with nasty. The game can be played with actions instead of words and is easier that way. With words, there is a strong tendency to produce heavily qualified statements like 'I think you're all right', or 'I don't like you very much'. One persists patiently.

The value of this exercise and others like it is that they rely on arbitrarily chosen attitudes and are, therefore, removed from areas of direct personality confrontation which arc dangerous. They are important in building relationships, because they incorporate the element of a chosen controlled reaction to another person, which is one of the basics of acting.

CHAPTER 9

The creative imagination and the use of fantasy

All the work outlined previously is designed to by-pass the intellectual, reflective, or pre-conceiving mind mechanisms and to overcome mental inhibitions through the release of physical energy. The training tackles specific problems in the actor's work. One must move slowly without pressure, only applying this when the actor makes, or seems to be on the point of making, a breakthrough by accidentally or subconsciously finding his own way to the sensations and awareness of them. One must be very careful not to reinforce the difficulties by concentrating intensively on them before the actor has the physical understanding necessary to correct them.

The work is helped by other activities which take the pressure off the actor completely. These activities seek to by-pass the conscious mind mechanisms by removing any idea that there is a problem to be tackled. They encourage the actor to give full reign to his imagination through free play.

Many years ago when the basis of our acting was much more emotional (not necessarily a good thing), the key words in actor training were *disciplining feeling*. The stress was on preventing emotional indulgence. The world, and the theatre, now seems a more inhibited place and the fashion is swinging back to *release*. Problems change from generation to generation. Only stereotyped mechanistic systems fail to take notice of this. One can only discipline what has been experienced.

Methods of self exploration have to be found, and at the core of these is the process of creative transformation, which is at the roots of acting.

In whatever terms theatre takes place, at the heart of it is a mystery, no matter how objective and scientific we may be about the actor's ways and means. Theatre centres upon the ritual transformation of one human being into another, conditioned by considerations of time, space and character which are not those of the person undergoing the transformation. Even in direct theatre situations, like the stand-up comic or the comedy duo, the performer finds a persona, or 'image', or 'style', through which to work or 'put it across'. The genius of Morecambe and Wise is not that they present themselves naturally, but that they present the characters they assume naturally. They are 'at home' in their characters.

There are many aspects of this ritual transformation and each actor's preparation for performance is individual to him. Some take a long time (Alicia Markova has said she took several hours to prepare for *Giselle*, moving gradually through stages towards the complete assumption of role). Other actors prefer to face 'a sudden death' in order to avoid rising anxiety. Some prefer hard physical exercise to warm up all the physical apparatus. Others lie down and relax or sleep. I am aware of a steady rise in energy, throughout the period approaching the performance starting several hours before the show, and I need to take the top off this energy by physically working out before a show so as to ease tensions. The effect of a perfor-mance on the nervous system of an actor has been estimated as the equivalent of the shock of a minor car accident. More scientific work could be done in this field, but the acting profession resents any prying into its secrets.

No serious actor treats the approach to performance casually. After-wards, most experience a sensation of being drained, or of being suddenly released from tension. In the latter case it may well be that this is due to a rise in energy and tension, when the role and action do not allow a strong release on stage. What is clear is that to some degree an actor has to 'unwind' or 'run down' after a performance.

The transformation involves many related processes, particularly the assumption of the objective aspects of role: costume, paint, mask and properties. But at the core is the actor's act of creative imagination. (This is not always complete identification with the role played. In the Brechtian sense the actor does not transform himself directly into the character, but into an embodiment of the character – the narrative role.) In this respect the actor becomes for the purposes of the performance a changed and heightened individual. If he did not, the performance would be (and regrettably often is) flat and ordinary.

One argument against a director appearing in his own productions is that he is involved in a mass of minor technical problems before the performance and has not the time and breathing space to fully prepare for the performance.

Ritual transformations and draining exercises

All the following exercises are preceded by the relaxation exercise described in Chapter 8, where tension is drained, by imagining it as a fluid, from the body. The actor is encouraged to be able to do this for himself, at will, and also to drain the mind of its temporal pre-occupations and conscious thoughts. Most actors and student actors find this very easy, with a little practice. The exercises must be open ended and last as long as they need to take, or as long as the actors wish to continue with them. At some point in every exercise, each actor will find a moment when, for him, the process of exploration has continued as long as he needs or wants, and he will, often quite suddenly, return to full contemporary awareness. Only harm can come from trying to prolong the work further, and the actor is required to move quietly to a seat and watch respectfully till everyone is finished. One person must stand outside the exercise for the security of the group. Occasionally one member of the group will get stuck in some part of the process. In the Evolution exercise described shortly, I have twice had actors stuck, unable to make the transition from four legs to two legs. Their total imaginative involvement made it impossible to apply objective rational knowledge to the problem. The problem is overcome by the leader, or some other member of the group, entering into direct touch relationship with him and, through talking, teaching him the objective rational ways of overcoming the problems. This is done gently and sensitively. It always talks the actor back to full, contemporary awareness.

With someone beginning to play the games for the first time it is advisable, if possible, to give the purpose of the game at the end of the talking, draining process. Occasionally, to give him the intention before the draining takes place fixes it in the actor's mind and inhibits relaxation. The advice is that if you are taking the exercises from this book, don't tell the group which one you are going to take. After the process has once been explored by the actors, they are usually quite able to participate without preconceptions.

Frankenstein The actors are asked to awaken at the flash of imaginary lightning that brings Frankenstein's synthetic monster to life. They explore the parts of the bodies from which they have been constructed, and how they are connected together and how they function. At this level it is a detailed and specific exploration of how the body is constructed and works. At an advanced level an attempt can be made to try to understand where the brain they have been given has come from; what sort of person owned it; and how the knowledge, thoughts and experiences stored there came about. At this level I have only known it be valuable for experienced actors. It is difficult for the novice to allow his imagination free reign in the areas of mind without intellectualising and falling back on objective conceptual understanding.

Evolution After draining, the actors are asked to explore the processes of the evolution of life; starting from protoplasmic slime; through invertebrates; through fishes and amphibians; through reptiles; through four-legged creatures; through erect two-legged creatures, to Man. It is a complex area of investigation, and each gets from it what he can in the way of experiences and, later, objective knowledge. The creative process of allowing the imagination free range leaves wide scope for exploration and learning.

A child growing up In their book *Children's Games in Street and Playground*, the Opies cite an instance when they were watching children play. They saw a small boy crouched on the pavement apparently oblivious to what anyone else was doing. When they asked the other children what he was doing, they were told he was a baby waiting to be born. I have taken this as a basis for an exploration of the processes of growing up. All the groups I have worked with have instinctively found it too personal to engage directly with their own childhoods, although this may be because I have never carried out this exercise with mature adult actors. Groups and individuals have always, for me, used either analogous identification with another child they knew closely, like a brother or cousin, or used amalgams of themselves and other children. Occasionally they have used the exercise simply to be childish and have ignored any thought of progressing through stages. This has only happened with university students. This does not invalidate the exercise for me. The use the individual can make of the exercise, at the particular stage of personal development he has reached, is the determining factor of value.

Preparation for performance. 'When I look at you I see . . .' This exercise was developed during a third year production of Gorky's *Vassa Zhelessnova* at Drama Centre. After draining, which took place in the setting of the play, the actors were asked to re-awaken in the characters they were performing in the play. They moved around the setting, looking at it, the furniture, and the other characters. In so doing, their reactions to the environment, material and human, in which they were to act, crystallised in their minds subconsciously. Post-discussion revealed that they were very clearly aware of their reactions without reflecting on them. The thoughts sprang instinctively into their minds. The exercise helped substantially to objectivise, integrate and revitalise all the work the actors had been doing over a long period of rehearsal.

The exercise has remained vividly in my mind and convinces me that it is one of the most powerful creative tools for building the acting ensemble. It can only be used within an ensemble as it relies heavily, as the other games and exercises do to a lesser extent, upon group involvement.

Minor games leading to objective awareness

There are a number of other games and exercises that work in this area although not so fundamentally. Most of them are used widely in actor training. Two free imagination games are **Monsters** and **The Seven Deadly Sins**. In Monsters the actors are asked to create their own individual monster, with its own shape, its own method of locomotion and its own sound. They work towards interaction with other players, and sometimes to amalgamation with them to create corporate monsters. A good starting point is the description, in *The Tempest*, of 'strange shapes' which inhabit Prospero's island. In The Seven Deadly Sins, actors assume the behaviour and sounds of the sin of their choice, and interact. Unless a great deal of preparatory work has been done, inhibited middle-class values tend to assert themselves, and the result comes out something like The Seven Petty Misdemeanors. **Animals** is used by other teachers. Some use machines, but this is too mechanistic and mind-restricting for me.

Imaginary activities – Walter Mitty

It is always interesting and often valuable to let actors give complete free reign to their imagination. That is, to put their day dreams and fantasy into action. Everyone, at some time, does this, usually when no-one is looking. We all play at being surgeons performing operations; orchestral conductors; gunfighters strolling the streets of Dodge City; D'Artagnan fighting his way out of danger. It is a highly pleasurable, and perhaps necessary, fantasy occupation. Vicariously and actively, it is at the roots of theatre. It is a subconscious activity and is usually repressed. I never make a head-on attempt to print out, as it were, the fantasy figures, but begin with lighter and more clearly defined activities. I usually begin with the game of throwing the ball round the circle, characterising it as heavy, light, a bomb etc. Maintaining concentration, I then ask the actors to create, through physical sensation, imaginary objects which have a particular size, shape, surface texture and consistency, though not necessarily a function or utility. The object is defined by what sensations in the body are enjoyable for the actor. The game can be developed by passing the completed object to someone else. This allows the players to alternate between doing and watching. The given object must never be defined in objective, mimetic terms or sign language. The sensation, not the conscious apprehension, is the raison d'être. The received object must be responded to, through sympathetic sensation, and then can be changed to suit the recipient.

Again maintaining concentration, the actor is asked to carry out some imaginary activity which he finds enjoyable, and from this he is asked to create some particular imaginary character from life, history, literature or drama. The final stage involves looking at the environment and the other players, and absorbing them imaginatively into the life of the character.

It is interesting to find out who chooses which character, from a totally free range of possibilities, and why. The reasons are never understood until you ask. Frequently one gets girls being Mary Queen of Scots or Florence Nightingale, which shows how well ingrained they are in the values of the educational system. At other times characters emerge who seem to be an important part of the personality structure. I first played this game with a group of professional actors during the time I was organising festivals for Centre 42. I had been haring round the country trying to perform miracles with inadequate resources, which, in effect, meant a constant struggle to stave off disaster. I was astounded that the imaginary character I came up with was Stonewall Jackson. Then I looked around my office and realised that with its small cot in the corner and its charts, maps, schedules, and instructions pinned to the wall it looked exactly like a campaign tent. On another occasion I found myself fighting for the North Vietnamese in an *American* tank. The cultural split in me obviously goes deep. A curious fact is that, once the fantasy figure has been discovered, it is never used again. Like morning mist it disappears in the light of day.

A further area of this work moves into the structuring of environments. Obviously every human being, as best he is able, structures his life-style and the environment he lives in to meet the needs of his personality and to express himself to the world at large. Some highly imaginative people construct highly individual décors for themselves. Other, less imaginative people construct from observed stereotypes. This fact is central to all considerations of marketing and the supply of public services, and is a source of informed comment upon society at any time in history and geography.

Actors can be asked to create environments out of the available furniture, fittings and space, as well as from the activities of the other actors. The environments can be actual or can be imaginatively structured. There is a lot of work to be done in finding out what makes people happy. I have done a great deal less work in this area than in most of the others because the need to carry it out has never been directly demanded by the teaching or rehearsal situation. I set it down here in case someone else wants to explore it.

The person opposite

Verbal print-outs of the back mind, leading to self-awareness, can also be worked at by seating the actors in two lines facing a partner. The leader begins asking questions, such as 'What do you like best about the person opposite?', 'What do you think he likes about you?', 'What part of the person opposite would you like to touch?', 'Where do you think he would like to touch you?', 'Where would you like to go with the person opposite?', 'What would you like to do there?' At no time do the actors vocally answer the questions. At every point in the questioning mirror reactions appear on the faces or in the bodies of the players, These are continuously questioned, 'Why did you smile?', 'Why did you fidget?', 'Why did you turn your eyes away?'. The game provides an opportunity to become aware of the instinctive processes of the back mind without reflection. I learned the game from the late Naftali Yavin, a games player of genius. I believe he learned it from another great games player, Ed Berman.

When I look at you I see . . . (2) The exercise described earlier in the chapter can be combined with the game above so that the line of the questioning leads to a print-out of the thoughts and reactions of the character the actor is playing. It is a means of integrating and objectivising the material taken in during rehearsal and private study.

What does it feel like . . . Fantasy exploration can be disciplined to serve the rehearsal in the excrcise above. There is another more general means of bringing discipline into the activity.

In response to external stimuli, the body/think reacts, and on the basis of the response makes a decision to act. It is required of the actor that he respond to imaginary stimuli. He is not in prison, or on a mountain top. In order to give a convincing representation of the actual situation, he has to provoke the authentic response from his body/think by imaginative means.

To help him to do this, or learn how to do this, and to be aware of what happens when he does it, a series of simple exercises are set up to phrase the imaginary questions to which the body/think will react.

The preparation can be the sequence of concentration exercises by which I approach the release of fantasy figures, or it can be the physical isolation exercises described in Chapter 8. The questions are then asked of the actor, 'What does it feel like to have your eyes?', 'What does it taste like to have your mouth?', 'What does it smell like to have your nose?'. It is at least arguable that the task of leading the actor to isolate movements in his body is best tackled through this method. The stress of the exercise is on *mind/body function* and not on *physical activity*. I think that if I did more work in this area, I would use it as a means of enabling the actor to carry out technical movement exercises, without self-consciousness. 'What does it feel like to bend your knee?'.

Usually I move into areas of imaginative response: 'What does it feel like to have indigestion?', 'What does it feel like to have a sprained ankle?', 'What does it feel like to have toothache?'. The scope of the questions is as wide as you care to make it, and can move into areas of feeling and emotion, because the concentration is on the mind/body processes that precipitate emotion, and there is no reflection on the emotion experienced. We often describe our feelings and emotions through metaphors, as though they were physical or kinaesthetic sensations, which indeed they are. We say 'My heart was in my mouth/sank to the floor/leapt/missed a beat'. One can incorporate all the physical metaphors of emotional sensation into this exercise.

When work has been done in this area, one can move into larger, or total areas of imaginative response: 'What does it feel like to be captain of a sailing ship?', 'What does it feel like to be a guerrilla fighter?'

It is important to make a distinction in this exercise between cliché and prototype. The nature of the cliché is that it is already total, and consciously defined before one employs it. A prototype is a structure based upon limited knowledge from which further investigation and development can take place. During our everyday lives, our brain is subconsciously processing information from a wide variety of sources. On the basis of this information we act. It is obvious, therefore, that the more information fed in during the acting process, by study of the text and the situation and from the experiences of rehearsal and performance, the richer will be the prototype produced. If the performance is 'fixed' at the Dress Rehearsal and the actors are asked to repeat the DR pattern at every performance, we have a theatre of clichés. If, in rehearsal, the actor works towards a precise and disciplined understanding of the dramatic situation and his specific part in it, then every performance will be a prototype for a performance which will never take place. The production, and the performances in it, will continue to develop throughout the run.

The investigation of prototypes is central to the imaginative play of children, and is indeed central to the learning process throughout life. Children explore roles of mothers and fathers, policemen and cowboys, from the limited information they possess. At the root of children's play is the question 'What does it *feel* like to be a father?' Their playing gains sophistication as they gain more observed information and then test it in imaginary practice. This is the only tool they have for understanding social and personal situations that will face them in the future, and for which they have no direct experience to draw on. It continues throughout adult life towards maturity. At certain points in our life we are faced with critical situations of social interaction or responsibility for which we have no direct experience on which to draw. What happens in adolescence is that the processes of testing prototypes becomes more of an intellectual activity than an imaginative exploration. We are going to apply for our first job. We try to write a script for the interview so that we can define an effective role for ourselves in the situation. We preconceive dialogue: 'He'll say to me, "Please come in and sit down. Now tell me why you want to join us?" and I'll say to him, "Well I feel I have a great deal of potential which is not being used in my present situation, and I want the chance to develop myself, to grow, and express myself creatively." In conclusion, he'll say, "You are just the man we've been looking for. Please start tomorrow"'.

We rehearse the dialogue, which is composed entirely of dead clichés and the result is that we are hindered from taking part in a flexible interaction with the other, and are left rather in the position of an actor holding a script for the wrong play. The understanding of this is, of course, a necessary part of acting certain characters in situations in stage plays. The process is closely tied to the sociological concept of 'Social roles' – the adoption of modes of behaviour which we preconceive will resolve tensions in a situation, or through which we can give a safe definition of dramatic fiction to any situation of social interaction, by defining clearly at the outset the terms on which interaction can take place. The works of Erving Goffman give lucid and detailed accounts of this process in action and should be an essential part of every actor's reading.

The reverse process of imaginatively exploring prototypes in the way children play is an essential part of acting. It is at the roots of two of Stanislavski's concepts. 'What does it feel like . . .' is very close to the magic 'If', 'If I were in this situation how would I act?' I find this can sometimes lead an actor into *thinking* about how he would act, instead of responding to the situation imaginatively, though, of course, responsible teachers working off Stanislavski would not allow the actor to get away with this in practice. 'What does it feel like . . .' leads directly into the subconscious use of the imagination.

The second concept of Stanislavski's that this process touches on is the characterisation of the external world to reflect the inner world of the character. Again, the approach is initially through metaphors. We talk of 'walking on air', 'being on top of the world', 'being dragged over red-hot coals', 'being up to our ears in work'. I believe that this is what Stanislavski intended by the phrase 'working from the outside to the inner' – not the adoption of preconceived external characteristics, but the imaginative characterisation of the external world either directly, or through analogies and metaphors, so as to induce in the actor the physical sensations which arc the key to the inner truth.

These metaphors provide a useful tool (i) for the actor, because they objectivise internal states of feeling in terms of overt physical sensation; (ii) for the director, because from them more complicated theatrical metaphors can be constructed with which to focus the action of units of the play; (iii) for the playwright, because they provide a realistic, but not naturalistic, dramatic structure for expressing content clearly and stylistically.

The maximum point of human discomfort for me is that point when I've waded into the sea and the waves arc lapping under my crotch. Do I take the plunge and get it over with, or do I run out again? Simply thinking about it makes me shiver. During rehearsals for Arden's *The Workhouse Donkey*, in the scene where the civic dignitaries are assembled with some embarrassment, for the opening of the new police headquarters, we used the metaphor of listening to the National Anthem dressed in one's best clothes, but minus skirt or trousers. We approached it via my sensation of standing in the sea.

The work of Albert Hunt in staging the Kennedy–Krushchev Cuban missile confrontation as though it were a classic Western (*John Ford's Cuban Missile Crisis*) and in presenting the life of Hitler in terms of the Oberammergau Passion Play (*The Passion of Adolf Hitler*) are examples of the potent use of metaphors in the construction of dramatic works.[1]

CHAPTER 10

Meetings and encounters

The work in this area normally begins with the conflict games, and the two games I am going to describe first are later used to illustrate what is happening in the other games. In the interest of clarity, I will describe the background exercises first.

The Chairs

The group is split into players and observers. The players are paired off and chairs are placed about three to four yards apart. Enough room is allowed between each pair of chairs to allow free movement round them. A simple sequence of action is established. One player moves the other from a sitting position in one chair to a sitting position in the other chair. The action is akin to a patient being moved by a nurse in a hospital, but should have none of the imaginary contextual overtones. The player being moved, neither resists, nor does he move voluntarily. He is led.

The action is repeated three times. The first time, the mover is asked simply to lead his partner from one chair to the other and to sit him on it. The second time, he is asked to think about something outside the situation whilst doing it. He might think about what he had for breakfast, or saw on the television the night before. The third time, he is asked to move his partner 'as quickly as possible', that is, to have a preconceived future intention. In the interests of safety, it should be pointed out that 'as quickly as possible' is a relative term. One can walk 'as quickly as possible' without running headlong.

At the end of the sequence, the roles are reversed and the actions repeated. The second group then carry out the exercise. The whole sequence is then repeated with one significant difference. In the second playing, the player being moved is asked to catch his partner's eye sometime during the process. This requires that the active partner should neither deliberately avert his eyes nor, himself, seek contact with the passive partner. He should simply carry out the process of moving his partner (a) naturally; (b) thinking outside the situation; (c) as quickly as possible. The effects of the exercise are then discussed.

These are normally recognisable, subjectively and objectively, as a break in the movement, a hiccough, or a direct stop in the process when eye to eye contact takes place in the second and third moves. There is a change of rhythm in the movement, a re-coordination of the body (i.e. the relationship between the head, neck, spine and pelvis). People often break into a smile or laughter.

The lessons to be learned from the exercise are clear, simple, and very important. In many ways I think it is probably the most important single exercise I use. One cannot make eye to eye contact, that is, enter into relationship with someone else, whilst the mind is either engaged elsewhere or concentrated upon a predetermined end result.

The implications for theatre are fundamental. This is the root cause of laughing, 'dying' or 'corpsing' on stage. The actor is self-consciously obsessed with his own part in the action; he is consciously concentrating on what he should be doing or intends doing (his objectives, motivations, the production moves, his character, the lines he has to say next, the effect he intends to produce). He catches the eye of another actor and he 'goes'. The elemental human contact drives everything else from his mind.

This demands that we look at our approach to the whole theatre situation, and our approach to work. If we consider that the theatrical activity is to rehearse a play to the point where we 'fix' it, and we see the purpose of the performance as the polished repetition of a past reality, then we can have no human contact on the stage, only pictorial and literal illustration. If the theatre is, as I believe, the art of human relationships in action, then we must consider the performance itself as the reality. Study and rehearsal are the preparation for a process, a springboard to action, and not the means of arriving at a fixed result. This is why, in order to produce recreations of seemingly spontaneous patterns of human behaviour, the actor must sink the study and rehearsal material into the automatic reflex activities of the back brain, and to work with an instinctive trust and confidence in the processes of the subconscious body/think. It is the only way he can meet other people in performance.

The overall principle in my work is to help the actor to a kinaesthetic awareness of his subconscious activities. This leads to the need to set up a situation in which the actor can experience the sensations of making contact with other people. One reason why this is necessary is that prolonged direct contact with human beings is rare in everyday life, and, when it happens, it usually occurs in emotionally charged situations.

Eye to eye contact

It is necessary to have an evenly lit room more than sixteen yards long. The group is split into players and observers. Partners face each other down the length of the room, at or about the point where each can look his partner in the eye and still see his feet. That is, each can take in a total body picture of the other whilst centring on each other's eyes. This can be done when the partners stand sixteen yards apart.

Players move slowly towards each other maintaining eye contact, kinaesthetically aware in the body/think of what is happening to them. At the points of strong reaction, they stop, and move backwards and forwards through these points, until they have a clear awareness of the physical nature of the reaction. The observers then become the players, and the exercise, and its effects, are discussed.

The process of approaching a partner in space is one of growing personal involvement and a lessening of environmental reference. The visual dominance of the partner increases as the walls of the room recede out of vision. There are several critical points at which strong physical sensations are produced in the body. These are usually found around twelve yards, five yards and two yards. The transition is not smooth but moves through clear separate stages, and the transitions are experienced physically as critical moments of decision, rather than as mental processes. At the transition points, the body re-coordinates slightly and this causes breaks and changes in rhythm, faltering steps and often a missed beat in the rhythm of walking. Each player experiences this, or is aware of it, in his own way. I myself am aware of sudden tensions and relaxations between the shoulder blades as I cross the transition points. (The exercise works in a totally different way for people with 180 degree vision, as they retain a balance between the room and the partner almost to the point of physical contact.)

On a second playing, starting from the same point, players are asked to move very quickly, or rush, towards each other. They are told to move to the right when they feel their safety is threatened. If this is understood, there can be no question of physical danger. They still tend to break to the right about five yards from the partner. (There is a break in rhythm at twelve yards but this critical point is easily overcome by the momentum of the movement.)

Through this exercise actors become aware of differing modes of relationship and of differing degrees of involvement at different distances. The exercise is then directed towards a theatrical problem.

It is often necessary, on large open stages, to be in very close relationship with another actor, although standing some distance from him. The reverse can apply on a small stage. Apart from the problems raised by playing on tiny stages, there are many situations in plays (for instance, in *Othello*) where characters are in close physical contact, but seek detachment. It has been an important realisation for all groups I have worked with that one can play intimate scenes without standing on the other actor's feet.

Theatre encounters

The theatre is the art of human relationships in action. This definition will apply to modern unstructured forms of improvised drama and rituals as well as to older established forms. In the theatre people meet, and plot is the result of their interaction. At the end the situation is not what it was at the beginning, because human beings have experienced a process of change. Change takes place in the audience individually through their meeting with the actors/characters/dramatist.

I have argued earlier that the audience primarily experiences a performance kinaesthetically, through sympathetic physical reactions in the body, and only later does it consciously reflect upon this experience. If this is so, then the strongest audience response comes when the actors are meeting and interacting on the stage, and imaginatively invoking in their bodies the kinaesthetic sensations of the dramatic encounter they arc portraying. If the actors are merely mechanically repeating the patterns of some past situation (as will happen if the production is 'fixed' definitively in rehearsal), or if they are consciously pre-occupied with reflective thoughts or intentions, then the audience cannot respond to the flow of interaction. All they can do is follow the stage pictures and the literal meaning of the spoken text. In the actual event, since the pictures move and actors speak the text – in other words, there is a *semblance* of true interaction – the audience experiences a series of contradictory pulls and tensions. They lose interest or understanding; they are uncomfortable; they switch off; they become bored and easily distracted.

A major part of actor training, then, should be the exploration of human relationships in meetings and encounters. Character, as Aristotle said, reveals itself in action. Without this precept, character becomes a static concept, and the social relevance of theatre declines.

Conflicts

The most violent and openly dramatic form of human encounter is the situation of conflict, which forms the core of so much of drama, and is a strong element in most plays. It is almost axiomatic in approaching the study or production of a play to ask where the conflict lies. No man is an island, and the internal conflicts of a character are occasioned by some pressure from the outside world, often the conflict between personal appetite and the demands of established social behaviour.

Touch your Partner Two players face each other. They are told their objective is to touch their opponent in the small of the back to score points, whilst preventing their opponent from doing likewise. No other deliberate physical contact is allowed. They cannot grab their opponent's hand or arm, or wrestle. The game is a simple, children's horse-play game. It is rarely played efficiently at first for the following reasons, all of which one tries to bring out in discussion afterwards.

Players rarely take account of their opponents; they look at the hands and not the eyes; they lack the balance between offensive and defensive possibilities that is there in the boxer or fencer; they tend to attack or defend for long periods, with no easy flow of alternating activities. They attack wildly, ignoring the risks involved; or they take out insurance policies against defeat by withdrawing from contact to a range where they are unable ever to score points.

The game reveals certain things about the personality of the player. Why does he act that way in that situation?

The characteristics outlined above can all be used to illustrate the difference between the conscious mind processes and the kinaesthetic body /think processes (which are what the boxer and fencer instinctively rely on).

It is the structure of the game that occasions much of this. The situation, in dramatic terms, is a *clash* of mutually exclusive interests, allowing little flexibility. Often it produces a physical clash in the action as the two players, both going for a point, collide with each other. But boxing is a clash of conflict and can reach high levels of skill in controlling balance and a very concentrated awareness of the opponent. We have therefore, to look at what inhibits these faculties, and again the reason is found in the game.

The game is enjoyable to play because of the energy it releases; it is exciting. I want now to outline the concept I introduced earlier in the book, that boredom is a necessary stage in the acquiring of physical skills. The game moves to a higher level of skill when, after several playings, the call is given to 'touch your opponent . . .'; the players are bored; no adrenalin runs; they look each other in the eyes, and they begin to play the game differently. They begin to play with each other, moving into areas of feint and deception, attack and counter attack, and the game begins to demand similar skills to boxing and fencing. In the first instance, the game is enjoyable purely for the subjective experience of taking part. In the second instance, the game is played for its own sake. A still higher level of skill comes when it becomes enjoyable for what can be expressed through it, that is, the use of it as a structured theatrical situation, but I will come to this gradually. It is important in games work to realise that the training potential cannot be extracted until the initial release of energy begins to dry up. The criticism I have of *ad hoc* warm up exercises is that they never capitalise upon the energy they release. Most warm-up sessions simply look for other release games when the energy flow fades and the actors begin to get bored.

The points of transition in games are experienced as moments of boredom, and what happens here is reflective of other human activity. In football, for instance, a boy will enjoy just kicking a ball about a field. It is enjoyable for the energy it releases. Eventually he becomes bored or dissatisfied with this. Two coats are put down to make a goal. Later two sets of coats are put down and the group splits into two teams. After a while this too bores, and the boy will only be satisfied with playing on a pitch in a match according to rules, and with the real rewards for success. At the highest level, the boy turns professional and the game becomes a way of life through which he expresses himself.

Every artist moves through these stages of transition, no less the actor than the others. The transition points, if natural, would be marked by the need to take child's play into plays; the decision to present oneself for training; then leaving drama school to work professionally. In practice the lines are blurred by anxiety at entering upon acting as a career in an insecure world and the fact that three years at drama school do not nearly complete an actor's creative and technical development. The transition points are not related to human development but are purely arbitrary and this causes problems in the theatre when the young actor is forced to compete at a high level of cool, objective, professional skill, when he is still learning the rules of the game and how to play it.

In theatre games there are several ways of making the transitions easier, but they cannot be rushed. Since so many areas of the work I do involve transitions from release energy to control and discipline, it becomes part of an established pattern of work and carries over naturally into each new area that is approached. The principle of reinstituting the body/think processes to the exclusion of the conscious mind processes is behind so much of the work that the actor is led into an instinctive knowledge of what is expected in any new game. One can simply wait for the actors to be bored. Principally, one works through introducing rules and disciplines after the first few playings. Children may have troubles with rules and discipline imposed on their play; adult actors rarely have. It is part and parcel of their lives and the transition is not difficult to provoke artificially. The fact that all the work is carried out in a theatrical framework, and is related in so many areas to rehearsal and performance, also gives the actor an understanding that the work is leading somewhere and he is often eager to press on.

In the conflict game, Touch your Partner, a rule can be introduced to limit the area of movement by fixing a certain position for the feet, and thus bringing the actors into eye to eye contact. It may be difficult for them to maintain eye to eye contact at first, but given free range of movement, eye to eye contact usually only happens when the actor goes looking for it. It can be pointed out that watching the hand is not an efficient way of playing the game, because it pulls the head down and forward, and the body off balance.

When the game is used as a simple image of a theatrical situation, rules and disciplines are fed into the game, gradually, from the dramatic situation itself. The games release energy that is disciplined in gradual stages, to enable the actor to build up to a complex relationship, instead of asking him to portray the whole situation at one shot. When rehearsing an improvised play, based on *The Cave of Salamanca* by Cervantes, we used this game in that way. A husband is leaving his wife. She is expecting a lover. She does not want to arouse her husband's suspicions by appearing cold, but she wants him out of the way quickly. The situation is further complicated by the fact that the husband has been denied his wife's bed for three months. He must hurry to catch the coach, but this is his only chance of physical contact and illusory sexual relief. In the play the leave-taking is prolonged. There is a complicated conflict of interests inside each person and between each of them. The actors could verbally talk out the situation in improvisation, but were totally unable to *act it out*. The humour of the situation lay in the physical action not the words. We began by the simple game of touching the partner's back. We progressed so that the object of the man was to have physical sexual contact with his partner. She was to avoid it. We then asked the girl to avoid the contact in such ways that she appeared to be encouraging it. A third actor called to the husband from off-stage to catch the coach before it left. The lover hovered in the opposite wings, and had to be pacified. In this way the game helped make tangible and physical what had previously been intentional and subjective. Other situations can be constructed to meet the demands of particular dramatic situations, using the same model.

The Coins More complex games can be found through which to explore different, basic encounters. The Coins is a variation of Touch your Partner. Players now hold a coin or small key on the flat of their left hand. The object of the game is to use the coin to distract the attention of the opponent from his own coin, so that you can snatch it. The body/think processes are crucial in this game. If you watch his coin, you lose the sense of your own coin and are vulnerable. If you watch your own coin, you lose the sense of his coin and will never snatch it. The only successful way to play is to watch the opponent's eyes and let the instinctive awareness of the body/think operate. The game sets up a more sophisticated conflict: that in which you must risk what you have in order to gain what you want. The relationship of Hedda Gabler to Judge Brack can be explored through this framework.

Group conflicts and period movement

The foregoing pattern of exercises can be extended into group games, and these can be used to work at general patterns of period movement. That is to say, the movement style of any historical period is dependent upon the means through which the individual pursues his ends, in conflict or co-operating with other people. What one might call the social rules of the game. Each period, and often each play, demands a game structure to meet its own needs. I will choose one to describe how it can be used.

The Jacobean Street Scene From the touch conflict game we move to the coin conflict game. The players are then asked to hold the coins on their hands without clenching, but to hold the hand behind the back. They must not run, nor break out of a walk. Nor must they protect the coin by standing nearer than two feet to a wall. The object of the players is to steal as many coins as they can whilst protecting their own, without clenching the fist. Once his own coin has been stolen, a player retires from the game.

The game relates directly to other games which explore 360 degree awareness of space, and is also a cooler version of the earlier hopping game, in which three players make and break alliances of two against one, by making spatial adjustments to change the relationships. Both these elements appear in a more complex form in this game.

The game moves on to another variation. The coin is removed in favour of a handkerchief tucked into the back of the belt and the game is played several times, feeding in rules until the following pattern is built up. Young bloods walk the street, provoking quarrels. The law demands that any duelling attack shall be punishable by death, unless the killer has drawn in self-defence. The players, therefore, try to provoke situations in which other players will be moved to attack them, or will back down from the confrontation and lose face. The skilful playing of the game involves extricating oneself from situations of provocation without losing face, or else finding 'innocent' counter-provocation which puts the boot on the other foot. It works well for *Romeo and Juliet*.

Other players play cutpurses, and try to steal the purses (handkerchiefs) from the belts of the bloods without being caught, killed or arrested. In this they can use whatever means they choose, e.g. flattery. Words are not allowed however until the game has been taken into, or near enough to, the rehearsal situation.

The amount of 360 degree awareness of space, and the carriage this produces, along with the relationship patterns defined by the rules, make it possible to build gradually towards a complex social situation, and to produce a general pattern of social movement for two groups of characters. This general pattern can then be made specific by feeding in rules taken from the individual characters and situations. The actor bases his work upon building up the body/think programme in stages, instead of conceiving cliché images of what pattern of movement the character should have. As such it is an analytical tool.

The Restoration Comedy Game In this game we work through the touch conflict and coin games to a more finely structured game. There are two players, a man and a woman.

The woman has the money in her hand. She is an heiress, and the money represents her dowry. It is her means of attracting a 'good' husband, someone who, in appearance and behaviour, is worthy of her. She must get him to woo her, and her objective is to manoeuvre him into such a position that she can trap one of his arms under hers. This is taken as a metaphor for dragging him off from town to a country house in Northamptonshire to settle down. To do this she must take risks with her money. If she holds too tightly to the cash he will not woo her, or his job will be made difficult. If she reveals her intention by directly trying to trap his arm he will be repelled by the danger.

The prospective husband is a younger son, accustomed to wearing the right clothes, drinking and gambling at the most fashionable clubs, racing with Old Rowley on Newmarket Heath, being seen and admired on the streets and at the theatre. To do this he needs money, which he hasn't got. He must charm and woo the girl to gain her dowry. In order to use the money for his own purposes, he must avoid, at all costs, being trapped by the arm. No words are allowed, but sounds may be used. At the start there are no other rules.

The game can be played a number of ways. It is usually best, at first, simply to let the players discover what they can in the playing. Later the game can be stopped whenever either player makes a mistake; if the man, for instance, is seen grabbing for the money, he loses dignity and is no longer an eligible husband. Slowly the discipline or rule conventions of the period can be fed in. In every age there are conventions of behaviour, for example in the areas of the body one can touch. In this way a gradual and detailed pattern of social behaviour is built up.

Sometimes, the player is allowed to continue after making a mistake to see what ways he finds of recovering from it. Human beings have made social gaffs in all ages and places, and the drama is full of situations which exploit this human failing. Sometimes, the game is set up like a relay race with a succession of wooers and heiresses taking over the roles, to try to sustain some development by capitalising on what they have observed in other players, and putting their observations to the test of practice.

Playing the game goes hand in hand with study and scholarship. Objective knowledge, gained from a study of the play and its social setting, is put into direct practice and used. What usually emerges from the playing is the general pattern of Restoration movement. The actual purposes of the movements and actions are constantly disguised and transformed into elegant gestures of wooing and deportment, producing light, airy, extravagant movements in space of the whole body and the limbs. In this way the movement style emerges directly from the actors' investigation of character and situation, and ceases to be an artificial mode through which he expresses his work.

The main rules of the game can be changed according to the situation and period one wants to investigate. In Farquhar's *The Constant Couple*, the girl and the man meet in a mistaken situation. The girl expects a wooer; he thinks he has come to a brothel. The main game is then a general springboard for a more complex specific situation. If the man were Al Capone, and the girl a vaudeville showgirl, the rules would be totally different, because the need, intention and interchange are different.

It is also necessary not to apply too strict a framework of rules too soon. The actor must first work out the approach that he can make before he moves on to selected alternatives. Trial and error is a productive method. Nothing succeeds like failure, because failure causes the actor to think, reassess, and try a different way. The rules similarly are not absolute. History and the drama is full of instances of human beings who broke the rules and got away with it – or didn't. In fact, an important aspect of working out of one's purposes within a framework of social rules and disciplines is knowing how to make the rules work to your advantage, how to bend and break them, and how to contain the other person inside them. Comedy of Manners is built on this. It takes skill and experience to put it into practice. This can be gained in the playing.

Laboratory work

The framework above can be used in a purely laboratory situation in which the objective rules are removed, and the only deciding rule is the response or reaction provoked from the other player, or players. Since these laboratory exercises are almost completely free and open-ended, and go whichever way the group wants them to go, they are difficult to describe. The value lies in the open-endedness. However, I will set out certain possible courses.

Triangles We explore triangular relationships. A game is set up in which a boy and a girl are together and another boy is alone. The one boy must somehow disturb the relationship so that he gets the girl and the other boy is left alone. No words are used, so the exercise relies on actions. At some later stage, words are used to show how they inhibit action, by allowing the players to preconceive their responses verbally and consciously. This is a major problem in the theatre. That is, finding ways in which the words spring naturally from the action, when the exact words are known before the action begins. The known text inhibits the search for the instinctive springs of the action, because it defines very clearly in the actor's conscious mind what the result of his actions will be, and what his reaction to the other actors will be.

No rules are established for the early playings of the game. The players are asked to find their own instinctive ways of acting and of reacting to what happens in the situation. Mistakes are registered when a negative response is provoked. For example, when playing the game recently, with a lone girl trying to separate me from a second girl, the girl I was partnered with pulled me violently away from a very warm smile-contact offered me by the lone girl. When I responded to the pull by looking at my partner, her face was hard and turned away from me. I felt I was being treated as a property, and not as a human being. I responded negatively to being pulled by breaking off the partnership and approaching the other girl.

As in the Restoration Comedy Game, this game can be allowed to proceed through mistaken strategies, to see how the player adjusts or recovers from mistakes made. Or it can be stopped and the mistakes discussed, with the player then allowed to continue playing and to try other strategies. Or a relay of players can take over the roles to try their approaches on the basis of what they have observed in the other players.

There is no one successful way of playing the game. The initiating player makes a move, which occasions some response in the player he wishes to contact or make an alliance with. The initiating player must then work on that response. If he fails to take cognition of it he will make a mistake. The discussion afterwards takes in the experiences of the group in similar situations. How they acted and reacted when trying to make contact with the opposite sex at parties and other social situations.

The game can sustain an apparently infinite number of playings, since the strategies and responses are so variable in any single situation. The basics can be varied: a girl splitting a boy and girl; a girl trying to split two boys; a boy trying to split two girls; a girl trying to take a girl away from a boy, and vice versa. It can be extended to one outsider trying to break into a group, and so on.

At the first playings, players are asked only to act and react naturally and instinctively. They are asked gradually to introduce discipline into the playing, first of all by trying different strategies to eliminate mistakes. Later they are asked to choose deliberately and imaginatively a specific approach and a specific reaction, that is, to play a part, and this moves the game towards dramatic situations and the controlled work of the actor. But the instinctive playing must always come first. The instinctive actions and reactions must be released before discipline is applied.

The game is a bridge to more complex dramatic situations, but I believe, in practice, it is necessary to explore the elemental contacts first, to bring the players into contact and relationship with each other. In Gorky's *Vassa Zhelessnova*, there is a scene in which a wife tries to make her reluctant husband take poison, in order to avoid a scandal that will harm the family. The scene is quite short and very tightly written and, in the course of it, the woman tries several different approaches, which are all clear in the text. It is difficult to get the actors to re-create the flow of demand and response in the scene, in other than intellectual and verbal terms, unless they can get away from the tightly structured text and give themselves time and room to examine the natural working out of the strategies and responses, which are highly compressed in the text. Other directors might tackle this problem by asking the actors to improvise in their own words. I prefer to approach it through this game structure.

As an educational tool for studying social relationships, this is a valuable exercise. It should probably be used in the educational system at large, or in sociological casework. For the actor, it provides a training in flexible contacts with other people, and directs his work to playing off the other actor's response. The disciplined areas of the work, which lead the actor to select his responses, are important in situations where one is working with other actors who do not respond naturally and openly to you, or refuse to enter into relationships with you on stage. It happens too often. The selected response to an imagined stimulus or demand is then necessary for the actor to work off. The exercise could be a useful bridge for young actors leaving the group atmosphere of a drama school and entering the world of weekly rep.

The game can also be structured to make freely tangible and objective the basic patterns underlying certain plays. Sartre's *Huis Clos* has a relationship pattern involving a man, a girl and a lesbian. Working on the game, the dramatic quality of the play was intensified by moving from *wanting* contact, to *needing* contact, to a desperate necessity to have contact. In defining the intention of the players in the game, the verbs one uses are of prime importance, because they condition the motive drive of the actors.

The game has a riveting fascination which compels the watchers and forces their attention easily and naturally to concentrate on every small action in the chain of demand and response. Once watching the *Midsummer Night's Dream* game where a boy wants a girl, who wants another boy, who wants another girl, who wants the first boy, which at that playing was particularly beautiful and exciting in its interplay of hopes and frustrations, I was moved to say, 'If the play can't be that exciting and theatrical, let's scrap the play'. Perhaps this is not so extravagant. Perhaps the seeds are here for a new experimental drama. Certainly the base is realistic and strong enough to support it. It would need time and resources to develop it, but I am sure it would be profitable to attempt. The main point, for now though, is that this activity should be central to the actor's training.

CHAPTER 11

Space

The work in this chapter has been developed for three purposes. Firstly, in response to young actors who have encountered problems in moving from drama school, where they have played in studio theatre spaces, to working in established theatre buildings. Secondly, in response to trainee directors, to explain the principles on which one 'sets' a play, that is, arranges the groupings and movements on the stage. Thirdly, to help professional actors explore on the one hand how they instinctively adapt their work to differing theatre buildings, and on the other hand how they imaginatively create situations on an open stage without the support of a topographic set.

The problems

The actor stands at the centre of a three-dimensional volume of space. In fact he stands at the centre of two three-dimensional volumes of space, the *actual neutral space* of the stage and the *virtual characterised space* of the setting of the play. Both of these concepts of space relate directly to another space area – the auditorium.

At various points in history the actor has been required to transform the real stage space into the situational space by the use of his imagination and body. At other times, the transformation has been made for him by other means. In a 'poor' theatre considerable demands are made upon the actor's physical and imaginative resources to effect transformations of space and time.

> Can this cockpit hold
> The vasty fields of France? . . .
>   . . . let us, ciphers to this great accompt,
> On your imaginary forces work.[1]

The intention of the Naturalistic set is to create the illusion that the play is taking place in the real setting of the situation. The actor is required only to effect the transformations of character. That is, not to *act*, but to *be* – or to seem to be.

At various points in history the stage and audience have occupied the same room, as they do in theatre-in-the-round. At others there has been a clear distinction between the two spaces, as there is in the Italian proscenium arch theatre.

Actors today do not possess the advantages enjoyed by actors of other ages who largely played in a very limited number of theatres with a constant stage/audience relationship. We work in pros. arch, thrust, apron, end-on and in the round. In these forms we move from 100 seaters to 300 seaters to 1,000 seaters. No two theatres ever look alike, or, more important for the actor, *feel* alike.

Dramatists in the past wrote for the theatre they knew. They wrote within its limitations, exploiting its strengths in structuring their plays, so that the actor could perform them effectively. Not only do we work in differing theatres, we engage with works which were written and conceived in terms of one particular style of theatre building, and we perform them in entirely different and often contradictory structures.

The development of sophisticated stage machinery during the nineteenth and twentieth centuries; the emergence of Naturalism, and its influence on subsequent drama; the growth of television and cinema as major sources of employment for the actor – all have tended to reduce the demands made upon the actor's technique. The trend is now moving into reverse, because of economic pressures on the theatre, because many directors and play-wrights are making more use of the actor and less use of elaborate settings, and because the work of artists like Barrault and Grotowski inspire a movement towards a 'total' theatre, based upon the maximum utilisation of the actor's resources.

The actor is, therefore, asked to respond to demands made upon him to produce skills which are little developed in him. Most of the actor training in this country is still trying to turn out actors for the old Naturalistic theatre and the old theatre of psychological realism.

Even within the unadventurous commercial theatre there has been constant critical complaint since the First World War that the theatre in this country is becoming ordinary; it lacks 'size'. A dearth is noted of 'big' actors who can fill a stage, or hold an audience, command attention – actors, in a word, who have 'presence'.

All of these problems are encountered regularly by actors and directors in their work. They are usually tackled pragmatically as they arise in the course of specific productions. A history of theatre architecture and scenic design in Britain over the last twenty years would reveal a search for more flexible and adaptable theatre buildings, and a movement away from decoration in the setting towards 'the creation and organisation of scenic space'.[2] A history of productions would reveal a definite trend away from picturesque 'groupings', towards a dynamic use of movement on the stage, and many examples of directors' ingenuity in breaking down the traditional role of the audience, which is to sit in one room, passively watching the drama enacted in another room through the 'fourth wall' of the proscenium arch.

Space has already been an important element in the work I have outlined previously. The erect posture, with potential mobility in all directions, gives the actor facility to use a wider area of space than the narrow segment bounded by the lines of his eye-sight. (It is usually necessary to prevent young actors turning to speak directly to the person they are addressing, although in life we more often than not speak to people *en passant*.) Ease of mobility around the central axis of the body implies that the actor is the centre of his own personal area of space, to which all other objects and people in space relate. I have argued that this is the natural condition of the human being; that pressures within the acting and theatre processes tend to disturb this; and that the kinaesthetic use of the body/think tends to reinstate it. We have not yet worked on kinaesthetic awareness purely in terms of space.

Personal space

Only at very rare moments are people aware of the space they stand in. This awareness is usually influenced by geographical or architectural factors. We feel 'free' standing on the top of a hill; we feel 'shut in' in small confined rooms. Our awareness of space is also defined by factors of character, mood and purpose, as well as by geography and climate.

We often express moods through physical, spatial metaphors. We are so happy 'we are on top of the world'. When worried or pre-occupied, 'the world closes in on us'. In desperation, 'we do not know which way to turn'. In confusion 'we are lost', 'we do not know where we are'. When we hold firm or fixed views on a subject, 'we take a stand' or a 'position', 'we refuse to budge an inch', 'we will not give way'. A person is 'approachable', or 'open'. His space area is relaxed and we can enter into it and into a relationship with him. He is 'withdrawn', he has retired into a very restricted space area; 'we can't get through to him', the limits of his space area are so sharply and clearly defined that they constitute a barrier to communication. The extrovert 'keeps open house'.

The 'arrogant' person 'tramples over people', that is, he intrudes into the privacy of other people's personal space without respect. We often form opinions of the character of people we see in the street, without direct contact with them, and we do this on the basis of what we see in their movement and the sympathetic sensations in our body/think. The arrogant person is characterised by a certain drawing up of the body 'to look down on people'; he has such a narrow space area that he can walk through a crowd as though nothing or no-one touches him; literally and metaphorically, he ignores the presence of people, 'brushes them aside'. He is 'up tight'.

In relationships, there are spatial metaphors of 'meeting half-way', 'finding common ground', and even 'coming together'. Subservience can be expressed as having no clearly defined centre but standing on the perimeter of someone else's space and relating directly to their space. The sinister sycophancy of Uriah Heep presumes that there is a contradiction in how he behaves. He appears to be subservient whilst remaining withdrawn within his own tight space. Master/slave relationships presume that the master has complete right of access to the space of the slave, who has 'no privacy'.

Stanislavski talks of the 'circle of concentration' of an actor. I understand that this also applies generally to people. We talk of people being 'broad' or 'narrow' minded. How wide and clearly defined is the 'circle of concentration', and what does it encompass? Again, using Stanislavski's approach of working from the outer circumstances to approach the inner truth, we can use these spatial metaphors to help us experience the body sensations that they express, by imaginatively re-creating them. They are a way for the actor to be objectively aware of states of mind, and a tool for him to use in creating and preserving character.

Before we can do this we must first make the actor aware of himself as the centre of a neutral three-dimensional volume of space, and then move on to characterising that space.

The following exercise is frequently used as a preliminary to observation training, but is also used as the basic exercise in space work. The actor is asked to stand in a room and to close his eyes (*illustration no. 24*). He is asked to listen to the sounds that come to him from different directions and at differ-

24 'He can experience the sensations of being "on centre"'

ent distances. Using the perspective of sound, he is asked to experience him-self as the centre of a three-dimensional volume of space. If the actor can do this – and the great majority easily can – the body is pulled into the erect pos-ture automatically, and he can experience the sensations of being 'on centre'.

The actor is then asked to preserve the sensation with his eyes open. He is asked to let his eyes wander round the room in all directions available to his eyes without turning his trunk. He is asked to perceive the perspective of objects in space.

The next stage is to be able to maintain the sensation whilst moving through the room, perceiving the changing perspectives of objects as he moves the position of his centre. This is obviously a natural and automatic activity. If we didn't do it we would bump into things, fall down stairs, crash cars. But to be *aware* of how the body/think works in this area takes work, and is subject to the usual interference by the conscious control mechanisms of the mind.

At any time when the sensations are lost or interfered with, the actor is asked to return to standing with his eyes closed listening to sounds, in order to regain the sensations.

In most of my teaching I have had the support of other teachers who have taught movement from an understanding of the work of Laban. The actors have, through this work, had an understanding of the possibilities of movement for the human body in space, and the divisions of the personal sphere of movement, or 'Kinesphere' (see diagram).

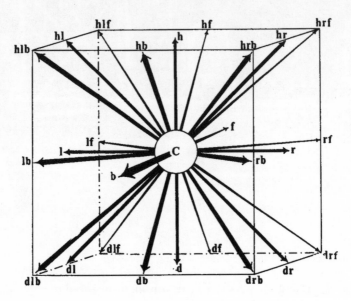

Space orientation

h = high	*hr* = high right	*hrf* = high right forward
d = deep	*db* = deep backward	*dlb* = deep left backward
l = left	*lf* = left forward	*hlf* = high left forward
r = right	*dr* = deep right	*drb* = deep right backward
b = backward	*hb* = high backward	*hlb* = high left backward
f = forward	*rf* = right forward	*drf* = deep right forward
	dl = deep left	*hrb* = high right backward
	hf = high forward	*dlf* = deep left forward
c = centre	*rb* = right backward	
	hl = high left	
	df = deep forward	
	lb = left backward	

The Kinesphere

All movement takes place by transferring the body or parts of the body from one position in space to another. Accordingly, each movement is partly explicable from these spatial changes of position . . .

Wherever the body moves or stands, it is surrounded by space. Around the body is the 'sphere of movement', or 'Kinesphere', the circumference of which can be reached by normally extended limbs without changing one's stance, that is, the place of support . . .

Outside this immediate sphere lies the wider or 'general' space which man can enter only by moving away from the original stance. He has to step outside the borders of his immediate sphere and create a new one from the new stance, or, in other words, he transfers what might be called his 'personal' sphere to another place in the general space.[3]

Where actors have not had this training, it has been necessary to introduce some work in this area. Work is also done on the clown 'grotesque' – contradictory movements in various parts of the body for comic effect. The clearest example is Groucho Marx. His eye-brows reach for the skies whilst his backside drags in the mud.

In the main, though, the work has moved directly on to the imaginative areas of the metaphors, and this has usually been carried out on the lines of the earlier exercise: 'What does it feel like . . .' We begin with geographical or climatic situations. Actors are asked to stand in space and imagine they are standing on the top of a high plateau surrounded by an infinity of sky, or in pouring rain, sheltering under a dripping tree. It is observable in these two situations that the actor first appears to be at the centre of a very expansive area of space, and, in the second, at the centre of a very tiny area of space. The sensations in the actor's body can almost always be directly related to his awareness of space, and he can soon begin to vary his awareness of differing volumes of space. The work is analogous to a footballer practising corner kicks, and most actors progress easily and quickly into a very subtle awareness of the possibilities of using space in their work.

Size

Directors are frequently concerned with the problem of 'size' in performance. What appears on the stage is often a pale reflection of what should be there. It fails to present a stage image which measures up to the forces at work in the play. Descriptively the play on the stage lacks 'electricity, magnetism, dynamic energy'. The problem is usually a lack of emotional intensity. The example which sticks in my mind is a production of *Othello* where there was general agreement among members of the audience that Desdemona was murdered because she lost a handkerchief. The tortured internal conflicts of Othello's trust and doubt, love and jealousy never appeared in the actor's performance.

'Star quality' is largely a question of 'size'. The star is 'larger than life' – 'the stage lights up when she appears'. But the star system also contributes to the problem by reducing so many of the actors to the subordinate role of supporting the star, and so diminishing the range of their acting.

Size of performance is determined by many factors, or by the absence of them, not least an insufficient 'depth of feeling', a lack of intensity of involvement in the activities of the character. I have already suggested ways of trying to overcome emotional inhibitions and barriers by physical means. We should also look carefully at the notes directors give when trying to cope with the problem of 'size'. They say, 'It needs to be bigger', 'It needs to breathe expansively', 'Give it more air', 'Open it out more'. The killing note is, 'It needs more *projection*'. This almost always leads to an idea in the actor's mind of forcing or pushing, which in practice reduces the size.

What is interesting about such remarks is that they are phrased in physical or spatial terms. Accepting the direct relationship between mind and body, there is some work that can be done to tackle the question of 'size', by a physical spatial approach. That is we try to find the physical means by which the 'big' actor succeeds in 'filling the stage'.

Some actors seem to possess an instinctive stage 'presence'. Others develop it as they gain security and self-confidence in their work. So much seems to depend upon the personality of the actor that there is clearly no magic formula by which 'presence' can be induced. All that we can do is to try to make the actor aware of some of the pressures which inhibit the full expression of his powers, and hopefully put him in a position where the natural strength of his acting can be used.

The earlier space work can be directed, in later stages, to an under-standing that stage 'presence' is very closely tied to being the strong centre of a personal space area. In this sense, we can speak of an 'egocentric' person, which is usually, falsely, what the world generally imagines the actor to be. Certainly, the clarity of the stage action depends upon the interaction of clearly defined characters, and awareness of space is an important part of this. When the actor has no clear centre position in space, from which he interacts with the other actors/characters, the stage action becomes blurred and the audience's attention meanders instead of flowing from focal point to focal point in the action. Let us examine some of the pressures which inhibit stage 'presence' in the actor.

Theatre space

The major factor affecting the actor's use of space is the architecture of the theatre. The actor, today, rarely plays long in any one theatre (quite apart from working in other media which make different demands upon him). He also, usually, rehearses in a totally different space from the one he will play in.

The body responds subconsciously to the particular space it is in. It feels different being outside a house from being inside it. We instinctively modulate our movements (and voice) to suit the space we are in.

The transference of a production from rehearsal room to stage is often painful for an actor. He feels lost. The sensations of working in a space to which he has become accustomed are taken away from him, and he is asked to work in a strange space which he doesn't understand.

Many actors, and all successful ones, are resourceful in instinctively 'getting the feel of the house'. It would be a very foolish actor who believed he could perform in a space or on a stage which he had not seen and 'walked' previously. Practically all actors arrive at a theatre early so as to get the 'feel' of it, and subconsciously they begin to adapt their work to the new situation. Technical crews on tour have difficulty keeping the actors off the set they are fitting up, for this reason. First nights on tour are always hated and are often poor performances because the actor has not had sufficient time to acclimatise to the house. For the same reason, dress rehearsals often bear little resemblance to opening nights, as the actors are struggling to adapt from rehearsal room to stage. Most intelligent directors take the pressure off the actor by making the first dress rehearsal on the stage a technical walk-through.

Since it normally takes a good deal of time and experience before an actor can adapt quickly to different spaces, we need to look for other ways of achieving this awareness and flexibility. Some of this work must be academic since we do not have access to a large variety of theatres during training, although this can be partly overcome by setting up laboratory situations.

Theatre architecture

The Greek amphitheatre, with its semi-circular auditorium, open orchestra for the chorus, raised platform stage, long entrances and exits to the side, and raised central entrance at the rear, is rich in its use of visual perspective. This perspective comes into play as the audience engages with the actions and reactions of the protagonists *through the chorus*, who move in the same area of space as the audience and stand between them and the actors in the drama. The chorus therefore has a special relationship with the audience through its spatial position. The main action is 'distanced'.

The Elizabethan theatre, with its wooden 'O', in which the actors and audience inhabited the same room space, used very limited perspective, but asked of its actors an awareness of almost all possible directions of space. Its great strength was the close actor/audience contact that the single space and jutting stage invoked.

The Italian proscenium arch theatre split the theatre into three areas: the detached scenic area, the auditorium, and the proscenium acting area, which was often an extension on the auditorium room. Later developments in the fan-shaped auditorium and the horse-shoe auditorium reduced the area of the proscenium and merged the acting and scenic areas, gradually creating two separate spaces: the stage and the auditorium. The proscenium theatre is often called the picture-frame theatre; when perspective was required this was created on stage by the scenic technique of false perspective, borrowed from the two-dimensional art of painting. The actors played towards the audience, often face on, against an elaborate representation of the geographical situation.

The gradual removal of the actor from direct contact with the audience, and the consequent restriction placed upon his contribution to the drama, was further intensified with the development of the almost circular auditorium. If one continues the line of the auditorium walls in the diagrams of the Nottingham Playhouse and the Yvonne Arnaud Theatre, Guildford, they meet just inside the stage area, giving a narrow elliptical shape which is part of both stage and auditorium. The architectural design almost removes the greater part of the stage area from direct contact with the audience and relegates it to the function of carrying scenery, material and human. The yawning chasm of the orchestra pit also intensifies the split between stage and auditorium.

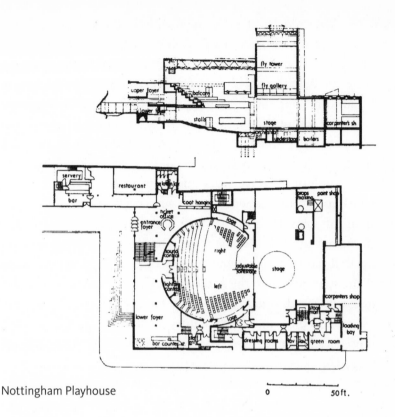

Nottingham Playhouse

0   50 ft.

The almost circular auditorium is very powerful for Variety and Music Hall. The slender interacting segment is a strong area for which singers and solo acts can contact the audience directly. The rest of the vast stage carries the spectacular effects, or is used for acts like dance, or juggling, which require no direct contact with the audience.

The proscenium arch theatre is practically useless for Greek drama, since it entirely destroys real perspective and creates almost insoluble problems of relating the chorus to the protagonists; if they stand in front of the actors, they obscure them; if behind the actors, they lose contact with the audience.

The pros. arch theatre creates problems for Elizabethan and Jacobean plays because of the difficulties of playing both intimate scenes and scenes involving violent conflict above the proscenium arch, away from direct contact with the audience. The balcony scene in *Romeo and Juliet* and the duel between Edgar and Edmund in *King Lear* are examples.

The persistence of the proscenium arch stage inhibits our theatre. Where new theatres have been built they have often been designed to overcome its limitations. The Mermaid Theatre dispensed with the proscenium arch and placed the acting area end on to a raked auditorium introducing some degree of three-dimensional perspective. Other theatres, like the Octagon, Bolton, and the Sheffield Crucible have been designed with thrust stages in fan-shaped auditoria. For the most part, though, because of economic stringencies, we are left playing in pros. arch, or variations of pros. arch theatres. Ways have to be found to overcome their limitations: lighting can be used to create perspective in space; the use of ramped staging changes the audience's perception of the stage space and helps project the actor into a closer relationship with the audience; and a similar effect can be achieved with the use of different levels in the stage setting, which can elevate the actor into dominant positions on the stage. Directors and designers have built over the orchestra pit, or around the proscenium arch, to project the setting from the stage area into the auditorium. The orchestra pit has also been built over with treads running down into the auditorium. The Berliner Ensemble designers in their nineteenth century pros. arch theatre have made a virtue of necessity by surrounding the stage area with a vast cyclorama cloth, creating a large open space in which the perspective of isolated scenic units and actors can more easily be perceived; but this works effectively only from the circles and galleries of the theatre. Many designers in this country have adopted a similar strategy.

For the most part, though, directors have relied upon creating an expansive stage area, in which they skilfully place their actors. If the pros. arch theatre foreshortens perspective, then one way to overcome this is to use very much more space, so that the fore-shortening is counteracted by a greater distance between the actors.

In working this way, the actor encounters certain contradictions which spring from the architecture of the theatre. Principally, he must be the centre of a space area which is removed in distance from the audience, while the building itself is designed to push him forward to the footlights.

Focus

The architecture of the nineteenth and twentieth century pros. arch theatre is designed to give a strong focal point at the front of the stage. The focal point of the theatre is usually found centre-stage about eighteen inches upstage of the curtain cut or setting line. Standing in that position one feels

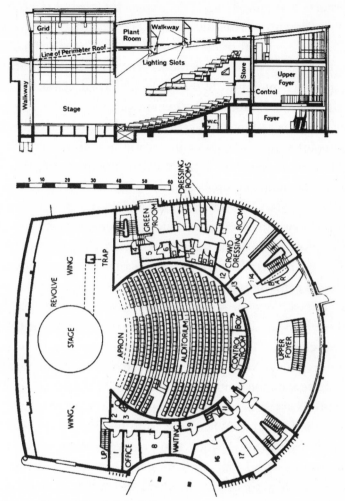

Yvonne Arnaud Theatre, Guildford

in relaxed and total contact with the whole auditorium. It can be experienced by moving up and down the centre line from the front of the stage until one finds the point where this happens. One feels 'strong'. Half-hearted attempts to build new theatres on the pros. arch pattern but with straight rows of seating tend to weaken the focus of the house, whilst retaining all the limitations of the pros. arch theatre. The fan-shaped auditorium tends to strengthen the focus.

The pressure of this focus can be felt by asking the actor to stand on the focal point and then, retaining contact with the audience, walk backwards upstage, opening out as he goes. That is, increasing the spatial size of his body gestures and movements. The architectural pressure of the building pushes him down towards the focal point against the movement he is making, and the natural reaction is to close up. The effect is like walking backwards up an ever-decreasing tunnel. The reverse effect is demonstrated in almost every Pantomime. In the final walk down, characters start at the rear of the stage and walk or run down towards the audience, opening out as they come. The architectural pressure works for them as they approach the focal point of the audience's concentrated attention, and projects them into such a warm, close relationship with the audience, that the heart expands and spontaneous applause breaks out. Every Pantomime producer knows that the final walk-down sets the seal on the show, and it will often rescue a poor show by sending the audience home happy.

Given a pros. arch theatre, the actor is asked to find the focal point of the state, and then to walk the stage trying out the sensations of various positions and paths through the space. The strong positions on the stage are those which face along the line of force towards the focal point. Movements along these lines, or along lines parallel to the diagonal of the stage are strong movements. Movements which cross these lines, or meander over them, are relatively weaker. The actor facing out front in an upstage position (except on the centre line) is in a weak position.

The actor is asked to walk directly across the stage from wing to wing, parallel to the footlights. When he does so the depth of the stage appears to diminish dramatically. When two actors walk across the stage from opposite sides, at different points in the depth of the stage, the stage appears to gain in depth until the point where they cross each other, when it diminishes suddenly.

Pairs of actors are asked to stand in the space, in various positions. The groupings are arranged to direct attention towards one of the pair of actors and then to see how attention can be focused on the other actor by changing his position on the stage. A third actor is added to the pair to see how the balance is changed when he stands in several different positions. The effects of the various groupings are discussed to assess how far the architectural focus of the stage is disturbed by placing actors in the space, and to what extent the positions of dominance, subservience and balance in any grouping is supported by, or relies on the architectural arrangement of space and the lines of force.

All the centring work described previously is now repeated on the stage to see how this is affected by being carried out in a theatre rather than in a room.

Every theatre space has its own character and must be approached pragmatically by the actor. The purpose of the work is not to provide the actor with a set of rules but to induce an awareness of space through body sensations. Obviously, though, some general principles do emerge.

Many small touring groups have to play in school halls which have pros. arch stages, with flat floors in both stage and audience areas. The actor at the rear of these stages always appears, to the audience, to be on the other side of a hill. The forestage dominates completely. Entrances and exits, or moves directly across the stage, parallel to the footlights, reduce the perspective of depth, and almost reduce the stage to being two-dimensional. In order to make an effective entrance from the lower wings the actor often has to move towards upstage centre and then turn down stage along the line of force towards the focal point.

Unraked stages sometimes give a subconscious feeling of walking uphill as the actor approaches the audience, if the front stalls are below stage level. The audience gradually comes into view beyond the lip of the stage.

Where both stage and auditorium have flat floors, and the stage has an apron, moving through the proscenium arch can be a disconcerting experience for the actor. The line of the pros. arch is felt as a barrier to be pushed through. Ways, and the right moment, have to be found to cross it decisively, or the differing relationships between actor and audience are experienced as an abrupt visual and physical shock. This is usually experienced by both actor and audience subconsciously, but it disturbs the action and reception of the play. Unaware of what is happening, the actor feels uncomfortable, and blames this discomfort upon deficiencies in the way he is playing, instead of understanding it as a spatial and architectural phenomenon.

Laboratory work

Because of the restricted opportunities for working in a wide variety of theatre buildings and forms during training, some work is carried out in a laboratory situation.

In a large rehearsal room, a square is marked on the floor with tape. At other sessions the shape is changed to an oblong or circle. All the work described previously is carried out in this neutral space. The non-playing actors sit at one end; on two sides; on three sides; completely surrounding the space. Token pros. arches are set up, and token aprons defined. The neutral space is therefore characterised to be whatever theatre form with whichever stage/audience relationship we require.

Set down like this it might seem of very limited value to the actor, since the space is far removed from the stages he plays on. In practice it has proved its value. A token pros. arch of no more than two chairs separating the stage space from the audience is quite sufficient for the actor to experience quite clearly the particular quality of stage/audience contact the pros. arch theatre gives.

All spaces have their focal points and positions of strength and weakness relative to this point. The focal point of the theatre-in-the-round is the centre-point of the stage area. I suspect that in productions this must be one of the least used points on the stage. It creates such an intensity of concentrated attention on any actor standing there that the audience tires if he stays there for long.

The focal point of thrust stages is towards the rear of the stage area on the centre line. A group of professional actors working with me in Cologne spent a considerable amount of time playing with the thrust stage, exploring the Shakespearian soliloquy. The focal point of the Elizabethan stage was upstage centre (towards the rear of the floor trap in *illustration no. 25*). It is possible that this work could assist scholars. The most important factor in reconstructing the nature of past theatre productions is to realise that they utilised a certain area of space, and a particular arrangement between stage and audience. It needs no elaborate paraphernalia to set up the space. More might be learned this way than by reconstructing elaborate settings inside existing theatre buildings which have their own obtrusively individual character.

This work should also be a necessary part of the training method of directors and designers of small touring companies, who have to play in a wide variety of theatre, and non-theatre spaces, in helping them to make the greatest use of the existing space in the presentation of their work.

Setting space

When work has been done on the nature of neutral spaces, design elements are introduced. The stage designer rearranges or divides up the stage space,

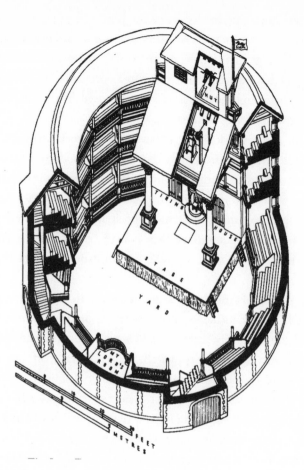

25 The Swan Theatre, *c.* 1594–96: scale reconstruction

creating smaller areas, in which the actor works. The director choreographs the production by allocating positions or movements to the actors in these spaces. Because this is largely an instinctive activity it appears to be very simple. The director will say, 'I think you'd be better if you moved the other side of the table'; the actor will say, 'I don't feel right here, can I move down a bit?' It is however a very skilful activity and theatre lore has many stories of legendary actors who were particularly brilliant in manoeuvring themselves into positions on the stage where they drew the audience's attention away from the other actors, towards themselves. 'Upstaging' is one such technique.

I have no wish to induce such selfishness in the actors I train; what is wrong is the use to which the skill is put. The ability to find the right position on the stage for the action of the play at a particular moment is a positive asset for both actor and director. Some directors work out the moves and groupings in advance, using ground-plans and models, and then choreograph the actors from their plotting. I prefer to try to lead the actor himself to find, through body sensations, his own instinctive way of using a setting and the spaces it comprises.

I always do some work along these lines in every production I direct. The setting and the furniture are there to be used by the actor, if the production is to have any unity or integrity. It is also a consideration to be taken into account when I analyse the play before talking to the designer. I begin by trying to get an arrangement of space that will help the actors. Decoration is purely a secondary factor. If the priorities are reversed, the actor's work must fit into the set, which diminishes the creative value and power of the actor.

The perception of the actor's movements in space is experienced kinaesthetically by the audience. The sensations are muted because they are only a part of the overall performance to which the audience is responding. Some plays are uncomfortable to watch, yet it is usually difficult to say why. One reason could be that the stage action lacks focus for the audience's attention; or that the setting does not create space areas which harmonise with the stage action. It has long been a technique of directing to increase and decrease tension in the play by working into or away from the 'points of interest' on a stage, or the focal points of certain areas of the stage space.

The Gates This is a very simple exercise, but seems, in practice, to be of absorbing interest to professional actors. It consists simply of setting two pieces of furniture in the neutral space, and letting the actors explore the areas of space this arrangement creates. The two pieces are usually placed about three feet apart and slightly up and down stage of each other. The actor is asked to explore and be aware of the sensations of the different areas of space, and of the variety of paths, and ways of moving through the gate formed by the two pieces of furniture.

The activity is fundamental to the work of the actor. The traditional advice to the novice is, 'Don't knock over the furniture, and don't stand in front of the star.' It is a cliché that the insecure or amateur actor moves about the stage from one piece of furniture to the other, groping for security, afraid to venture into open areas of space. This also applies to pools of bright light. Insecure actors have the best lit knees in the business.

Moving through the gate gives all the psycho-physical sensations of a decision made; that is, when you are aware of the sensations. The manner of moving through the gate affects the quality of the decision. Hovering in the gate creates sensations of discomfort and indecision. Strength, speed, direction of path and rhythm of movement are the physical means of qualifying the decision.

The point of the downstage corner of the downstage piece of furniture, which effectively marks the dividing line between two areas of space is experienced as a point of extreme discomfort.

A full interior set contains a number of 'gates' and, at first sight, an actor has difficulty taking in all the small areas of space that the setting encompasses. He is also, usually, pre-occupied with the process of adapting the work done in the rehearsal room to the theatre building. If we can give him some awareness of what is involved in walking a set we can materially help the process of adapting.

The Gates are my favourite and most absorbing toy. I never tire of playing with them. A great many actors I have worked with have spent hours happily playing with them. They are the core of all the choreographic and setting rehearsals in my productions. They are a tool through which I analyse and come to understand the action embodied in the text, and which I use to express, project or reinforce the psychological activities of the characters. The more I play with them, the more I learn.

Situational space

Using the stage or laboratory space, exercises are mounted to show how the actor's use of his body can characterise space.

The creative genius of Joan Littlewood's work lies in the fact that she achieved her effects through the use of the actor's creative and physical resources, and with a minimum of scenic devices. In *Oh What a Lovely War!*, for instance, six actors, using only small items of costume, reconstructed a Belgian cavalry charge in which the horses leapt trenches and were driven back by machine-gun fire, regrouped and charged again, to be caught in barbed wire and mown down and slaughtered. I have never taken part in a production which made greater demands on the actor, and I have never been happier in the theatre.

In one of my own productions, *Julius Caesar*, I marked the area of

Brutus's tent by a ring of armed soldiers on guard. During the course of the following scenes in the play, the soldiers, in their own rhythm, and at varying speeds, relaxed and slowly slumped from the upright alert guard position to a drooping body position; to kneeling; to gradually lying down to sleep. The visual effect, taken with a gradual lowering of the lights, was one of candles burning low, guttering, and finally dying out, throughout a long night. The consequent recovery, in the morning scene, was an image of a camp springing to arms.

The stage action was thus realistic and stylised; it was a metaphor which, taken with the action of the scenes inside the tent, gave them their setting, and commented on the state of mind of Brutus in particular. His energy drains away during the quarrel and the nightmare. It attempted to provoke a complex physical/psychological/emotional response in the audience. It also saved a lot of money on the setting, by using one of the theatre's greatest resources, the actor's psycho-physical imaginative powers.

Working away from the rehearsal/production situation, laboratory exercises are set up on this pattern. The Doors is the principal one of these.

The Doors Two actors are asked to stand in space, upright, facing downstage about five feet apart, on a line parallel to the footlights. A third actor stands several yards behind them, further away from the audience. At a signal, he walks between the pair of actors. As he passes through the 'door' of which they are the frame, the two static players turn, in the rhythm of his movement, to face upstage, by turning on the 'inner' foot.

The effect is of the one actor moving from an outside to an inside room, with a door closing behind him. The optical illusion of the action is to thrust the lone player into close contact with the audience as the 'door' closes. No use of the imaginative powers of the actor is asked at this stage. The action is purely physical.

The implications of the exercise are discussed, and the sensations aroused in the players and the audience, particularly the degrees to which the watchers begin to interpret, from the simple action, a dramatic situation, and the physical shock and sense of heightened response when the moving actor is suddenly projected into a new relationship with them.

Several variations of the game are tried out. The actors framing the door turn outwards rather than inwards, when the other player passes through them. The reverse process is tried. The moving actor walks upstage through the door, away from the audience. The door is set on the diagonal instead of on the line parallel to the footlights.

The purpose of the exercise is to examine how the character of the neutral space can be changed, simply by the positions of actors in space and simple patterns of movement, without any use of the actor's imagination.

The next stage of the exercise asks the actor to vary the quality of his movement through the door. He is asked to move quickly with a strong rhythm, or slowly with a light rhythm. Again the audience response is discussed, how they interpret decisiveness or hesitancy from these movement qualities, and how this affects their projected understanding of the situation, and the character's frame of mind.

The moving actor is asked to open out as he passes through the door, to give the impression of moving from confinement to release. This is often simply done by asking him to imagine passing from darkness to sunlight. The process is reversed. The variations in turning inwards or outwards by the door players, and the different positions of the door, are tried on all occasions to examine qualitative differences in the audience response and in their interpretation.

The actor is then asked to work towards specific real or dramatic situations in order to define the activity more clearly. Hamlet's escape from the prison atmosphere of Elsinore, which leads to 'O, from this time forth,/My thoughts be bloody, or be nothing worth!', and Lear's various entrances to and exits from the castles of his sons-in-law and his subsequent disorientation in the storm, are good examples.

Occasionally, the doors participate in the action. They are asked to play guards, or they become bar-room loungers through which the first player pushes his way into a Western Saloon. They act as swing doors.

Finally, the door players are removed, to show that the actor can carry out all the activities quite clearly without the support of the door players. It's all in the imagination, or, rather, the body/think. Work moves on to more complicated exercises involving either specific situations or else situations taken from plays. Since *Oh What a Lovely War!* is close to me, I use scenes from that play. I also return to the Chinese Peking Opera scenes, *The Fight in the Dark* (see Chapter 4) and *The Boatman Crossing the River*. Usually beyond this point one waits for specific productions to make their demands on the actors.

CHAPTER 12

Theatre narrative and the tenses of acting

It is relatively easy to show that the actor can create on the stage specific situations without the use of scenery to depict the setting. It is not easy to explain how he does it.

We may say he uses his imagination. He imagines himself to be on a battlefield and acts accordingly. But this will not do, for several reasons. Firstly, it is much too generalised and abstract. What is the 'imagination'? If we said to an actor, 'You are not using enough imagination', what could he possibly do? One director's note is, 'You have to believe in what you're doing', but is this any clearer as a motivation to the actor? The point, in any event, is not that the actor should believe in it, but that the audience should be convinced. It is simply begging the question to say that if the actor believes in it, the audience will too.

A convincing representation or image of the scene demands discipline from the actor. We cannot, within a production, simply rely upon the hit-and-miss processes of 'free play' in the actor, particularly when the scene involves several actors, and the shape of the action is dependent upon the rhythms within which they interact. Joan Littlewood has described the difference between this work and 'plotted' productions as the difference between playing jazz and strictly scored music. Jazz gives more scope for improvisation but it also requires more sensitivity to the other players. There is much more 'give and take'.

In order to make the representation clear, certain technical disciplines may be required of the actor. The cavalry charge in *Oh What a Lovely War!* (mentioned in Chapter 11) requires the actor to be both horse and rider, and when the bullets hit the charge, the horses bolt and the rider tries to control the animal. A very specific movement was required to show this. It would not suffice simply to imagine one was riding a horse in the way children play. With the legs close together the horse was lost. The rider had to sit on the horse for the horse to be present in the scene. This required turning the thighs out wide at the pelvic joints, and keeping them turned out during the whole of the action. This in itself did not suffice. When the legs and thighs turned out, the horse became triangular if the feet were turned out naturally in line with the legs. To keep the barrel shape of the horse, the feet had to be turned to face directly to the front. In this position, the easiest way to walk is to put the ball of the foot on the ground first, but this gives a lift to the movement, which again narrows the horses back by narrowing the turn out at the pelvic joints. To maintain the shape, the heel had to be placed on the ground first. The movement is difficult to maintain and places a considerable strain on the legs.

The scene is quite short and involves very violent action and, because five other actors are involved in the scene, very precise choreography is needed to avoid bumping. Having learned the choreography, the actor must then 'use his imagination' and 'believe' in what he is doing. The actor in the scene has to weld together the action of the horse, the actions of the rider, the choreography of the paths about the stage, the geography of the situation, including the leaping of the trenches, the impact of the bullets, and the differing reactions of horse and rider to the bullets.

In practice the actor and director can work either of two ways on this scene. The separate parts can be taken in isolation and then gradually put together in stages, or the charge can be started as an improvisation and shaped through various stages. In the actor's mind a programme is built up which becomes more and more complex, rather in the manner of a computer programme in which signals trigger off new activities. But the actor's 'programme' is more flexible in that it must constantly adjust in the situation to what the other actors are doing, or to slight changes within the situation itself. The actor is not a mechanical instrument.

The technical process can all be explained without recourse to abstract terms like 'the imagination'. The director asks the actor to make certain movements; these are rehearsed over and over again, and changed or modified. The actor works to make the movements automatic and instinctive, so that he can carry them out without conscious thought, and then gets on with the job of making that activity live. His mind engages a sort of overdrive which enables him to believe in the situation whilst carrying out a series of very complicated artificial activities.

Whatever the nature of this 'belief', it is clearly an attitude of mind. Some people have it and others clearly do not. It is akin to children's play and to adult fantasy, but both those activities are free-ranging and undisciplined. Whatever the actor does, he does with great discipline and sensitivity to others. In trying to elucidate this attitude of mind I must make it clear that it is purely an *explanation*, and not the basis for a *method*.

The explanation I offer is that we 'print out' the tape that is recorded in the back of the actor's mind during rehearsals. Since this tape contains a consecutive sequence of events and activities, it will be in the form of a *subconscious narrative*. I suggest that there is running through every actor's mind a subconscious narrative that has been built up during study and rehearsal and that, as this narrative runs in the mind, it triggers off physical activities in the body. One could say that the problems I dealt with earlier, of conscious control interfering with the activities of the body, arise because the narrative is being held in the conscious front mind, and therefore there is no direct connection with the muscles of the body, so the automatic triggering of physical activities does not take place. Nor is there any feed-back from the body, which is what helps the mind to adjust the programme and keep it flexible.

The other factor that keeps the programme flexible is that the actor, in preparing for the role, has taken in more material about the situation than he needs, or has looked at it from alternative points of view, so that there are choices within the programme which can be called on if required.

My explanation for this in-built flexibility was prompted by a specific situation. In 1964, I returned to Theatre Workshop to take over from another actor in *Oh What a Lovely War!* at Wyndham's Theatre. Because she was busy elsewhere, Joan Littlewood was unable to rehearse me in the show and in fact I had only around three hours rehearsal before I went on. I had done so much work with her at that stage, that I had a clear idea from watching the show what she intended to happen at the points when I would be on stage. What I had, however, was a finished *result*, which had to be broken down into processes of action, if it was not to inhibit my work.

A further complication was that the cast had worked hard during rehearsals to come to terms with the actual historical situation of the First World War. The show had been built upon extensive improvisations by the actors, which I had missed. As it happens I was almost brought up on the Great War through close contact with a survivor and I still had his collection of books and magazines, along with others I had collected since. But this too was material in finished form – *result* material. I still had to break it down and re-synthesise it, so that I could act off it without reflecting on it. I looked for some way in which I could sort out the impressions in my mind and select the images and sensations that I needed for the performance. I conceived that to carry this out I needed some sort of narrative line to tie the various thoughts, ideas, visual impressions and factual information together. The idea was right, but the form of the narrative I chose turned out at first to be totally wrong.

I put myself in the situation, as I thought, and began the imaginative narrative in the *first person, present tense*. In this way, I considered I was following Stanislavski in saying, 'If I were in this situation how would I act?' I started improvising narrative whilst carrying out the physical actions involved.

Thus I began to move and narrate: 'I am a soldier in the First World War, on a route march up to the front. I am passing dead horses, overturned ammunition carts, ruined houses', and so on. I waited for the physical reflex reaction and it never came. I tried again: no result. I was tempted to give up, and just go on and do the show technically and take a chance on things coming alive in the show. But I had enough experience to know that the actor's performance is only ever as good as the material he has absorbed. If he doesn't know what he is playing, he can't act. He's just a clothes-horse for a costume.

I began to look seriously at what I was doing – a grown man, alone in a room, trying to imagine himself a soldier in the First World War. I began to reconstruct the narrative in the *first person, past tense*, since it seemed, on looking at it, that I wasn't a soldier in the First World War. I began 'I was a soldier in the First World War on a route march up to the front, etc, etc.' Better, much better. I began to get something of the feel of it, till I hit a snag.

In the first person, present tense narrative the feeling had been wrong, but I had not known whether I was simply having difficulty getting into the swing of things until it had finally collapsed on me when I tried to introduce fresh information about myself into the narrative. Thus, when I tried, 'I am a soldier on a route march in the First World War, and I have a limp . . .', the entire First World War disappeared the moment I thought about the limp. It made life very difficult. In the second version, 'I *was* a soldier in the First World War and I *had* a limp,' The War and the limp seemed to alternate in my mind. I couldn't get them together. I tramped round the room in and out of the war, alternately marching and limping. By this time, the First World War seemed to have been going on for ever, and I began to worry that the show might close before I solved the problem. I went back to the drawing board.

If it was obvious that I wasn't a soldier in the First World War, it must be equally obvious that it wasn't *me* anyway. *He* might have been a soldier, I certainly was not. I began again in the *third person, past tense*. 'The soldier was on a route march in the First World War.' It worked, and a sensational thing happened: *the limp appeared in my body before the words formed in my mind.* The body/think reflex activity happened before the 'print out' formed. I was immeasurably relieved; I could act again.

I later used this example in teaching. I went through the stages again, and discovered another important fact about it. In the *I am* narrative, any glance at another person destroyed the narrative. In the *I was* narrative, I could take other people in, on the periphery of my vision, and describe them as other soldiers, resting or wounded. In the *he was* narrative, I could meet them and involve them instinctively and imaginatively, and could interact with them.

I also found that, whereas in the first two narratives any corrective note applied destroyed the whole, and I had to go back to the beginning to construct a new image which was the *result* of preconceived thought, in the *he was* narrative, I had complete flexibility to modify the *processes* whilst I was carrying out the activities. I was only limited by the amount of knowledge stored away in the back brain programme, and this could be increased or modified without stopping to reflect or ponder.

I learned several important lessons from approaching the actor's problems this way. I understood that the use of Stanislavski's 'If I were in this situation . . .' is not concerned with an internal transformation. The moment one says, 'If I were', then it is clear that one is not and never has been in that situation. The event and the actor personally are not at issue. What is at issue is the dramatic recreation of the situation accepting the otherness of time, place and character. Throughout history, actors writing about their work have tended to fall into two groups: those who said they believed they were the character they were portraying, and those who understood they were only actors playing a part. I was confused about this, since the former seemed to be a highly dangerous, undisciplined process, and the latter a cold technical activity. I never believed that any actor ever adopted either extreme. How could any actor play a major classical role without being acutely aware of the difference between his life experience and that of the character. How could any actor sustain a major classical role to which he did not commit himself entirely? I began to understand that a balance could be reached which relied upon an acceptance of the otherness of the character one was portraying, and a total personal commitment to recreating the character. The actor is not the character, but no-one can give his performance for him.

I also began to understand what Brecht meant when he talked of 'estrangement' or 'distancing' as it applies to the actor and his role. In fact, he talks of third person, past tense acting in the Epic Theatre. I had arrived at Brecht by way of the back door. But I began to understand that the difference between Brecht and Stanislavski was relative, and not absolute. Because of the overt socio-political intention of Brecht's theatre, he laid much more emphasis on the otherness of the character's behaviour than Stanislavski, who laid more emphasis upon the actor's personal involvement with the re-creation. But the difference is simply a question of degree. Stanislavski lays stress on the social behaviour of the character. Brecht, in an illuminating note to an actor after a performance, says, 'Last night you gave me all of the social comment, and none of the character'.

I believe that all actors instinctively strive to achieve this balance between objective activity and subjective involvement. Certainly, I know no actor who would actually claim he was Lear, and I know no actor who would not be horrified if he were told he was 'just like himself' on stage.

This has also led to my making a strict demand on actors in rehearsal. The action must always precede the word and never should the word precede the action. The verbal 'print out' always arises after the mind has originated the impulse of the body movement. This often arises in early stages of rehearsal, because the actor reads and/or learns the words before the action has been worked on and so the words are uppermost in his mind. I try, through direction, to get the process in the right order as early as possible, to prevent future problems.

The tenses of acting

There was one very good reason why I started to construct my narrative in the present tense. Joan Littlewood has always referred to playing off the pre-conceived result as *past-tense acting*. The thought process was already in the past, over and done with, before the action commenced. This seemed to me such a clear description of what was happening that I accepted it without questioning deeply enough what the relationship was between thought and action, and what the actor was actually doing in the *present tense*. In any case there would seem to be a paradox in which I have written in saying that, in order to perform, my mind/body programme has to be in the *past tense*.

I have constructed group exercises to try to make this clear. Actors are asked to improvise being soldiers in a war situation. A hill has been overrun and captured; it has to be cleared of debris, bodies, wounded; the fortifications have to be repaired against possible counter-attack; supplies have to be brought up. Whilst improvising, the actors are asked to run a silent narrative through their heads, in three successive versions: first person present; first person past; third person past. The instructions are also given to them in these terms: 'clear the site'; 'I told them to clear the site'; 'the sergeant told them to clear the site'.

All the phenomena noted in the earlier chapters recur. Through the successive stages, the head/neck/spine/pelvis relationship alters. The back gradually straightens during the successive versions, the head rises on the neck, which lengthens. The actor becomes the centre of his own space, relating with other actors, instead of being on the periphery of a space centred somewhere in front of him. The range of movement and mobility dramatically increase. He progresses from an introverted position to an extroverted position.

I go back to the earlier exercise of The Chairs (in Chapter 10), in which actors discovered it impossible to meet whilst thinking outside the situation (for example, of what they had had for breakfast), or when trying to move a partner as quickly as possible. We can say that reflecting on breakfast puts the material, or the event, in the reflected *past*; moving a partner as quickly as possible puts the intention into the *future*. Meetings can only take place in the here and now, the *present*, the simple activity of moving the partner.

The confusion that led me to begin my narrative in the present tense arose because I had not clearly accepted in my mind what the activity was. The activity of the actor is not the illusory *reliving* of an imaginary event, but the *re-enactment* in the present of an event which we accept as gone for ever, in which we personally had no part, and which is no longer at direct issue. Whatever terms we work in, the actual event is the performance of a play by actors. This may seem absurdly simple to point out, but the truth is that some very confusing descriptions of theatre have been put about and, certainly in the minds of young actors there is no clear understanding at times of what they are doing. A great number of words have been expended on terms like 'suspension of belief, or disbelief'. The core of the theatre performance is not mystery or magic, but technical discipline.

Compound tenses

I have done some work on compound tenses. It has usually arisen out of work on voice dynamics and relates more to what an actor does with a text, rather than to the acting processes pure and simple.

There is a difference in the dynamic quality of the voice, causing, or resulting from a sensation in the body, between telling a story which does not involve the listeners in a *shared* body of experience, and one that does. That is, I sound and feel different when I say, 'I remember during the war we slept in air-raid shelters' (the *personal historic*), and, 'Do you remember during the war when we slept in air-raid shelters?' (the *racial historic*). The tenses of action are clearly defined by the experience or activity, and do not always coincide with the strict grammar of written language. The first example, the personal historic tense, might well be phrased by someone recalling the experience in this way: 'During the war we slept in air-raid shelters', which is in the straight past tense. But the fact that he is recalling experience, colours the voice differently to a straight statement of objective fact.

The bigotry of the fanatic may well be caused by his desire to move from the present scepticism of his listeners to a *future state* of conversion and total belief faster than the processes of rational argument will allow. His concentration on the future aim or intention and his pursuit of it, regardless of the processes of cause and effect, denies him all flexibility. He speaks and acts as if in a *future tense*, although his words, grammatically, are often in the *mperative*, 'we must . . .', 'only believe . . .', and so on. It matters greatly to the dynamic quality of voice and body whether he intends some future conversion, or an arousal now to immediate action, although it is likely that the same words would be used in either case.

The qualitative difference in the voice is usually tackled directly by work on character motivation and intention. Like most of the other work I do, though, I believe the actor achieves a greater technical control in re-creating the activity if he has a physical awareness of what it felt like when he first carried it out.

The problem arises quite often and acutely in chorus and prologue speeches in classical plays, where the actor/character addresses the audience directly and has no clear intention beyond giving information to the audience. The relationship of the speaker to his material, particularly in terms of time and space, makes a considerable difference to the dynamic quality of the speech. The Chorus in *Henry V* talks to the audience about things that have happened, things that are happening, and things that are about to happen. He is confidant, historian, eye-witness and prophet, and on the successful manipulation of these roles depends his success in persuading the audience to transform in their imaginations the bare stage into the progress of the wars. The prologues in Greek tragedies frequently entail the recitation of long-past history and traditions, the present state of play, the future hopes of the character.

Functional roles

There are certain situations in which people communicate information to other people. The purpose behind the communication, the contents of the communication, and the situation in which the communication takes place, give to the communicator a functional role for him to play.

Examples of these functional roles would include: Priest, Propagandist, Accused, Witness, Commentator, Raconteur, Sage, Survivor, Teacher. Each has a particular attitude in time and space to the event or experience he describes, and consequently a general dynamic quality in the voice and body which distinguishes his role from the others. The dynamic qualities are influenced by the precise instrumental purpose of the speaker, by the exact nature of the information he communicates, by the physical nature of the situation in which the communication takes place, by his own character or personality, by his attitude to his work or to what he has to say, and by his relationship to the people to whom he speaks. All of these would influence the general physical movements of his body and the dynamics of his voice that are induced by the role he undertakes.

But the general dynamics do underlie the activity. We would not mistake a sports commentator for a priest, or a propagandist for a survivor. And the fact that the factors above do influence or modify the observed movements of the body and the dynamics of the voice is my reason for believing that the actor can, and should, work to be able to reproduce, through kinaesthetic sensations, the ways in which these factors operate, so that he can mimetically recreate in public convincing representations of patterns of human behaviour.

This is necessary because there is one important functional communicational role that I have omitted from the list – the actor. The actor may at any time be called upon to portray any of the functional roles I have listed, but there are pressures which bear specifically upon the actor in his work.

The role of the actor has never been clearly defined. He has been compared at various times with the priest and the teacher. Some people have seen him as a sort of raconteur, as an eye-witness, as a propagandist. Sociologists have tended in the main to assign him a neutral expressive role. He is simply the instrument through which the literary content of the drama is communicated to an audience. The adoption of any of these concepts of the actor's role places specific pressures on him. I do not complain that theatre has political content, but I object to the actors preaching to me.

The fact that an actor reads and studies and rehearses a play or part until he knows it backwards, pushes him towards adopting a position of 'putting it across' to an audience, getting the message over. The simple fact that he appears nightly in front of a paying public who have come to see and hear him, seems to thrust this functional role upon him more strongly. The actor must be aware of how these pressures operate on him and be able to counteract them – because the work of the actor is to present convincing patterns of human behaviour and interaction in public, and that is a totally different activity.

There is a simple proof of the difficulty of counteracting these pressures. Outside of functional roles, each situation in which people communicate produces its own dynamic quality – an interrogation is vastly different from a conversation. I have collected twenty-eight different situations which have their own specific dynamics, doubtless there are more. One of them always gives the actor problems. I have rarely, if ever, seen a convincing representation of a telephone conversation on the stage.

Narrative training

There is no specific exercise for working in this area, one simply does it. I began the work with the actor Brian Murphy when we were both appearing in *The Hostage*. Because we were in that play we took the situation of an

IRA ambush and 'we told the story' into a tape recorder, from the point of view, successively, of: a man who had taken part; an uninvolved witness; someone writing the history of the event afterwards; a witness at a consequent trial; a commentator watching it. There are many situations in *The Hostage* where each of these positions, or close analogies, are required by the text and action of the play. We worked at the correct use of language and voice dynamics for each situation and role.

I would still recommend it as an acting exercise, and, of course, I have since discovered Brecht's use of this technique. It is often necessary with student actors, and always with university students, because the bias of our educational system is heavily 'literary'. That is, the result of the use of the mind and imagination should be something which can be written down. It seeks *definition* of thought and not *expression* of thought.

These exercises, if done with young people, almost always produce literary results, and a great deal of critical work has to be done to make them aware of this. Along the way they should learn a great deal about the structure of language and acquire an increased ability to express themselves.

The clown

One side benefit I have gained from the work on tenses is a clear under-standing of the work of some great clowns. Buster Keaton seems to spend most of his life in the immediate present tense. He reacts only to what happens, as it happens. He never seems to reflect, nor to pursue any future intention. Much of his physical comedy derives from his instantaneous reaction to whatever person or event he makes contact with. Even when in a hurry, his movement is never rushed. He runs normally, but very fast. Harpo Marx has no past and no future. If a girl crosses his path, as he pursues another girl, the sight of the new girl alone is enough to make him instantly switch tracks. The old girl is forgotten at once and the new one pursued. He never catches the girl; the pursuit is what is enjoyable.

CHAPTER 13

Communication improvisations

I rarely use free improvisation, preferring to use some games activity as a structure within which the actors can improvise.

The principal use of improvisation, as far as I am concerned, is to overcome the actors' failure to penetrate the text to the actions which underlie it. The words make sense, but have no real meaning. The actor manages to make Lear sound like the London telephone directory. It is very much the problem of 'size' that I described earlier, but this time it arises out of a specific limitation in the actor. The actor learns the text and the text somehow inhibits the use of his imagination. He clings to the text and nothing but the text for security. I have seen it happen in productions where improvisation was used early in rehearsals. The actors improvised and carried out some highly imaginative exploratory work on characters and relationships, and then, once they had the scripts in their hands, they clammed up and simply 'played the text'.

I said earlier that the problem of 'size' was usually encountered by directors as a deficiency in emotional expression. The words had no feeling behind them. Whatever the cause of the problem, very many directors clearly attribute it to the words inhibiting the actor. They tackle the problem by taking the words away from the actor, and by making him play the scene or situation without them. This is the main reason for using improvisation.

Often these improvisations take the form of asking the actor to take the situation and to make it up in his own words as he goes along. Many directors set up these improvisations early in the rehearsal period, before the actors have worked on the text at all. I prefer not to, because, to repeat what I have said earlier, the actor at this stage has little information about the scene he is playing until he has worked on the script, and the activity lacks discipline and structure. A great deal of the work might well be totally wasted effort if the actor cannot relate what he did in the improvisation directly to the structured scene to which he returns.

My second reason for not using this method is that the improvisations often turn out to be no more than verbalisations. The actors talk like parrots, reiterating haphazardly everything they can recall about the situation, without listening to, or more than marginally responding to, the other actors.

I can recall once trying to set up an improvisation (though I can't remember why) in which an unemployed actor waits for a phone call from a film producer to know if he has a part or not. The engineer arrives to cut off the phone unless the bill is paid immediately. The landlady is the only source of possible money, and the actor owes her six weeks' rent already. The conflicts and possible alliances in the situation are stimulating, but the framework turned out to be too free. It gave no firm direction to the actors. The result, as I recall it, was that each of the three actors stood around and endlessly *explained* what they were doing and why. The explanations destroyed the processes of interaction between them and created a completely false situation. Everyone revealed exactly what their intentions and justifications were, something which practically never happens in life. When we want someone to do something to our advantage, we seek strategies through which we might achieve our ends. We work in terms to which we think the other person will respond positively; putting all the cards on the table is very rarely one of these. Human beings are astonishingly devious and versatile in constructing dramatic fictions through which we try to manoeuvre and control the responses of others.

The strength of a games structure, for me, is that the specific encounter, exchange or conflict can be isolated, worked on and taken directly into the situation of the play. At certain times, for specific plays, I have worked on the ways that confidence men construct dramatic fictions, but the intention then was to emphasise the use of words and actions to disguise intentions, not to reveal them. The actor was given a specific intention or purpose to pursue in the scene, where verbalisation was not possible. I have also used the works of Erving Goffman as the basis for general training exercises. These are full of examples of dramatic fictions through which people try to define the levels and processes of interaction with other people. The work of some sociologists, and particularly Goffman, should be fed into actor training, since this is an area of study and discovery about human relationships which was almost totally unavailable to Stanislavski when he was writing. I have used Goffman's work mainly as background information from which to draw the rules and disciplines that are fed into the games structures, but they can be used as the basis for improvisations. Most of his work is, however, concerned with dramatic fictions which *restrict* the range of contact between people in any situation and are, therefore, of little use in tackling the problem of 'size',

Some directors try to tackle the problem by constructing analogous situations in which the actor is free to improvise, I have rarely seen this done successfully. The analogy often provides as many problems as the scene itself. Whatever analogy for Macbeth's murder of Banquo we can find in a student actor's life is bound to be of diminished power against the original act. As a directing technique it is valuable to suggest to actors analogies to the dramatic situation which they can grasp, but I have never found it necessary to set these up as improvisations. Once pointed out to the actors, they manage to absorb them into their work quite easily.

Directors sometimes ask actors to play scenes in their own words. In my experience this leads to verbalisation both when the situations are too free and when the sections of the play which are improvised are extended. This method was used extensively by Joan Littlewood, very productively, but she worked on small units or even isolated moments in the play. She began with the actor's own words, and the text seeps into the rehearsals gradually.

To free the actor from the inhibiting influence of the text, she sometimes assigned one prompter to each actor. The prompter fed the lines to the actor, about half a line before he needed them. The actor took the lines without worrying about what he had to say and was free to get on with the action of the scene. I have seen her use the method very successfully, but it has never worked for me.

Another method, which I have used, and seen used successfully, is to get the actor to speak the 'sub-text', that is, the thoughts that underlie the dialogue. Many modern playwrights, Chekhov pre-eminently, employ an opaque style of writing in which the characters conceal from each other their true feelings, or the true depth of their feelings. Unless the actor brings to his performance a deep sub-textual understanding of the inner life of the character, the dialogue becomes flat and expressionless. The dialogue must not be allowed completely to obscure the inner life of the character, but must be a restraining hand upon the full expression of the feelings embodied in the character. It is useful to take the actor away from the text in these plays to allow him full free range of expression of the inner thoughts and feelings of the character, upon which the structured scene and dialogue will later depend for its underlying impact and significance.

This technique is widely used by actors to sustain thought-lines between stretches of dialogue. They speak the thoughts of the character to preserve a continuity of activity throughout the scene. It is also used by actors to build up the 'interior monologue' of the character. Some directors work individually with actors to build up a narrative line of thought and reaction which will underlie the scenes that the actor plays,

The actor can also be assisted in building the 'interior monologue' by having other actors play out parts of it. In rehearsal the other actors speak parts of the character's thoughts when the character has conflicting thoughts, or has to overcome internal obstacles to act. An example of this are the many scenes in French farce when a character who has been cuckolded determines on revenge. He has to triumph over the disgrace in order to act. The other actors keep reminding him verbally of his disgrace by literally calling him cuckold, or describing in graphic detail the event which made him a cuckold. The actor absorbs the memory of the external insults and pressures into his performance.

In the Mrs Pankhurst scene in *Oh What a Lovely War!* the actress has to combat a variety of hostile attitudes to what she is saying. These are manifest in the comments of the crowd listening to her, but, in order for the actress to be heard, these comments have to be restricted and to punctuate her speech. In rehearsal much more voice can be given to the opposition, to make it a continuous destructive wave, over which she must lift her voice. Once objectivised, the sensations of overcoming this opposition become an integral part of the actress's performance.

Nonsense improvisations

One method used in some drama schools, and by some directors, to overcome inhibitions in the actor caused by the words, is to remove words altogether. The reasoning is that if the actor cannot get through the words into the sub-textual action he can do this if the words are no longer there to hinder him. The words are taken away from the actor and some easy verbal substitute is given him in their place. Unfortunately other blocks can come into play.

Exercise 1 Three actors play out the following situation. Two are driving a car when the car breaks down, causing a traffic jam. The third actor plays a policeman who comes to investigate and clear the jam. The only words that can be used are those of a nursery rhyme like *Jack and Jill*. The problems become clear. One cannot say one thing and think another. One can think, 'We've run out of petrol', and *then* say, 'Jack and Jill went up the hill', and there is some carry over of meaning. But after that the actor gets lost in the flow of talk.

Even if the actor goes away and rehearses the scene (that is, preconceives a substitute text), he still gets lost. Once he says something, he finds there is only room in his mind for one thought at a time. If it is rehearsed the exercise is self-defeating anyway, because it is no longer an improvisation. Tried with numbers instead of nursery rhymes, the same problems still emerge.

Occasionally the actor finds some fun in playing around with nursery rhymes in that situation and some energy comes from fooling around. This evaporates on repetition. I allow the actor all the possible alternative ways of trying out the improvisation, so that he understands that it is the structure of the improvisation that is at fault, and not his playing.

It may seem that time would be wasted on such a futile exercise, but for some reason this approach is quite often used. A second exercise sometimes reveals the reason.

Exercise 2 Once again, nursery rhymes or numbers, or some other simple formula, is given to the actors. Two actors sit in the corridor of a police station, waiting to be questioned for their separate offences. They attempt conversation. If this doesn't break down, for the reason given in the first exercise, there seems to be a glimmer of a solution to the problem.

The actor generates an emotional tone or colour through the words. He strikes or adopts an emotional attitude to the situation and this colours whatever words he uses. Communication is impossible because we communicate through words, but a generalised emotional charge or attitude is expressed, and the other actor can often respond to this. The exercise collapses in a welter of generalities. The actors lose energy after a certain point, since they have no specific content in the situation to sustain them. However, the actor has generated some emotion, and the object of the exercise is now to get him to generate this generalised emotion through the text when he returns to it.

It is depressing to record that, firstly, actors often do this, and it is known as 'playing the emotion and not the action', and, secondly, it is a part and parcel of many actors' working lives. When the script is itself undramatic, as it is in many soap operas and television serials, the actor is left with the job of making it interesting and alive. There is no 'sub-text' to penetrate through to, and the actor 'sells the show' by projecting emotional colour into the text to make it appear dramatic. American television actors, in such works as Peyton Place, have developed these techniques to a fine art.

In appealing to sympathetic, generalised, emotional responses in the audience, the mind is numbed, and drama reduced to the level of an emotional warm bath. When the techniques are applied to a text by a dramatist who knows his job and has done it, like Shakespeare, it takes all the guts and intellectual rigour out of the play. The effect is as if the actor were painting the text by numbers: 'My lord, I come from Westmoreland, in deepest purple'; 'My greeny-yellow mind will hatch its plots'; 'Red is the colour of my mounting rage'. Try it yourself.

Emotional colour

Emotional colour exists in literary metaphors like 'a brown study', 'a black mood', 'green jealousy', and it should remain there. There is, obviously, emotional colour in the actor's performance, but it must be the precipitate of action and arise from a clear specific response to the text. The words define the specific nature of the actor's intentions and actions. Specific emotions arise out of specific actions and reactions. Painting by numbers is not creative.

I try to take this generalised emotion to its extreme by using an exercise I learned in drama school. It is France 1944. A girl is arrested for being out on the streets after curfew. Whether she is innocent, or a member of the resistance covering up, is left to the actress playing the scene. She is brought before the chief Gestapo officer, who attempts to break down her alibi during interrogation. The actors have only one phrase they can use: a line from Edward Lear, 'They went to sea in a sieve.'

The situation is highly charged and gives full range for tearing off into a passion. The playing often gives off a great deal of emotional heat as the two actors try to break down the other's resistance, or resist the other's pressure. But if the improvisation is allowed to run on for any length of time, problems begin to arise. Since neither understands what the other is saying, it is difficult to sustain the action beyond a certain point. When this point is reached, two courses are open to the actors.

The Gestapo officer is led to the point where he must cool the emotional tone, and then the energy immediately begins to drain away. It is harder, once the emotional temperature has been lowered, to raise it again. And yet the only other course open to him is to intensify the action, and this takes him into areas of overt physical violence, sadism. Usually, when this point is reached, an instinctive inhibition in the actor is encountered and the exercise suddenly stops for him.

The girl is similarly led to a point where she must either cool the emotional tone and lose energy, or intensify it, which leads her to introvert the energy and takes her into areas of hysterical masochism, or emotional masturbation. Playing the exercise, one can often see the actress's eyes appear to 'click' off as she introverts the energy.

Carrying out these exercises personally depresses me, but sometimes it is necessary, with young actors, to slam some doors in their faces in order to prevent wasted effort on unproductive solutions to problems. The solution to the problem of 'size' does not lie in putting generalised emotional charges behind the text, but in intensifying the action, and the text is necessary to define the specific nature of the interaction between characters. The action and the word must be integrated; it is not profitable to separate them.

Curiously though, there is one area of work which lies outside these considerations. Perhaps because at the root it is a mirror of the problems of linguistic communication.

Non-existent languages

Pure gibberish I have never found useful, but non-existent languages have been. There are some difficult scenes in drama in which non-existent language can be used to help, and other areas in which the actor is driven to explore the need to communicate by methods other than words, and to understand the communications of others.

As an example of a difficult scene, I shall choose the Buckingham Palace scene from *Oh What a Lovely War!* The scene takes the form of a fluid, improvised party, out of which little vignette scenes emerge. Characters relate against a background of action which is seen but only rarely heard. Rehearsing, the actor seems to get tied down if he has to improvise the non-existent dialogue. He can do it, but he gets bored with carrying on doing it, and the level of the action drops. There is also a danger that the actor, once bored, invents 'funny' or 'amusing' ways of playing the scene, and 'sends it up' in parody. He invents gags or jokes to keep himself from being bored.

Rehearsing the situation in parallel, or directly, in mock-Russian, removes from the actor the problem of what he should be saying, to make small talk, and lets him get on with the job of exploring the mimetic situation in a play manner. Once the trivial words are out of the way he can use his imagination, and both the physical action of the scene and the use of gesture become surprisingly larger and spatially more free. It takes unnecessary problems off the actor and lets him get on with his work.

As an example of a situation in which it is difficult to make sense of what the other characters are saying, let me take *An Italian Straw Hat*. The play runs through a whole series of mistaken identities and situations. Having the script, the actor must rid himself of everything he knows about the situation in order to play it. It is a recurrent problem of the actor's work, that he must continually put out of his mind that he knows what the other actor's response to his line will be. Here he has to rid himself of the entire knowledge of situation and content.

To help him explore the sensations of this experience, a series of parallel improvisations can be set up in which no-one does know what the situation is, and must therefore direct all their attention to observing what the results of their actions are on others, and trying to work out what the other is trying to communicate. The communication is always specific. The reception is always confused. In this respect, it is a mirror of everyday communication. We are constantly trying to express ourselves clearly despite an inadequate control of language, 'struggling to find the right words'. We are constantly trying to find out what the other person really means, what is 'behind' what he is saying.

In *An Italian Straw Hat*, Fadinard, searching for a replica of the straw hat his horse has eaten, enters the Baroness's soirée and is mistaken for an Italian tenor and compelled to sing for the guests. A tourist straying through the wrong door in a foreign country to be greeted by a reception committee expecting Gigli is a parallel to start from. Define the parallel as closely as you need.

An extensive exercise in this vein was devised by the actors during the West End run of *The Hostage*, to keep the show fresh. The play contains many situations in which characters try to understand exactly what the other characters mean by the words they use, and how far one can trust them to do what they say, since they are so often contradictory in their statements. This particularly applies to the hostage himself, the British soldier, Leslie.

A situation was set up in which a concentration camp has been simultaneously liberated by American and Russian forces. Both armies have withdrawn to prevent international friction, and the inmates are left in limbo. They are torn between the hope of being sent to America as refugees, and the fear of being transferred to a work camp in Russia. They come from all parts of Europe and, for the purpose of the exercise, no-one speaks anyone else's language. They are used to a situation in which one is exterminated when one is unfit for work, and in which one's clothes are removed before death. Into this camp are sent two Swedish Red Cross officials, whose job it is to ascertain, quickly, the possibility of a typhoid or cholera epidemic, and to select those people who are free from disease for emigration to America. They are required to judge the nutritional standards of everyone in the camp, and to estimate requirements of medicine and clothing. I have used the exercise since as training in non-verbal communication.

In the first playing, when the actors literally do not know what is going on because each group is given the instructions separately, the actors tend to concentrate on the processes of communication, they try to make sense of what is happening. Repeated, they explore the situation. There is no limit to the exercises one can devise for specific dramatic situations. It requires skill to structure the situation to concentrate on the specific issues involved.

The major exercise I use in this area is intended to explore the processes of communication between human beings leading up to speech. The actors split into pairs and undertake the draining process described in Chapter 9. One actor is designated as Miranda, and one as Caliban. The draining exercise for the Miranda actor is a simple relaxation, but the Caliban actor attempts to totally drain away all that he physically and mentally understands of the processes of speech and language. In practice this is not as difficult as it might seem. When the draining is complete the Caliban actor will open his eyes and Miranda will attempt to teach him language. This entails an exploration of all possible means of communication between the two actors working towards the point where linguistic communication is possible. Obviously the point will never be reached where words can be exchanged, and it is of vital importance that the actor playing Miranda does not use words, as the mind of the Caliban actor will instinctively respond to them and the game will be broken.

CHAPTER 14

Work on text

When I first began to act, words terrified me. I remember painfully being told by Joan Littlewood that every time I opened my mouth I destroyed all the work I had done in the previous half hour. For some fortuitous reason, I had a clearly demonstrable ability to make myself useful by purely physical means, creating the situation, environment and ambiance, in which others could get on with the acting. I became almost resigned to being a dumb actor. I looked back wistfully to the days of Buster Keaton, and decided I had been born outside my time.

I am very clear now why I had problems. Until I understood what it was that I was doing wrong, the problems were insoluble and self-reinforcing. I became 'voice conscious'. That is, I kept listening to the sounds my voice made, to check if they were right. The voice mechanism corrects itself by a combination of aural feedback and physical sensation, which are mutually interactive, and part of the reflex processes of the body/think. To listen to the voice with concentration brings the process into the conscious reflective front of the mind, and inhibits the body reaction.[1]

Sometimes I became so terrified that I rushed or gabbled; I tried to get to the end of the line almost before I had begun it, to get it over quickly. This dragged me into an alternating sequence of past tense/future tense activities. When I had no words, I found I could meet, relate, react to the other actors on stage without any problems, and, as far as I can tell, with sensitivity. Given words, I lost touch with them.

The initial problem for me was that I spoke *lines*, and did not work through the body processes which produce words, I literally *learned lines*, and when the moment came on stage, I *spoke lines*. I conceived the whole line as a fixed entity, and it became a *result*, not the verbal expression of an action. I even know that at times I had a mental picture of the line in my mind before I said it.

Indeed the actor talks of *learning lines*. Since most major roles require a concentrated period of solitary graft to learn the script without wasting rehearsal time, the actor develops a series of technical tricks to help him.

There is a wide range of such devices. One of the simplest and most obvious is to memorise the lines from the order in which they are set out on the printed page. One often cannot remember the line but it comes at the bottom of a right hand page, and one struggles to visualise the page. What is after all a matter of typographical convenience with little regard for the flow of thought or the relative significance of words and phrases becomes ingrained in the performance.

Learning lines leads naturally to speaking lines. The mind can accomplish the action of turning typographical symbols into speech much more quickly than it can conceive the thoughts embodied in the words. The same is true of our facility to repeat lines recalled by memory. When this happens the movement of thought within the line becomes streamed out, generalised and preconceived. The normal human activity of expressing thoughts in words is a constant search for the right words and concepts to define the thoughts. When the activities that constitute the normal process of articulating thoughts are not worked through, the audience cannot sympathetically participate in them, and the spoken word is taken only at the level of its literal meaning. Theatre becomes inadequately spoken literature.

The physiology of speech

Many actors find themselves subjected to 'technical voice training'. There is a false concept at the core of much of this training, which is there out of pure convenience, and contradicts the normal processes through which speech is produced. The actor is encouraged through 'rib-reserve' breathing methods to maintain a reserve supply of air in his lungs by keeping the ribs swung out. 'Rib-reserve' is a good training to strengthen the muscles that control breathing, and for co-ordinating the actions of the intercostal muscles and the diaphragm, but it is an unnatural way of controlling the breath. It can help flexibility and strength to be developed in the muscles, but it creates problems of unnecessary tension in the body if used in performance. Allied to it is the concept that voice is produced by a constant stream of air being passed through the vocal chords. The concept is invoked to help the actor work upon the control of a sustained tone in the voice, but it is totally alien to the structure of the English language and to the physiological processes which produce voice and speech.

(The opposing) theory maintains that when the pulmonic air-stream mechanism is in action, the air is not (as one might think) expelled from the lungs by a constant, regular muscular pressure, producing an even and continuous flow of air. What happens, rather, is that the respiratory muscles alternately contract and relax at a rate of roughly five times a second, so that the air is expelled in a succession of small puffs. Each contraction, together with the resulting puff of air, constitutes the basis of a syllable. In the view of those who hold this theory, therefore, the syllable is essentially a movement of the speech organs, and not a characteristic of the sound of speech, though in any given language the sound will contain clues, of the most varied kind, to the occurrence of the syllable-producing movement.

This syllable-producing movement of the respiratory muscles has been called a chest-pulse (because the intercostal muscles in the chest are responsible for it), or breath-pulse, or syllable-pulse (the term pulse being used because of its recurrent and periodic nature). At least one such movement must be involved in whatever we may say: a syllable is the minimum utterance, and nothing less than a syllable can be pronounced.

The syllable, then, is essentially a movement, and one which, in most cases, is an audible movement. It is not necessarily always accompanied by sound, however, and it is possible for a chest-pulse to take place quite silently, producing an inaudible syllable. Such a chest-pulse occurs, for example in the speech of many English-speaking people when they pronounce a rather perfunctory *thank you* so that nothing can be heard except *'kyou*. The movement of the respiratory muscles for the first syllable, which is auditorily missing, persists, however, as the speaker will often admit when his attention is drawn to the possibility.

A chest-pulse may be produced by exceptionally great muscular action; it is then a *reinforced* chest-pulse, and it gives an extra powerful push to the lung walls. As a result a stronger puff than usual of air is expelled from the lungs, and this very often causes, among other things, a louder noise. A syllable produced by a reinforced chest-pulse is called a stress-pulse. A speaker of English can, for example, easily make himself aware of the extra effort he makes when he reaches the stressed syllable in the word *university*, especially when the word is pronounced vigorously . . . The pulmonic air-stream mechanism, therefore, is seen to be a complicated one. It consists of the periodic syllable-producing movements, recurring at a rate of five puffs a second, and at intervals a reinforcement of these movements, producing the stressed syllables. These two processes – the syllable process and the stress process – together make up the pulmonic mechanism, and they are the basis on which the whole of the rest of speech is built.[2]

Failure to observe the phonetic structure of the language we speak, by streaming sound, results in words whose literal meaning we understand, but which phonetically do not exist in the English language and are a distortion of it. The effect on actor and audience is catastrophic.

The ear is important to the speaker as well as to the listener. Any activity involving a succession of skilled movements has to be carefully controlled while the movements are being executed, and for this we need a continual stream of information about the progress, at every moment, of the activity. This information is provided by what has come to be called *feedback*: almost instantaneous reports from various senses, to that part of the brain responsible for initiating the movements, on how successfully the latter are being carried out. Probably there are no movements more skilled than those we make for talking, and we regulate many aspects of these movements by what is called 'auditory feedback' – we listen to their effects in the form of sound, and judge their success by that. Hearing is not the only sense concerned in monitoring the movements of speech, however, for an important part is played by the sense of touch, and a still more important one by the muscular or kinaesthetic sense (the 'sixth' sense). If feedback information from any of the above sources is cut off for some reason, it is difficult to talk properly.

The sound of speech, on the one hand, and the movements producing the sound, on the other, are in fact closely linked for both speaker and hearer. Speaker and hearer are usually looked on as two distinct and separate roles in conversation, but in fact each partakes somewhat of the activities of the other. The speaker, as we have just seen, is simultaneously also hearer (he must be, for the normal conduct of speech); but the hearer, is in a way, simultaneously also speaker (at least when listening to his mother tongue) in so far as he 'empathetic- ally' enters into the speaker's sound-producing movements, sometimes even making tentative movements of a similar nature himself . . . Everything to do with the mechanics of talking has, with normal people, become quite unconscious through long habit and indeed it is necessary for the efficient functioning of spoken language that this should be so. We are not conscious of making the producing move- ments, nor of monitoring our own speech for the purpose of control- ling it. If the production of the sound of speech were not automatic it would cease to be a satisfactory medium for language because its production would monopolise thought instead of conveying it. We need, as speakers, all our attention for *what* we are saying, and we have none to spare for *how* we say it. In the same way we need all our attention, as hearers, for what is being said and we ignore the mechanics of its production.[3]

The problem is once again to take the actor's mind off what he is doing, to let the natural processes of the body work effectively. It is not a simple one. The text is after all what we start with in rehearsal. It directs the form and shape of the action more than anything else. In other words, the theatre, by its very nature, puts the cart before the horse. In life, thought and action precede the words, in theatre the word is the starting point. We cannot rely purely on the natural processes of speech because theatre is performed in artificial circumstances, conversations have to be heard at a distance of 70 feet or more, and some texts are by their nature artificially structured.

I don't want to beg the question of voice training, which is clearly necessary since the actor must develop more than usual levels of vocal strength and skill; I could wish though that more voice training was related directly to language, and less to the production of artificial sound in abstract. The first step in the right direction has been taken by Cicely Berry in her book, *Voice and the Actor*,[4] and I would therefore refer anyone interested to that book. One other clearly scientific work exists, but only in German.[5]

Whatever work I carry out with the actor I do through the medium of text. One can take words to work on, to show the actor how the phonetic structure of the language is produced by the body processes, but it is not profitable to substitute the 'five puffs a second' air-stream theory, for the 'continuous stream' theory. The object, as Abercrombie points out, is that speech should be automatic and instinctive, and the actor should think about what he is saying, and not how. Therefore, the work with the actor has to be related directly to the meaning of the words he speaks, bearing in mind the technical and physical processes that are involved in speaking.

For this reason, I also reject, at least in early sessions, working on quantitative and qualitative metre and stress patterns. This may be useful for the director to reveal how the poet has structured the speech, and what choices and alternatives he gives the actor. When the actor has the shape of the speech, through an understanding of content and meaning, this can help him to be more precise. But I would not use so technical an approach early in work.

Reinstating the natural processes of speech

Since the actor has no problem communicating with other people in everyday life, it requires no extraordinary technique to teach him how to do it on the stage. The task is to remove the artificial obstacles which speaking a text place in his way, and to allow the natural processes to come into play. The first task is to slow down the speech until he speaks at the speed at which he can normally conceive thoughts, so that the two processes become integrated again. Often a very simple adjustment of speed will suffice. It is axiomatic of every actor's and director's work that the actor effects fine shifts of pace and speed to allow the audience to take in what is being said. The less the intellectual content in the line, the quicker the dialogue can flow. Ultimately, the hope is that the speed at which the actor himself can conceive thought and express it in language will correspond with the speed at which the audience can receive it.

I ask the actor to put a brake on the speech. For illustration, I use the idea of a fixed-wheel bicycle, where you push against the pedals to slow the machine down. The actor is asked to find the speed at which, while speaking, the images and thoughts flow naturally, with each given full weight in the back reflex area of the mind; to find the speed at which things *happen* naturally. This also helps tackle the problems of 'size' in playing, and also the problems of penetrating text to find the sub-textual actions and activities. Once the natural processes can be reinstated, the associative interaction of thought in the mind and feeling in the body comes back into play, and the image or thought produces the physical sensation, and the reactive chain of sensations inform the words.

> It is an extraordinary thing that when you use volume without great sensitivity, you not only iron out the subtlety and manoeuvrability of your own voice but you actually create certain mental tensions so that you cease to think specifically. The size must be found through coming to terms with the particular ideas and feelings of the character and, therefore, with the words that are used . . . There is also the extraordinary sense of discovery of the separate existence of each thing [in the text]. With it you can preconceive nothing. You must listen [i.e. be physically responsive] for what it says. Because, in the end, it relates to one's own existence, it can only be given meaning if it is allowed to 'touch down' on one's own private sense of physical being. It is this that must inform the voice.[6]

Once we have slowed the speech down (or sometimes in order to slow the speech down), there are several ways of breaking up the line into its separate parts. One is to use the punctuation that the dramatist or editor has put into the text. By speaking the punctuation in the line, one gives full weight to the pauses which break up the line. It is easy to assign time values to commas, full stops, semicolons, etc.

With classic texts one runs into problems of editorship, and the fact that editors and publishers tend to set out text according to the strict rules of written grammar. This does not always coincide with the way people speak, but it helps the actor to make decisions about what pauses, and length of pause, he wants to make in the speech. And it leads him to an analytical examination of the structure of the text, so as to discover its precise meanings and intentions.

Speaking the punctuation often reveals certain surprising things about the overall rhythms of the speech, by showing the juxtaposition of short and long phrases, and often clearly reveals the use of long against short vowels through which the pace and rhythm of the speech manifest themselves.

Naturally, no-one can find the time to go right through a major part this way, and it is not necessary to do so. One normally only uses the device when one hits snags. Apart from this, when it has been practised over a relatively short section of text it can become a normal reflex action. The brain is programmed to work this way on all texts it meets, and will often do so naturally with very little training.

A second method, which gets closer to the specific nature of the thought behind the word, is to introduce questions to break up the actor's thought patterns into demand and response. To start with, another actor supplies the questions. Later it is easy to do it for oneself. Thus:

If (what?) Music.
If <u>Music</u> (what?) be.
If <u>Music</u> be (what?) the food.
If <u>Music</u> be the <u>food</u> (food of what?) of Love.
If <u>Music</u> be the <u>food</u> of <u>Love</u>, (what shall I do?) Give me.
If <u>Music</u> be the <u>food</u> of <u>Love</u>, play on, <u>Give</u> me (what shall I
give you?) <u>excess</u> of it

The words I have underlined are where the process produces the strongest kinaesthetic response in me; they therefore take the major stresses. It may be different for others. The alternatives are not infinite, but they are there. Each must find his own way.

One problem this method also seems to clear up is that of the silent stress, which is an important part of the structure of English verse. Silent stresses never appear printed in the text; the gaps between the words are always constant. The results of not taking the silent stresses are very curious. I had an actor get stuck with the problem of,

Did from the flames of Troy upon his shoulder
The old Anchises bear,

The line is balanced, to get the meaning:

> Did/fromthe/flamesofTroy/uponhis/shoulder/
> Theold/Anchises/bear,/

The sense is clear when balanced this way. Unfortunately the actor kept getting stuck in a lighter more sustained rhythm and we always seemed to end up with 'Did from the flames of Troy/upon his shoulder/The old Anchises bear', conjuring up images of a small Asian mammal which habitually rides on a man's shoulder.

The *Twelfth Night* line balances: 'If/Music/bethe/food/ofLove, play on,/Giveme/excess ofit.'

The method needs some refinement in particular areas. We do not always speak literally. We almost never, for example, say '*bread/and/butter*'. Since the term refers to a total entity, a slice of bread with butter spread on it, we usually speak it as a single concept – almost in practice as one word: 'breadandbutter'. In the Cassius speech that I have marked, there is no pause in the phrase 'flames of Troy'. Since it is Aeneas who is being talked about, there is no need to establish the separate existence of Troy. 'Flames of Troy' stands as one concept. The exceptions to the rule are very easy to discover once you have applied the rule.

Shaping the speech

Every actor has his own methods of shaping a speech, according to which key words must be emphasised to bring out the full meaning clearly. The foregoing exercises help shape the speech, but there are other ways which I use for difficult texts.

The hierarchy of words I arrange words in an order of importance. The order is established by the associated effect they have in the body through the kinaesthetic feedback. 'And', for instance, produces next to no effect in me, because it is a conjunction which simply links thoughts, ideas and images.

Verbs come at the top of the list because they refer to activities, and are therefore closely associated with the process of action in the body. I look carefully at the use of verbs, their tenses and forms. 'I *thought* I *was doing* the right thing' produces a very different response in me to '*Cry* havoc, and *let slip* the dogs of war'.

The verbs are usually the most important parts of a speech because they reveal and define the action that the dramatist has embodied in it, what is happening and in what terms. As an example, I give below the first section of a translation of the prologue to *The Phoenician Women* of Euripides.

> JOCASTA: You who *cut* your way through heaven's stars,
>   *riding* the chariot with its welded gold,
>   Sun, with your swift mares *whirling* forth our light,
>   evil the shaft you *sent* to Thebes that day
>   when Cadmus *came* here, *leaving* Phoenicia's shore,
>   he who *wed* Cypris' child, Harmonia,
>   *fathering* Polydorus, who in turn
>   *had* Labdacus, they *say*, and he *had* Laius.
>   My name [*is*] Jocasta, as my father *gave* it,
>   Laius [*was*] my husband. When he still *was* childless
>   after long marriage with me in the palace,
>   he *went* to Phoebus *asking* and *beseeching*
>   that we *might share* male children for the house.
>   But he *said*, 'Lord of Thebes and its famed horses,
>   *sow not* that furrow against divine decree.
>   For if you *have* a child, him you *beget*
>   *shall kill* you, and your house *shall wade* through blood'.[7]

There are many aspects of this speech that need working on to get the clear shape of it, but the verbs bring out, at least, the relationship between the speaker and the content she is communicating to the audience. The sense that the weight of the past tradition, which is by now only hearsay ('they say'), unites with fate to create the present predicament of Thebes and Jocasta – this sense only becomes clear when we examine closely the verbs she uses, and their tenses. There is a total re-orientation of the speech somewhere after line four. The sun (Phoebus) is addressed directly in the first four lines, but then Jocasta addresses the audience. She informs them that she is Jocasta and, by line thirteen, Phoebus is referred to in the third person. The prophecy is given its full force by being given in the future tense, to show that its working out is still happening now. The effect on the audience depends upon the changing tenses of the verbs. The rest of the speech continues to switch suddenly between the past tense of tradition, the present tense of the contemporary situation, and the unfulfilled predictions for the future. The audience understands the past events which have led to this point, the present hopes and fears of Jocasta, and waits with anticipation the future outcome of events.

General teaching work in this area always involves a study of a number of dramatists or scripts to examine the use of verbs by dramatists, particularly the use of active tenses as against passive or reflective tenses. Compare:

> But I don't understand you, sir. Is a sentence of exile to be my reward?
> Exiled all my life? Think of it yourself, sir! To leave everything I have
> in England, and never to see it again! It's unthinkable.[8]

with:

> A heavy sentence, my most sovereign liege,
> And all unlooked for from your Highness' mouth.
> A dearer merit, not so deep a maim
> As to be cast forth in the common air,
> Have I deserved at your Highness' hands.[9]

Nouns hold the second place in the hierarchy of words since they embody images that the body responds to, or reacts to, kinaesthetically.

Adjectives and *adverbs* define the precise nature of nouns and verbs. When distinctions have to be made they often take a stronger stress. The same is true of pronouns and personal pronouns. It is a minor problem that actors sometimes give adjectives and adverbs a higher place in the sentence because they indicate degree. The worst example of this, which distorts the English language at present, is the use of superlatives: 'We had a *super* time', 'It was an *excellent* performance'. Obviously, no dramatist of any quality will be as generalised in his dialogue as this, but actors, given an adjective or adverb of degree in a sentence, will at times hit it hard at the expense of the noun or verb it qualifies, and the precise sense of the line is generalised, or lost.

Hollywood Cherokee Hollywood has developed to a fine art the technique of constructing languages which can be clearly understood, but sound as though a foreigner was speaking them. Hollywood Cherokee is one of these, and it is an ingenious way of finding the main stresses, or key words, in a sentence. You leave out everything that is not absolutely vital to the meaning, and string together what is left, without syntax. Thus, 'Before the morning breaks, my braves will make many white women widows' becomes in the mouth of the 'Cherokee', 'Before morning, many women widows.'

The example is probably not a good one for us because it is a static statement. The verbs have little importance. It's bad dialogue, but the principle can be applied elsewhere. Thus:

> From the high citadel we saw the host,
> white-shielded men of Argos. They left Teumesus,
> they rushed the ditch to set the town on fire.[10]

becomes

> From citadel saw host. Left Teumesus, rushed ditch,
> set town on fire.

The approach is not absolute, simply a framework within which to work out what you want to do with the shape of the speech.

Upper case, lower case, parentheses One other way of breaking down a difficult text is to look for the main line of the speech, and metaphorically print this in upper case, or CAPITALS. The subsidiary parts take lower case, and the interjections are put in parentheses.

HORATIO: THAT CAN I;
            (at least the whisper goes so.) OUR LAST KING,
            (Whose image even but now appear'd to us),
            WAS (as you know), BY FORTINBRAS OF NORWAY,
            (Thereto prick'd on by a most emulate pride),
            DAR'D TO THE COMBAT; IN WHICH OUR VALIANT HAMLET –
            (For so this side of our known world esteem'd him)
            DID SLAY FORTINBRAS; WHO, by a seal'd compact,
            Well ratified by law and heraldry,
            DID FORFEIT, with his life, ALL THOSE HIS LANDS
            Which he stood seiz'd of, TO THE CONQUEROR;
            Against the which a moiety competent
            Was gaged by our king; which had return'd
            To the inheritance of Fortinbras,
            Had he been vanquisher; (as, by the same covenant,
            And carriage of the article design'd,
            His fell to Hamlet). Now sir, YOUNG FORTINBRAS,
            Of unimproved mettle hot and full,
            HATH IN THE SKIRTS OF NORWAY, (here and there),

SHARK'D UP A LIST OF LAWLESS RESOLUTES,
For food and diet, TO SOME ENTERPRISE
That hath a stomach in't; WHICH IS NO OTHER,
(As it doth well appear unto our state),
BUT TO RECOVER OF US, by strong hand
And terms compulsatory, THOSE FORESAID LANDS
SO BY HIS FATHER LOST: AND THIS, (I take it),
IS THE MAIN MOTIVE OF OUR PREPARATIONS,
The source of this our watch, and the chief head
Of this post-haste and romage in the land.[11]

It is useful to do this with some very involved speeches, actually to get the gist of what is being said. Audiences will tend to get lost in them if the actor has not got his priorities clear.

Movement in speech

'Speech may be said to consist of *movements made audible*.'[12] The major effort in producing speech is made by the muscle groups which control the pulmonic air-stream mechanism and the articulators in the mouth. But no muscle, or group of muscles, can act in isolation. The whole body apparatus is involved, in maintaining balance, in producing the impulses which initiate and characterise the sound produced, and in controlling it through the kin-aesthetic 'feed back'. Usually these movements in the body are imperceptible, or exist as kinetic sensations in the speaker and hearer. Some groups of people or individuals allow a much freer range of body movement accompanying speech – their gestures are larger and more emphatic. Mediterranean people have a popular reputation for doing so. The British are more restrained.

It is possible to extend the range of movement made to accompany speech – to give it freer rein during rehearsal in order that the actor can experience it more strongly, and later bring to the voice the same considera-tions that we brought to the movement training of the actor, of balance and the alternating flow of movement, gathering and scattering over stance. In fact, there are good reasons why this should be done. Not the least of these is the practice in drama schools of dividing voice and movement training, as though they were totally separate activities. Ideally they should be taught with a high degree of integration and, if it is unreasonable to expect anyone person to be expert in both fields, the teachers in each area should be capable of practising in the other, so that they are aware of all the demands and pressures of the actor's work, and not just of their own speciality.

There is also a tendency in voice training to work on abstracted sounds, and for text to be brought in at a level where some degree of interpretation is required. A pyramid is often built up in the young actor's mind, the top of which is the classic text. This induces some anxiety, because the pyramid is one of increasing difficulty. To break this, very basic voice work needs to be done on difficult texts. The text is the raw material of acting not its highest achievement.

This problem is complicated by acting methods which concentrate on the inner life and actions of the character, in the hope that the vocal delivery will instinctively right itself. This approach is largely based upon Stanislavski's ideas and practice. I don't doubt the efficacy of it in a large number of cases, but it has to be understood in conjunction with a great deal more of his work. It will not stand in its own right. I have spoken earlier of how the partial or misunderstood application of Stanislavskian concepts can throw the body off balance, and how this produces tensions and disturbances in the voice. The Stanislavski concept of the 'through-line' is very much based on psychological development in the character, and this simply will not suit a number of texts which are 'gestic' in construction and have no psychological through line. It might well work for a wide range of Shakespeare's speeches, but rarely for those of Marlowe and the Greeks. Shakespeare and most later writers have a thought-, character-, or action-line running through the speech, to which the text can be related as a spine. The Greeks and Marlowe and the French Classic dramatists have a disturbing tendency to juxtapose separate thoughts and actions, to produce a cumulative effect on the audience.

> To be, or not to be, – that is the question: –
> Whether 'tis nobler in the mind to suffer
> The slings and arrows of outrageous fortune,
> Or to take arms against a sea of troubles,
> And by opposing end them? – To die, – to sleep, –
> No more; and by a sleep to say we end
> The heart ache and the thousand natural shocks
> That flesh is heir to, – 'tis a consummation
> Devoutly to be wished. To die, – to sleep; –
> To sleep! perchance to dream; ay, there's the rub; . . .[13]

Not all Shakespeare is this straightforward, but there the developing thought-line is clear, and balances the actor through the speech. The thoughts flow naturally from one to the other, and each being a preparation for the next. Not so Euripides:

JOCASTA: I heard your Phoenician cry,
> girls, and my poor old feet,
> trembling, have brought me out.
>
> My child, my child, at last I see you again.
> Embrace your mother's breast with your arms,
> stretch forth your face and your dark curly hair,
> To shadow my throat.
>
> Oh, Oh, you have barely come,
> unhoped for, unexpected, to your mother's arms.
> What shall I say, how phrase the whole
> delight in words and actions
> That compass me about.
>
> If I dance in my joy shall I find the old delight?
>
> Child, you went as an exile; your father's house
> was left in desolation, your brother's doing.
> But your own yearned after you
> Thebes itself yearned.
>
> And so I weep, and cut my whitened hair.
> No longer, child, do I wear white robes,
> I have changed to these dark gloomy rags
>
> And the old man in the house, the blind old man,
> since the pair of you left the house,
> clings to his weeping desire. He seeks the sword
> for death by his own hand, he casts a noose
> over the roof beams mourning his curse upon his
>   children.
> He is hidden in darkness and steadily wails his woe.
>
> And I hear that you have paired yourself in marriage.
> the joy of making children.
> In a stranger's house you have taken a stranger bride,
> a curse to your mother and Laius who was of old.

Doom brought by your wedding.
I did not light your wedding torch
as a happy mother should.

Ismenus gave no water to the marriage;
your coming to your bride was never sung in Thebes.
May the cause of these sufferings perish, be it the
   steel
or strife, or your father, or a demon-rout
In Oedipus' house.
For all their grief has fallen upon me.[14]

The speech is not written with any through line, but moves in sections, often with very sudden and unprepared for leaps between the sections. There are three main areas of attention; Jocasta's subjective feelings, Polyneices' past experience, and Oedipus; and they are all self-contained for the most part. The speech splits into two main parts beginning with the intense, subjective joy of Jocasta's reunion with her son, and ending with the intense, subjective misery of Jocasta trapped in the sufferings of the house of Oedipus. The switch between the two sections takes place inside one line: 'If I dance in my joy shall I find the old delight?' One can imagine another poet writing the speech to maintain a constant balance between Jocasta's joy and misery, but Euripides chooses to separate them, because in the situation no balance or compromise or reconciliation is possible. The appearance of Polyneices brings a joy which cannot last, and heralds a catastrophe which cannot be averted. It is essential for the full effect of the speech that the actress avoid 'bleeding' one section into the other. The joy must not cover the pain, nor the pain obscure the joy; there must be no smile through the tears. Each section independently must be given the full force of the feelings embodied in it. Any consistent through-line will mute the force of the speech.

Similar problems arise in Marlowe:

Black is the beauty of the brightest day;
The golden ball of heaven's eternal fire,
That danced with glory on the silver waves,
Now wants the fuel that inflamed his beams,
And, all with faintness and for foul disgrace,
He binds his temples with a frowning cloud,
Ready to darken earth with endless night.

Zenocrate, that gave him light and life,
Whose eyes shot fire from their ivory bowers
And tempered every soul with lively heat,
Now by the malice of the angry skies,
Whose jealousy admits no second mate,
Draws in the comfort of her latest breath,
All dazzled with the hellish mists of death.

Now walk the angels on the walls of heaven
As sentinels to warn th'immortal souls
To entertain divine Zenocrate.
Apollo, Cynthia, and the ceaseless lamps
That gently looked upon this loathsome earth
Shine downwards now no more, but deck the heavens
To entertain divine Zenocrate.
The crystal springs, whose taste illuminates
Refined eyes with an eternal sight,
Like tried silver run through Paradise
To entertain divine Zenocrate.
The cherubins and holy seraphins,
That sing and play before the King of Kings,
Use all their voices and their instruments
To entertain divine Zenocrate.
And in this sweet and curious harmony,
The god that tunes this music to our souls
Holds out his hand in highest majesty
To entertain divine Zenocrate.

Then let some holy trance convey my thoughts
Up to the palace of th'empyreal heaven,
That this my life may be as short to me
As are the days of sweet Zenocrate.

Physicians, will no physic do her good?[15]

One can imagine another dramatist beginning with the philosophical
principle:

'If she should die, then what should life be worth?
My kingdoms and my conquests brought to nothing
By the brief mortality of man,'

and then debating the possibility of transcendence over death. But Marlowe does not do this. He shows Tamburlaine attempting it. He begins with the black realisation of Zenocrate's impending death, and then suddenly leaps into a series of extravagant images of Zenocrate's transcendence into immortality. At the peak of these images the focus shifts abruptly from Zenocrate to Tamburlaine himself. Then, in the last line, Tamburlaine comes down to earth and practical realities. Each section, and even word, in the speech, carries its own weight and importance, and if one fails to find the precise balance through the line from specific thought to thought, or specific image to image, the sense of the speech is lost on an audience.

The first line in this respect is very difficult. Had he written 'The beauty of the brightest day is turned to deepest black', there would be a natural balance through the images, but he doesn't. No generalised intention, thought or image will bring out the evocative power of the line; it will simply smooth it out. The application of Stanislavski's 'super-objective' or through-line will ruin the whole speech. What is required of the actor is an acrobatic balance which swings him from image to image, thought to thought, and to do this the speech has to be analysed by the actor to find the precise moments at which to make the leaps, bridges and transitions from one to another. Compared with Shakespeare, it is like using stepping stones as against climbing a ladder.

The actor can go sadly astray caught between a concept of difficult text as the pinnacle of achievement and the hope that if he gets the character's inner life right, the text will take care of itself. It patently won't.

Technical work on text

One hopes that the work outlined earlier – breaking up the text and slowing down the speed of speaking – will bring the actor to the point where normal speech processes take over and work instinctively; however there is work that can be done to reinforce this. This is often necessary because the balance of the body is disturbed by the activity of speaking text, for all the reasons I have just given.

The basis of this work is to remove the mental processes by which an actor 'builds a character', and to work from the concept of the actor as a resonant instrument through which the speech is articulated, in the same sense that movements applied to a musical instrument produce music. The more sensitive the movements, the more expressive the sound produced. In this respect the actor is both instrumentalist and instrument.

The instrument The first task is to tune the instrument and to make the actor aware of the range of sounds that his body will produce naturally.

The expressive quality of the voice is directly influenced by the positioning of the larynx against the vertebrae of the neck. If I lift my larynx to a higher position in the throat I can produce a sound very close to that of Bluebottle in the *Goon Show*. Imitate Bluebottle and the larynx rises. This is the easiest way of demonstrating it. Drop the larynx in the throat and a deep, 'dark brown' voice is produced. Most actors have experienced the problem that the anxiety of the approaching performance causes tension in the body and the pitch of the voice rises. Actors will often say 'I must get my voice down', and they adjust by feel to their natural placing – the centre of the voice.

Objectively, the placing of the voice can be traced to a note on the piano by asking the actor to speak normally and then tracing the centre note of his voice. This method is employed for instance, in the training of actors, voice teachers and speech therapists parts of Germany. The actor can be asked to try out a variety of placings until he finds the one which he *feels* is most comfortable. Having found it he is asked to sing 'Ah' in that place and then to read through a long passage of text or a newspaper on that placing, and possibly on that single note. When he has found his correct voice centre, the actor works to preserve the sensation so that he can return to it whenever he needs.

To place the voice too high or two low inhibits its full range. I am aware, from observing myself and others, that when the placing is wrong some instinctive reflex mechanism in the body/think automatically takes the actor away from areas of danger in musical pitch, by inhibiting him from going into high or low areas of pitch, where his voice is off-balance. However, this instinctive activity has little productive value since it is not related to text and meaning. When it happens, the actor will suddenly move into an upward or level inflexion when the natural flow of speech should produce a downward inflexion, or vice versa. The actor can overcome the inhibition by consciously forcing the voice. The result is weakness and strain.

A large part of the problem arises from musical education in schools, and from the terminology which specifies 'high' notes and 'low' notes. One is told to sing *up* or *down* a scale, and this instinctively sets up spatial ideas of high and low. Other languages have entirely different terminologies for describing the phenomenon of musical pitch.

In thinking *up* whilst singing *up*, the child, or actor, often shifts the *placing* of the voice with each note. It is perfectly feasible and practical to think *level* when singing up a scale. It is not difficult to think *down* when singing *up* a scale, and vice versa. The result of the first is a maintenance of balance. The result of the second is to emphasise the force of gravity, with a consequent gain in strength and often resonance (though not flexibility) through stronger contact with the ground. It is noticeable that untrained singers 'reaching' for a high note often go up on their toes.

I have a theory, which I cannot begin to prove until I have done much more work on it, that with every strong thought impulse, or major new idea, or change of direction in the voice, the voice returns to the musical pitch that coincides with the centre placing of the voice, and that this is accompanied by a recovery of the body to a state of balance. What leads me to believe this is that it can be applied to a specific acting problem with corrective results. The problem arises both in extended passages of text and between actors, when the actor begins a new sentence, thought, or line, at the same pitch as the previous one finished on. Actors have a consistent tendency to pick up the pitch of the previous speaker's last word, and even to pick up his rhythm. This tendency upsets the balance of the actor's voice and takes him into dangerous areas of extended musical range. The solution I have found is, at these points, to bring the actor back to his centre note.

One manifestation of a wrongly placed voice, which can be isolated to give a clue as to what is happening, is that the actor who has placed too high appears physically and vocally to be bearing down on the line of the speech. Placed too low, he appears to be pushing up into the line of speech.

The alternating current of speech There is an ebb and flow of movement within speech, which the streaming of sound inhibits or contradicts. One aspect of this has already been described by Abercrombie: '. . . What happens . . . is that the respiratory muscles alternately contract and relax at a rate of roughly five times a second . . . (to form the basis of the syllable).'

Balance, in any physical activity, is a process of oscillations to either side of a notional centre. In Laban's terms movement is an alternating flow of movement in and out of the centre, gathering and scattering. In physical sports such as fencing and boxing, the lunge must be followed by a recovery before the next lunge, if balance is to be maintained. Continual extensions without recovery result in overbalancing and a drastic weakening of the strength of the thrust. This leads to a desperate tensing of muscle groups to maintain strength and balance, which in turn leads to strain, general weakness and lack of mobility.

Something of the same sort happens with actors who stream sound and speak lines. It is the plague of teachers and directors who have to work with young and inexperienced actors that they continually drop the ends of lines, being unable to maintain strength (that is, balance) through the line. One cannot work on the alternating contraction/relaxation of the syllable puffs, because the movement is too small for the actor to control. The earlier exercises, designed to break up the text into its component parts, attempt to produce this balance naturally by reinstating the normal processes of speech communication. Some work can also be done by listening to tapes of people speaking and by trying to understand how the gather/scatter alternation manifests itself in ordinary speech patterns. The actor is asked to imitate and be aware of how the sensations appear in his body.

Although speech is an alternating flow of gathered and scattered impulses, at times one or the other predominates in the activity. That is, the major stresses of the line fall on either the gathered or scattered impulses, and the off stresses (recoveries or relaxations) fall on the other. In physical terms this is the difference between an outward or inward directed flow of movement. In vocal terms an absurdly simple example lies in the difference between calling in the cat and shooing away birds. In the former the gathering impulses predominate, in the latter the scattering. Purpose or intention induces the effect. It can be induced at will.

Every actor knows that, in playing in large auditoria, the clearest audibility is never achieved by trying to push or project the voice to reach the furthest seat, but by pulling or drawing the back of the auditorium to you. A gathered impulse has a clearer focus than a scattered one, which soon dissipates its clarity in space. An actor who speaks softly with a gathering impulse can usually be heard more clearly with less effort than one who shouts. This depends, though, on the whole range of the vocal apparatus being used economically and not on a small part of the resources being used, as is the case in conversation.

Actors who have not learned this technique by pragmatic trial and error frequently fall into certain traps. In 'speaking lines', or projecting the voice, they allow the scattering impulses to predominate by default, and to recover they make massive gathering impulses at the ends of lines or sentences, when they usually take the breath. This is exactly the reverse of the bel canto opera singer who uses only gathering impulses; he always appears to be 'singing in', not out, and takes massive relaxation recoveries at the end of the phrase, accompanied by vast intakes of breath. It has been said of the great Italian bel canto singers that they could sing a high forte note and not trouble the flame of a candle held an inch from their lips. The system is too inflexible for the actor, but it is good discipline for breath control.

The actor who phrases his line in this way, leaving the 'gathering' until the end, will disturb the natural flow of the language. The gathered/ scattered impulses should alternate throughout the line, according to the action embodied in the text. The constant alternation also ensures an automatic reflex series of small in-breaths throughout the line and topping-up breaths which materially assist in sustaining breath through difficult speeches and passages, and make an artificial breathing system like 'rib reserve' totally superfluous.

The first impulse is of vital importance to the actor who has problems with speech. It is a matter of choice, largely directed by the content of the speech and the situation in which it is spoken, as to whether the first impulse in any line or section is gathered or scattered. However, if the actor has become accustomed, through habit and use, to a predominantly scattering activity, the first scattered impulse sends the line away from him and, if this is followed by a second scattering impulse, he never gets control over the line until a break in the speech, when he needs a massive recovery to bring him back to a central balance. One can often see the physical effect of this in a young actor, as he pushes the line away from him and the body comes forwards off-centre. He is like a jockey trying to ride round Aintree sitting on the rump of the horse. Instead, I ask the actor to take a grip of the reins on the first impulse, that is, to make a gathering movement.

If an actor predominantly scatters, then the gathered impulses are the ones that need working on. The scatters come naturally to him as relaxation from effort. By taking a grip of the reins, as it were, at the outset, he is able to ride the rhythm of the speech more securely and with balance, and to keep control of what he is saying.

To bring the actor on centre, and to make him keep contact between the centre of the voice and the centre of gravity in the body, I literally ask him to ride the speech as one would a horse. Horses, bicycles and racing cars are ridden and driven by the seat of the pants. I ask the actor to 'sit on the speech', and often to forget about speaking the speech through his mouth and let it come out of his backside. (A similar but more subtle approach to resonance has been used by Grotowski, who has asked actors to make the sound in various parts of the body. It is not scientific, but the actor's use of his imagination, in this respect, produces the right results in practice.)

Depth of sensation Elementary to all the foregoing is the task of leading the actor to the sensations of flexible, centred balance so that he can work from the right balanced position instead of striving to find what he has lost, or is not experiencing. This necessitates the correct relationship between the head, neck, spine and pelvis, and particularly the removal of dis-coordinations of these parts of the body by tension stops along the spinal column. That is, the upper body pivots on its primary hinge, the upper part of the pelvis opposite the horizontal centre of the body, whilst the line of the entire body is close to the optimum line of the vertical centre running from the ear to the anterior of the ankle joint. Practise work can be done in this area, and the sensations help in rehearsal and performance when the need for wider mobility makes a conscious sense of balance difficult. In *Voice and the Actor* Cicely Berry goes into detail about one of these ways of working, which I also use. The actor is asked to lie flat on the floor with the knees bent upwards. The back muscles are isolated and relaxed so that they spread and are supported by the floor, with the pelvis turned forward and upwards, leaving the hollow of the small of the back flattened on the floor. It is important that the neck is long and not shortened at the back, nor over-extended by straining (*illustration no. 26*).

There are two other ways. The sensations of the prone position can be taken to a sitting position where the actor sits into the upright back of a chair and slides down it without displacing the pelvis. His seat therefore covers the maximum area of chair room and the point where the spine articulates out from the pelvis is supported by the back of the chair, leaving the spine strongly supported without undue strain or tension for balance. The hip joints should be opened to the point of maximum relaxation, and the legs should stand directly straight from the knees to the ankles.

The last method is to ask the actor to stand with his back to you, legs apart, and again with the hip joints opened as far as they will go without any strain. Placing your fingers in the top of the groin, parallel with the horizontal centre, ask the actor to bend the upper body from where he feels

26 'The actor is asked to lie flat on the floor . . .'

the fingers, and to hang from that position naturally (*illustralion no. 27*). Care must be taken to see that the actor does exactly what he is told and does not first move from a secondary hinge, higher up the spine, or change the action in mid-movement by moving first from the centre and then changing to start a different movement from higher up the back. Supported by the primary hinge, and your fingers, the spine should hang with the minimum tension to prevent a collapse of the upper body; then you are ready to begin on the text.

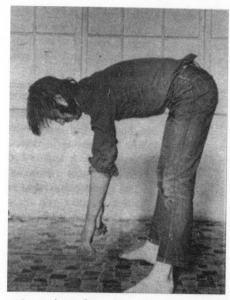

With optimum and minimum tension in the upper body, the muscle groups are free to respond to the thoughts and images expressed in the text through the words in which they are embodied. The kinaesthetic sensations are uninhibited and vibrant. The body/

27 '. . . to hang from that position naturally'

think is untrammelled and the actor can be led to what the metaphor expresses as 'depth of feeling and conviction'. The sensations run freely and resonantly right down through the whole torso to his guts. Once aware of these sensations, the actor must learn to control the power physically to re-create them in less advantageous circumstances in rehearsal and performance.

Changes of direction Since speech is the result of movements made in the body, and all movement is the shift of the balance of the body's weight in space, it should follow that speech itself has a spatial dimension. Changes of direction in thought can be interpreted as changes of direction in space. The classic vernacular metaphor, 'on the other hand . . .' indicates a clear spatial change of direction. There are others: 'On top of all that . . .', 'he strayed from the point . . .', 'he collected his thoughts . . .'. The actor, too, knows what is meant by the 'throwaway' style of delivery.

Rationally pre-developed thought follows narrow, straight lines, as in a lecture, where the speaker sets up a cause-and-effect narrative to prove the results of an experiment. First we have A, then we add B to A, and the result is a chemical reaction, in which C is given off as a gas and D is the precipitate. Very few human patterns of thought do this, and even in this example, the logical development of the thesis can lead to a 'build up' as the climax of the experiment is reached. 'Gas' could take us into a high dimension because of its airy associations, and 'precipitate' could drop to a low dimension because of its earthy associations.

C is given off as a gas

The result is a chemical reaction in which   and

Then we add B to A

First we have A   D is the

precipitate

The speech does not swerve from the same straight line, but varies in the use of the high and low spatial dimensions. It must be clear, though, that I am referring not to the inflection of the speech, but to its dynamic quality.

The spatial movement patterns of speech can be clearly heard in normal speech. What can be done is to make these movements actual, that is, to take what is a relatively small shift of balance in the body and give it the full range of body movement that it implies. In releasing it, the actor objectivises what is happening on a subjective level, and is better able to bring it under fine control when he reduces it again to the level that the performance requires.

The exercise described earlier – helping the actor to be aware of 360 degree space and his possibilities of movement in all dimensions of space – is an important part of this work, and it is tackled by translating the thought patterns of the speech into the spatial terms of the diagram on page 140. With speech we are particularly concerned with the orientation of the body centre in space.

I will give two examples of how this work can be carried out.

INFANTA: Shall I consider still my birth and rank
Which make my love a crime?
Or shall I listen, love, to you whose claim
Makes me rebel against my royal time?
Unhappy Princess, choose,
For either choice must lose
The hope of happiness. My Royal grace
Would mock me as I kissed Rodrigo's face.

Pitiless fate that sternly separates
My glory from desire;
Why must the choice of courage that is rare
Bring to my heart this hot, despairing fire?
Oh God, how many tears
My heart must blend with fears
Until this long torment can end forever
And either quell my love, or my love sever.

Too long have I been scrupulous.
Why must I condemn by choice?
Although my birth gives me to kings alone,
To claim Rodrigo's name I can rejoice.
Striking two kings down,
He will achieve a crown,
His wondrous name of Cid – does this not prove
That he should rule a princess and her love?

Yet worthy of my birth, he is Chimena's.
I give him to her at love's decree.
Not even her father's death could make them hate,
Though from her duty now she cannot flee.
I dare not hope for bliss tomorrow

> From his crime or from my sorrow,
> Since ruthless fate, to punish me, foresees
> That they shall keep their love, though enemies.[16]

The speech is based upon two conflicting forces working within the Infanta – her sense of honour and her desire for Rodrigo – which cannot be reconciled. This is the lateral spatial dimension. The vertical spatail dimension is the rise and fall of hope in the Infant. Because the soliloquy is spoken facing the audience we accept the diagonals as the lateral divisions of space. The movements of the speech are (or could be) these:

1. From the centre along the right front diagonal:
    'Shall I consider still my birth and rank . . .'

2. Falling back along the right front diagonal to the centre:
    'Which makes my love a crime?'

3. From the centre along the left front diagonal:
    'Or shall I listen, love, to you whose claim   . . .'

4. Falling back along left front diagonal to centre:
    'Makes me rebel against my royal time?'

5. Centre rising vertically:
    'Unhappy Princess, choose,'

6. Centre relaxing to fall:
    'For either choice must lose
    The hope of happiness,'

***7. Centre advanced forward (since the position of despair is not acceptable to her and some argument must be found that will settle the tensions):
    'My Royal grace
    Would mock me as I kissed Rodrigo's face.'

8. Centre advanced forward (since the argument does not settle the tensions but rather intensifies them) with strong pulls along both diagonals:
    'Pitiless fate that sternly separates
    My glory from desire;
    Why must the choice of courage that is rare
    Bring to my heart this hot, despairing fire?'

9. Centre sinks vertically to its lowest point (despair) possibly
through the Infanta sinking to her knees:
'Oh God, how many tears
My heart must blend with fears
Until this long torment can end forever
And either quell my love, or my love sever.'

***10. Centre rises and moves forward to new position with major shift
of thought:
'Too long have I been scrupulous.
Why must I condemn my choice?'

11. Centre rising with the developing argument towards the high
front dimension:
'Although my birth gives me to kings alone,
To claim Rodrigo's name I can rejoice.
Striking two kings down,
He will achieve a crown,
His wondrous name of Cid – does this not prove
That he should rule a princess and her love?'
(At the end of this section the centre should have reached the
limit of the extension in space, high front – the height of hope.)

12. Centre falls from high front extremity to stance:
'Yet worthy of my birth he is Chimena's.
I gave him to her at love's decree.'

13. Centre moves out along right front diagonal (since the death of
the illusory hope makes the position untenable):
'Not even her father's death could make them hate,'

14. Centre falls back along right front diagonal (with the realisation
that there are obstacles to Chimena marrying Rodrigo, which
opens the situation again):
'Though from her duty now she cannot flee.'

15. Turbulence at the centre (caught between the desire for
Rodrigo and the necessity to renounce him, and between the
hope of time making love a possibility, and the fear that a
reconciliation between Rodrigo and Chimena will prevent it
happening); the centre is pulled all four ways at once creating a
wringing sensation:

'I dare not hope for bliss tomorrow
From his crime or from my sorrow,
Since ruthless fate'

16. Counter tensions in the body; the centre is moved to rise in hope
    which the circumstances contradict (hoping against hope):
    'I dare not hope for bliss tomorrow
    From his crime or from my sorrow,
    since pitiless fate, to punish me, foresees
    That they shall keep their love, though enemies.'

The movements marked * * * are the only moves which I would of necessity
plot into the scene, because they indicate major shifts of position in the
thoughts of the Infanta. The other moves I might well, in a production,
make actual in space, or keep kinetic in the body, depending upon the
theatre and the actress playing the role. I would make all the movement
actual in rehearsal.

The movements out from the centre in any direction in space are not
unbroken straight lines, but are naturally subject to the alternating flow of
gathered/scattered impulses. Unless this is maintained, that is unless the
movement maintains contact with the centre, then the use of any concept
of movement in the voice in spatial terms will result in pushing, and sending
the speech away from the actor. This is of vital importance in movements
which fall back from the extremity or perimeter towards the centre. In
practice I have come across a tendency in the actor, once the extension in
space has been reached, to relax the tension which maintains contact with
the centre, and to allow the speech to droop or drop off on the periphery.
That is, instead of the line of speech going so:

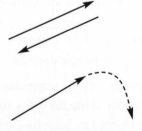

it goes so:

The second example I want to use is the Death of Zenocrate from
Tamburlaine. The speech is as follows:

What, is she dead? Techelles, draw thy sword
And wound the earth, that it may cleave in twain
And we descend into th'infernal vaults,
To hale the Fatal Sisters by the hair
And throw them in the triple moat of hell,
For taking hence my fair Zenocrate.
Casane and Theridamas to arms!
Raise cavalieros higher than the clouds,
And with the cannon break the frame of heaven.
Batter the shining palace of the sun
And shiver all the starry firmament,
For amorous Jove hath snatch'd my love from hence,
Meaning to make her stately queen of heaven.
Whatever god so'ever holds thee in his arms,
Giving thee nectar and ambrosia,
Behold me here, divine Zenocrate,
Raving, impatient, desperate, and mad,
Breaking my steeled lance, with which I burst
The rusty beams of Janus' temple doors,
Letting out death and tyrannising war,
To march with me under this bloody flag.
And if thou pitiest Tamburlaine the Great,
Come down from heaven, and live with me again![17]

The poet's images give the immediate clues to the directions, moving firstly through the stages down into hell, to the realisation of the loss of Zenocrate. The feeling of loss in death (mirrored in other images in the play) transmutes into images of eternal life, and the tension between loss and idealisation leads to a climb to heaven through various stages, to recover Zenocrate from the Gods. The sensations of impotence transform the battle into a pleading in heaven, and then to a search for supernatural allies, and the impossibility of this leads to the final human pleading for the return of that which is lost, out of pity. That is, at the height of ambition Tamburlaine the Great breaks down, in the face of death. (The next line from Theridamas is 'Ah my good lord, be patient. She is dead, And all this raging cannot make her live.')

The movement of the speech in the body must, firstly, travel in the forward downward direction from the centre, to the maintained 'For taking hence my fair Zenocrate'; secondly rise through the centre and climb through the attack in stages, to the weak extended passage about Zenocrate with the Gods; and thirdly climb through the raging attack to 'bloody flag'. At this point, the voice breaks at the limit of one's extension, and the actor physically crumbles during the last two lines. The major problem is to keep contact with the central balance of the body to prevent the speech falling off along the periphery with consequent loss of control.

With any writers of the calibre of Marlowe, I find myself saying to actors, 'If you can find the movement in the verse, you will find that the poet does 60% of the work for you. To start from a position of "what are we going to do with this?" puts you in a position of trying to do his job for him'.

I am not sure that even if I had done more work on this I could describe it any better. My understanding of it is based on a collection of some two to three hundred tapes I have recorded of people communicating facts, arguing convictions, recollecting experiences they have lived through, and on work with actors on text. The tapes have demonstrated to me that there is a great deal more dynamic physical movement (and use of musical range) in everyday speech than ever seems to find its way on to a stage. Once, in rehearsal, I played some of the tapes to the cast and said that that was the quality of speech that I wanted in the production. 'And where,' asked the senior actor present, 'will you find the actors good enough to reproduce it?' That is the job.

CHAPTER 15

Technical work

Almost all of my teaching has been done either with actors who have had technical training in movement, or with the support of other teachers who were working in the more technical areas of movement training. Approaching technical movement through games has been relatively easy for them to assimilate into their general pattern of work. They have seen the value of an energy-releasing activity that will prepare the way for technical exercise, that will also provide a means for the actor to continue his training and keep up the condition of his body when he has not acquired the technical expertise to do this on his own initiative and that will further help him cope when no experienced movement teacher is at hand to lead his technical work.

In working on my own body, I use technical exercises. Having gone through all the games work, I can work technically on my body without becoming in any way distressed. I can isolate the actions I am working on. Only when I have had a lay-off from physical work do I return to the games work to get back into the swing. There is always a resistance to starting work again after a lay-off, and the games release the energy needed to get started again. I will also take technical classes with actors where there is no experienced teacher to hand to lead the work, or, sometimes, because the actors demand it. To some actors the games work seems like 'playing around', and the technical classes demonstrate some earnestness of intention.

The technical exercises I use are a mixture picked up from Laban and from various forms of dance training or athletic and gymnastic training. It would take another book to set them all out, but in the present context it is sufficient to say that I work from principles that are close to those on which the games work is built.

If some games element can be built into the work, then I build it in.

Skipping is a good exercise from stamina training and one which, again, takes actors back to the pleasure of play and of competition – who can make the highest number of skips without a break. Actors can be asked to sing while skipping, or to hold conversations with other actors, or to play the long rope skipping games they played as children – anything which takes the attention away from the activity itself.

Dance steps Various steps and movements can be 'played around with'. There are only five types of jump possible. The number is absolutely limited by the number of legs we have. You can jump from one foot to the other; from one foot to two feet; from one foot to the same foot; from two feet to one foot; and from two feet to two feet. There are no other permutations possible. A great amount of physical work can be done by pointing this out to a group and letting them play around with the possibilities. If they want and are able to, they can move on to jetées, cabriolets, assemblées etc. When they've played around with the basic jumps, one can introduce turns into the jump or ask them to throwaway the leading leg and follow it with the other, rather than launching themselves off the supporting foot. You can ask them to perform star jumps or to do circus turns, like jumping over the crouched bodies of one or more persons kneeling in the centre of the room. This way it is fun, not work, although by slightly changing the movements they are doing, you can begin to purify the movement and work towards technical expertise.

Early in my career, I spent some time working back-stage with a ballet company. I used to practise the steps, in private, to amuse myself. A surprising amount stuck. Nothing would have persuaded me to stand at a barre and take part in a class, but I learned a great deal just 'playing around'. I used to think 'That's an interesting movement, I wonder how she does it', and I would go away and try to find out.

The basis of this work can be the old children's game of **Follow my Leader**. The faults made by the 'followers' can be joked out, rather than seriously corrected. I find it easier than standing in front of a class demonstrating movements for a class to follow. Unless the movements are absurdly simple the class has difficulty in breaking down the movement into its component parts. Working on dance steps by doing it alongside them, I can carry them through the basic action of the steps, and then complicate it, in a gradual progression. Once they have grasped the principle, they can work to improve and perfect it. Most choreographers working with actors use this method, and most actors enjoy it and can show great ability. If, to start with, the actors are shown something they can use in the theatre, they will work hard to be able to do it.

The lever class The body moves, of course, by the interaction of contracting groups of muscles, at the instigation of impulses originating in, and controlled by, the nervous system. But it is too difficult to contact the muscle groups. It is more advantageous to begin with function and activities than it is with muscle action. If the muscles are hard to isolate, the actions of the joints are quite simple.

In all the exercises I carry out in class, I work to take attention away from muscular effort by concentrating upon the lever actions of the joints. Where possible I use a fixed surface to lever the joint against. Going up on tip toes, for instance, the class are not asked to raise the body, but to press down on the floor. The heel may be raised either by contracting the muscles of the calf, or by pressing down the toes on to the floor, using the ball of the foot as a fixed point to lever against. For me the former method produces undue tension in the calf muscles. The latter doesn't.

The floor is the most important surface to lever against, and as many exercises of the pelvis and torso as possible are performed lying on the floor, with the anti-gravitational muscles relaxed. Habitual contractions of the back of the neck can be worked on, lying on the floor with the small of the back flattened and the knees raised. The head is gently raised to its normal vertical position, keeping the shoulders on the floor, and holding it there as long as is comfortable, before returning to rest. The muscles which normally contract are thus extended, and vice versa. The principle should be employed wherever possible. If there is an undue tension anywhere in the body, exercises should be introduced to work on contracting the complementary groups of muscles, which will elongate those in which the habitual contraction occurs.

Pelvic impulses There is one technical exercise I use which does not fit these earlier patterns. It has an imaginary stimulus and is thus closer to the games activities. The exercise seeks to get the actor to make uninhibited and uncontrolled impulsive movements at the body centre. That is, central impulses affecting all the limbs and parts of the body simultaneously. The exercise is performed on the floor. Actors are asked to respond to the beat of a drum, or a thump on the floor, as though they were being kicked alternately in the stomach and at the base of the spine. On being kicked in the stomach, they contract all the limbs into the centre to completely cover the soft parts of the crotch, stomach, breast and face. On being kicked at the base of the spine, they shoot all the limbs out as wide as possible. When secure in the exercise without 'binding' any of the movements, they are asked to try out for themselves central impulses of gathering and scattering, of differing strengths. The principle involved is to move from free, uncontrolled movement to controlled movement. The actor is helped to an awareness of uninhibited gathering and scattering impulses at the body centre.

The actor as social scientist

The theatre has throughout history been seen as an image or metaphor of life in the society outside: 'All the world's a stage', 'Totus mundus exerceat histrionem,' 'The Great Stage of human life', 'The world . . . a stage, where every man must playa part'. In recent years a succession of social scientists, like Gotffman and Parson and Sills, have taken theatrical concepts and terminology as a model through which to analyse and study wider aspects of social behaviour and interaction. The concept of 'role playing' is now a central part of sociological analysis and vocabulary.

The dramatists have always been taken seriously in this respect. Academic institutions have been set up to study the sociological knowledge that can be gained from the study of play texts, and dramatists have advertised the seriousness of their purpose by directly stating the analogy. But nobody has taken the actor seriously, and he, after all, is the man that actually carries the play on to the stage. I should like to strike a blow for the actor.

It angers me when the crucial importance of the actor's work is diminished, both inside and outside the theatre, by treating him as simply the mouthpiece for the dramatist's words, or the expressive instrument of the director's concept. The actor is the theatre, and the sooner we give it back to him the better. I mean this literally as well as metaphorically. The greatest period of our drama was when the actors controlled the theatres by owning shares in the company. Now that so many theatres cannot survive without subsidy, some way has to be found of letting the actors have a direct responsibility for those theatres.

The chief obstacle is the image that society has of the actor as feckless, irresponsible, impractical and unreliable; an image that, regrettably, too many actors accept without question. I would argue that actors are the great underachievers of our society, and that society has not yet found how to extract more than a minute fraction of the value that the actor holds for society.

There is no such activity as 'acting'. The actor presents aspects or images of human behaviour and interaction on the stage, through his presence and controlled relationships with other actors. Life is never portrayed on the stage, only images of life; and the range of the theatre's imagery, and of the actor's resources, is rich and wide. But the physical and mental processes through which the actor works are common to all human beings.

The actor can be said to operate between two poles of activity; the child's explorative play on the one hand and paranoia on the other. The child *explores*, imaginatively, situations of time and space that he has not directly experienced. He is close to the Stanislavski concept: '*If* I were a cowboy . . . what would it be like?' The child is not interested in critically *defending* the results or effects of his play. If you try to introduce discipline to the play and say 'Policemen don't act in that way' you introduce factors which are outside his playing and he will tell you 'I was only playing'. The play activity is destroyed by the imposition of external criticism. This only develops later in early adolescence, often with disastrous results, splitting the child into a doer and a critical self-observer. Inhibit creative play and you stunt the adult; this is the ultimate justification for drama as a subject in schools at all levels.

The paranoiac believes himself to have an identity other than the one society gives him. The cliche is that lunatic asylums are full of people who are convinced that they are Napoleon.[1] They are not interested in *exploring* what it would feel like to be Napoleon. Such an investigation would immediately question the whole basis on which they act, and through which they have resolved personal and social tensions. They *are* Napoleon, and their whole life is an elaborate set of *defensive* actions which make the whole phenomenon of their living fit the central thesis.

These two attitudes are notional extremes of human action and reaction. In between lies the whole range of modes of social behaviour. I have suggested earlier the processes by which we rehearse dialogue for critical situations like interviews for jobs. We also test our techniques in practice and then take them back to the drawing-board to analyse the results and then resynthesise them. We try to pick up a girl at a party. We fail. We go back home and analyse why, then try next time with a modified approach until we find one that works. Then we try to apply this to all situations till it fails, and back we go to modify. This process continues way beyond adolescence and way beyond the simple example I have given. Maturity gives the flexibility to handle situations as they come. Confidence is gained from successes across the board. It is also true that we imaginatively explore areas of our personality in fantasy activities or 'fooling about'. I have suggested earlier that we adopt restricted roles in response to anxiety situations in which we cannot act fully. This is an essential part of everyday life. We construct endless series of dramatic fictions to cope. The clearest example of this is the army, where elaborate structures are set up to force the human being into the limited role of the good soldier who reacts to extreme situations by simply obeying orders and doing his duty. We become someone, who in totality we are not, in response to social pressures.

I have also suggested that the two processes merge in the creation of fantasy figures which help resolve personal tensions brought about by our encounters with our environment.

All of these processes lie at the roots of the actor's craft. The actor in a way is an amalgam of the child and the paranoiac. As a creative artist he constantly explores imaginary situations in time and space, which are not of his own devising, in order to find out what it feels like to be in them. From these he gets his sensational (in its literal meaning) material for performance. Since his name appears on the programme as, say, 'Baron Tusenbach', he has to defend in public the proposition that he is someone other than the person whom society knows or recognises him to be. He also engages creatively in all the strategies of human action and interaction which are general in the life of society. In fact he may be said to be the most experienced and adept performer of the whole human gamut of social skills and activities. If he is this, and I believe the accomplished actor has this potential, then we must take the actor very seriously indeed. He is capable of bringing back from his explorations a mass of sociological information, and he does this experientially, not from the detached, impersonal and limited viewpoint of an outside observer.

Those sociological role-playing exercises which I have witnessed have always struck me as bad directors directing bad actors in scripts by bad playwrights. The human processes of action and reaction are either little understood by the sociologists, or they have little skill in re-creating them. The one who possesses the requisite knowledge and skill is the actor. I will go to my grave believing that the actor could be the most important experimental social scientist in the world. But, as I said, actors are the great under-achievers of our society.

Theatre into education

The second aspect of my work which goes beyond the strict confines of theatre is when it becomes a tool for educational exploration and development. Actor training deals with the whole human personality and all its interactive processes, mental, physical and emotional. The same is true, but more crucially so, when one is working in the educational field.

In 1966 I became Lecturer in Theatre Practice in the Department of Drama and Theatre Arts at Birmingham University, in order to get time and breathing space to make my work as systematic and as scientific as I could. A great deal of my work therefore has been developed in an educational establishment. I don't believe this limits it theatrically. It all springs directly from my practice as a director and actor, and even while lecturing I have been able to work professionally for short periods outside the department, so that, throughout, my work has been fed back into the professional theatre for 'testing'.

What has happened in the process of relating professional experience to the demands of teaching is that the processes of acting which I have described throughout the book have also been shown to be relevant, even central to the processes of education – that is, the individual development of the personality. But it needs a more sympathetic and flexible educational institution than exists at present, to explore a territory which I only began to open up.

The department's intention in taking me to Birmingham was to raise the standard of practice. The department's policy was that the study of Drama and the Theatre Arts should be the study of practice in these fields, and a professional was needed to teach the practice. In the event no significant change was effected in the first three years I was there, because the teaching all took place within a normal university course-structure. The limited exposure of students to the demands of practice, which mainly took the form of two-hour sessions each week, did little more than reveal their limitations.

At the end of three years a new teaching structure was set up which allowed students to work with me, optionally, outside normal teaching hours. To take part, students had to commit themselves to meeting the demands made upon them, without reserve, and they were given no guaranteed pattern of work. It was understood that the work of the group would be directly related to the abilities and needs of the individuals in it. There would be no academic justification for the work outside that of creating opportunities for the individual to develop his practical capability. If this meant we spent the whole year on simple basic physical exercises, then this we would do. We would not mount *Hamlet* just because it would be 'nice' or 'interesting' for the students to perform Shakespeare, if they also happened completely to lack the ability to tackle the practical problems it posed.

The work was arduous, involving students in more than 35 hours a week work outside the normal Departmental courses. Central to the work was the concept of the Scholar/Clown.

As long ago as the mid-1930s, Allardyce Nicoll called for a link between scholarship and professional practice to the mutual advantage of both. But the two worlds have remained apart. The academics mistrust the actors, and to the theatre profession, 'university' is a dirty word. With the most slender resources imaginable, we took on the work of making the link.

The concept of the Scholar/Clown involves a person who not only understands the scholarly aspects of Drama and the Theatre Arts, but can put them into practice. To this end the work of the group was integrated as far as possible. No piece of work was self-justifying. Everything had to be related to the use to which the group and the individual could put the study. And that use had to be very clearly defined either in terms of immediate application or in terms of the professional theatre that waited for them when they left university.

It was also understood that, in the circumstances, the ensemble was the best teaching instrument. The group had to define very clearly the common ground that existed between the members. It became clear early on that no political, religious or philosophic common ground existed between us and that all we did have in common was a concern for the human condition . . . Hence, the grandiose and rather pretentious title, 'The Theatre of Man', was adopted as the basis on which we could build the ensemble.

The work took shape from three templates. Firstly, we took Oskar Schlemmer's drawing of a man in three-dimensional space (see p. 216) as our symbol. We used the concept of man standing at the centre of actual space as a basis for exploring the possibilities of the human body as an expressive instrument. Secondly, we took the concept of man in his social and environmental space as the source of the material which the theatre should present. We studied the world around us, and the life experience of other ages as reflected through history and drama. Thirdly, we took man in theatrical space, through which we could study and understand the form, structure and style by which dramatists, directors and actors had articulated the 'very age and body of the time, his form and pressure'.

Oskar Schlemmer's drawing of a man in three-dimensional space

Lecture, seminar, research, practical exercise and production came together when these three templates were merged or superimposed on each other. The results of this work are still with me, six years later. One of the consequences is that, since then, I have been forced to examine the content and structure of plays in a more critical light. I no longer think of 'good' plays and 'bad' plays in purely theatrical terms, after having had to justify each piece of work presented to the group in a much wider framework. I feel I have entered into a personal relationship across the ages with other actors and dramatists, particularly Euripides, for whom I have developed a very deep personal love and respect. The work made us look at each play as the end-product of one man's sitting down at a particular moment in time and space, and committing his thought and experience to words. Seen in this way, the somewhat abstract nature of the play-text becomes finite and tangibly comprehensible.

Many actors experience this to some degree. To them the study of the history and practice of their craft becomes a vital part of living and working. Through this activity we understand our place in history and society, and we can see our work in the historical and developing per-spective which is sometimes crushed by the pressures of the time we live in. I believe that, given this opportunity to study through practice, many an actor would whole-heartedly become a Scholar/Clown.

But, because it was carried out in a university, the most important result of the group's work lay in the opposite direction. Since the processes of acting are so inextricably linked to the processes of personal and social behaviour, the work became a frame within which the student could come to terms with his own personality and that of others. The integration of objective scientific knowledge and experimental practice led us to a concern with the growth and development of the individuals within the group, which is after all the fundamental purpose of education. Work which had been developed originally as a means of training the actor became in fact the basis of a possible educational method. Its achievements were considerable, not the least being that we disproved the university's opinion that more practical work meant poorer examination results. On the contrary, we raised the grades. However, by concentrating upon the individual, or his needs or the means necessary to help him realise something of his potential, we ran counter to too many of the traditional educational concepts. The experiment could not be contained within the normal university structure and the work was stopped. For me at least, and I think for many of the students who took part, the case had been made that the structure was wrong if it could not accommodate the work.

The future

All the work set out in this book is absorbed into my own professional practice as an actor, director and teacher. I assume that it will continue to develop as I go on working. Having written it all down I realise that I will experience a certain difficulty in getting the literary form of the book out of my mind and returning to simply getting on with the work. At this moment the form of the book acts as a limitation to free thought and response: which is why I would advise anyone who takes this book as an aid or starting point for their own work not to accept the validity of anything set down in it, but rather to use it critically in the first instance; that is, to try to prove mistaken my hypotheses and explanations. The work set out is my work and no-one else's. It does not 'belong' even to those actors who have worked for long periods with me. Whoever takes the work from me immediately makes it his own and from that moment accepts the responsibility for whatever he does. He also is entitled to the full credit for whatever use he can make of it. The work that the book describes only exists when I carry it out. The content of the book is nothing more than the ideas it puts into circulation, and whoever can use them is welcome to them. The success of the book depends entirely on how useful the ideas prove to other people.

It would be pleasant and exciting to think that the two further areas of work I have outlined in this conclusion could some day, somewhere form the basis for a body of sociological, educational or theatrical research of a practical nature over a sustained period. I should be very excited and grateful to participate in such a programme, if it ever came about.

Appendix

The nervous system

The nervous system is often divided into two; the old brain and the new brain. The new brain consists of the rind or bark of the brain, the cerebral cortex and its auxiliary structures. It has no direct connection with the muscles of the body; they are affected by the intermediation of the old brain, i.e. the cerebellum, bulb, spinal cord; in short, all that remains of the central nervous system when the cortex and its appendages are removed. Tho old brain is concerned chiefly with reflex actions and message conduction to and from the cortex.

The cortex, responsible for what we call higher activity, is therefore called the new brain, as it is supposed to have evolved subsequently to the more primitive structures of the old brain.

All the activities of the nervous system can be roughly divided into three categories: conscious activity, reflex and automatic activity, and vegetative activity. It is understood that these activities correspond to the new brain, the old brain and the vegetative system.[1]

The significant facts to note are (a) that the new brain overlays the old brain which is at the base of the skull, which leads me to feel the activities as front and back, and (b) there is no direct connection between the new, front brain and the muscles of the body. For conscious thought to be turned into actions and activities, the intermediation of the old, or back, brain is necessary.

In ordinary life, if one wishes to move his arm, he simply does so; however, the distance between the decision and the execution is large. The conscious self makes the intention, and the execution is relegated to an automatic process that is essentially unconscious. For one cannot take the time to consciously contact the proper series of muscles in the proper order for every single act made during the day. The cost in concentration and energy would be obviously impossibly high; therefore, it is evident that much action must be relegated to the automatic 'systems' of the brain.[2]

Notes

About Theatre Games

1. Keith Johnstone, *Impro: Improvisation and the Theatre*, London, Methuen Drama, 2007, p. ix.
2. Ibid., p. 115
3. Richard L. Gregory, *Oxford*, Oxford University Press, 1987, p. 727.
4. M. Feldenkrais, *The Elusive Obvious*, Capitola, CA, Meta Publications, 1981, p. 91.

Chapter 1: The work of the actor

1. Constantin Stanislavski, *My Life in Art*, trans. J.J. Robbins, Harmondsworth, Penguin, p. 524.
2. D. Magarshack, *Stanislavsky on the Art of the Stage*, London, Faber, 1967, pp. 75–6.

Chapter 3: Thought and action

1. Quoted in A. J. Manser, *Sartre*, London, Athlone Press, 1966, p. 48.
2. *Ibid.*, p. 120–1.
3. M. Feldenkrais, *Body and Mature Behavior*, New York, International Universities Press, 1970, p. 108.
4. R. Magnus quoted in *The Resurrection of the Body – The writings of F. Matthias Alexander*, selected by E. Maisel, New York, Dell, 1969, pp. 199–200.
5. Feldenkrais, *op. cit.*, p. 94.
6. Feldenkrais, *op. cit.*, p. 36.
7. Feldenkrais, *op. cit.*, pp. 75–6.
8. Feldenkrais, *op. cit.*, p. 101.
9. W. Barlow, *The Alexander Principle*, London, Gollancz, 1973, pp. 21–2.

10. Feldenkrais, *op. cit.*, p. 74.

11. Feldenkrais, *op. cit.*, p. 74.

12. An example of sympathetic audience response occurs in a recent project initiated by the Department of Drama and Theatre Arts in Birmingham. Every performance of a local production was tape-recorded to chart audience response. The strongest audience response was recorded in a scene during which an actor came on stage and nightly pushed his voice into a hoarse bellow. For ten minutes after this scene begins the tape records fidgeting in the audience and a great deal of coughing and clearing of throats. It is a common experience that when one is listening to someone speaking with a tight throat, or with blocked sinuses, one experiences the need to clear one's throat or blow one's nose.

13 B. Beckerman, *Dynamics of Drama*, New York, Knopf, 1970, pp. 145, 150.

14. Manser, *op. cit.*, p. 52. Jean-Louis Barrault puts it this way: 'Emotion is a state which the actor must never be conscious of. One can only become conscious of an emotion which has already passed, for the act of consciousness dissipates the actual emotion'. (*The Theatre of J.-L. Barrault*, London, Barrie and Rockliff, 1961, p. 51.)

Chapter 4: Actor training

1. Feldenkrais, *op. cit.*, p. 109.

Chapter 7: Categories of games

1. Roger Caillois, *Man, Play and Games*, London, Thames and Hudson, 1962, p. 157. Under *simulation* Caillois includes all play activities which involve disguise, wearing a mask, playing a part (including, of course, theatre).

   An example of *simulation* and *vertigo* in combination might well be a secret society whose rituals involve transcendental drugs and ceremonial robes – witchcraft. It would also include modern, experimental, anti-establishment theatre groups who try to destroy the audience's accepted role in the theatre, and sweep it into participating in experiences it has no preparation for, nor any defined role in, such as touch exploration.

2. Caillois, *op. cit.*, p. 65.

Chapter 8: Release of physical inhibitions

1. Feldenkrais, *op. cit.*, p. 86.

Chapter 9: The creative imagination and the use of fantasy

1. Accounts of both these shows are in Albert Hunt's *Hopes for Great Happenings*, London, Eyre Methuen, 1976.

Chapter 11: Space

1. *Henry V* Chorus 11–12, 17–18.
2. G. Woodruff, 'Design and Equipment', in J.R. Brown (ed.), *Drama and the Theatre*, London, Routledge and Kegan Paul, 1971.
3. Rudolf Laban, *Modern Educational Dance*, London, Macdonald and Evans, second edn., 1963, p. 85. See also: R. Laban, *Choreutics*, London, Macdonald and Evans; and J. Winearls, *Modern Dance*, London, Black, 1968.

Chapter 14: Work on text

1. 'Voice consciousness' is a regular problem among student actors. Voice training makes them more self-conscious than any other area. They cannot see how well or badly they perform physical movements; they can always hear their own voices. A great deal of voice training work is performed in abstract. It is an artificial activity which somehow does not relate to any other human activity. Movement training relates to physical education and to dancing, but voice training is on its own. The most successful way I have seen used of breaking down 'voice consciousness' is in the work of Emil Froeschels. Froeschels works on the principle that there are no separate speech organs, that the organs that produce speech are common to the processes of chewing and eating, and that they share the same centres in the brain. His speech therapy methods are based upon 'chewing'. The method appeals to me because it takes the actor's mind off what he is doing, and centres on a process associatcd with pleasure and not with anxiety. (The method is used in Germany, which is where I first encountered its use in the training of actors; see Egon Aderhold, *Sprecherziehung des Schauspielers*, Berlin, Henschelverlag, 1963.
   I have listed some of Froeschels' publications in the bibliography.)

2. David Abercrombie, *Elements of General Phonetics*, Edinburgh University Press, 1967, pp. 35–6.
3. Abercrombie, *op. cit.*, pp. 22–3.
4. Cicely Berry, *Voice and the Actor*, London, Harrap, 1973.
5. Aderhold, *op. cit.*
6. Berry, *op. cit.*, pp. 131, 118.
7. Euripides, *The Phoenician Women*; trans. E. Wyckoff, University of Chicago Press, 1959, p. 73.
8. Gordon Daviot, *Richard of Bordeaux* Part II. Sc. iv.
9. Shakespeare, *Richard II* I. iii. 154–8.
10. Euripides, *The Phoenician Women*, p. 115.
11. *Hamlet* I. i. 79–107.
12 Abercrombie, *op. cit.*, p. 24.
13. *Hamlet* III. i.
14. *The Phoenician Women*, p. 82.
15. *Tamburlaine* (Part Two) II. iv.
16. Corneille, *Le Cid* V. ii; trans. J. Schevill, in Eric Bentley (ed.), The Classic Theatre, vol. IV, New York, Doubleday, 1959.
17. *Tamburlaine* (Part Two) II. iv.

Conclusion

1. This may not be a cliché if we examine its roots in the nineteenth-century conflict between the philosophical ideal of the great self-determining individual and the practical frustrations of the interchangeable worker, or 'hand'. Anyone who wants to understand how involved and tortuous are the shifts of the human personality to rationalise phenomena which appear contradictory, or which cause emotional disturbance, should refer to Bruno Bettelheim's books, particularly *Love is not Enough*.

Appendix

1. Feldenkrais, *op. cit.*, p. 15.
2. A. Pesso, *Movement in Psychotherapy*, University of London Press, 1969, p. 45.

Bibliography

Games

Caillois, R., *Man, Play and Games*, London, Thames and Hudson, 1962.

Acting

Barrault, J.-L., *The Theatre of Jean-Louis Barrault*, London, Barrie & Rockliff, 1961.
Brecht, B. (ed. Willett, J.), *Brecht on Theatre*, London, Methuen, 1964.
Brecht, B., *The Messingkauf Dialogues*, London, Methuen, 1965.
Stanislavski, K.A., *An Actor Prepares*, Geoffrey Bles, 1937.
Stanislavski, K.A., *My Life in Art*, Harmondsworth, Penguin, 1962.
Stanislavski, K.A., *Stanislavski on the Art of the Stage*, Faber, 1967.
Stanislavski, K.A., *Building a Character*, Methuen, 1968.

Movement

Alexander, F.M. (ed. Maisel, E.), *The Resurrection of the Body*, New York, Dell, 1969.
Barlow, W., *The Alexander Principle*, London, Gollancz, 1973.
Feldenkrais, M., *Body and Mature Behavior*, New York, International Universities Press, 1949.
Laban, R., *The Mastery of Movement*, London, Macdonald and Evans, 1960.
Laban, R., *Modern Educational Dance*, London, Macdonald and Evans, 1962.
Pesso, A., *Movement in Psychotherapy*, London, University of London Press, 1969.
Winearls, J., *Modern Dance*, London, Black, 1968.

Voice

Abercrombie, D., *Elements of General Phonetics*, Edinburgh University Press, 1967.

Aderhold, E., *Sprecherziehung des Schauspielers*, Berlin, Henschelverlag, 1963.

Berry, C., *Voice and the Actor*, London, Harrap, 1973.

Froeschels, E., and Jellinek, A., *The Practice of Voice and Speech Therapy*, Boston, Expression, 1941.

Froeschels, E. (ed.), *Twentieth Century Speech and Voice Correction*, New York, Philosophical Library, 1948.

Theatre in General

Beckerman, B., *Dynamics of Drama*, New York, Knopf, 1970. Brown, J. R. (ed.), Drama and the Theatre, London, Routledge and Kegan Paul, 1971.

Bentley, E. (ed.), *The Theory of the Modern Stage*, Harmondsworth, Penguin, 1968.

Sociology and Social Psychology

Bettelheim, B., *The Informed Heart*, London, Thames and Hudson, 1960.

Bettelheim, B., *Love is not Enough*, New York, Collier, 1965.

Bettelheim, B., *Truants from Life*, London, Collier-Macmillan, 1964.

Goffman, E., *Asylums*, New York, Doubleday, 1961.

Goffman, E., *Interaction Rituals*, New York, Doubleday, 1967.

Goffman, E., *The Presentation of Self in Everyday Life*, New York, Doubleday, 1959.

Goffman, E., *Relations in Public*, Harmondsworth, Penguin, 1971.

Goffman, E., *Stigma*, Harmondsworth, Penguin, 1964.

Philosophy

Buber, M., *Between Man and Man*, London, Fontana, 1961.

Buber, M., *I and Thou*, Edinburgh, T. & T. Clark, 1937.

Manser, A., *Sartre, A Philosophic Study*, London, Athlone Press, 1966.

Index

The minimum specifications for the successful operation of this DVD-ROM are:

- Pentium 4 2.8 GHz
- QuickTime 7+ player installed (available as a free download from www.apple.com)
- 4 x DVD-ROM
- Graphics card min. 32 Mb
- Sound Card
- 512 Mb RAM
- Minimum resolution 1024 x 768
- Windows XP2+
- Media player (available as a free download from www.microsoft.com)
- Mac OSX

Please close down other applications whilst running this DVD-ROM.